Music for the Common Man

Music for the Common Man

Aaron Copland during the Depression and War

Elizabeth B. Crist

OXFORD
UNIVERSITY PRESS
2005

OXFORD
UNIVERSITY PRESS

Oxford University Press, Inc., publishes works that further
Oxford University's objective of excellence
in research, scholarship, and education.

Oxford   New York
Auckland   Cape Town   Dar es Salaam   Hong Kong   Karachi
Kuala Lumpur   Madrid   Melbourne   Mexico City   Nairobi
New Delhi   Shanghai   Taipei   Toronto

With offices in
Argentina   Austria   Brazil   Chile   Czech Republic   France   Greece
Guatemala   Hungary   Italy   Japan   Poland   Portugal   Singapore
South Korea   Switzerland   Thailand   Turkey   Ukraine   Vietnam

Published by Oxford University Press, Inc.
198 Madison Avenue, New York, New York 10016

www.oup.com

Oxford is a registered trademark of Oxford University Press

Library of Congress Cataloging-in-Publication Data
Crist, Elizabeth Bergman.
Music for the common man : Aaron Copland during the
depression and war / Elizabeth B. Crist
    p. cm.
Includes bibliographical references.
ISBN-13 978-0-19-515157-2
ISBN 0-19-515157-7
1. Copland, Aaron, 1900– 2. Composers—United States—
Biography. I. Title.
ML410.C756C75 2005
780'.92—dc22   2004029062

Epigraph source: Carl Sandburg, *The People, Yes*
(New York: Harcourt, Brace & World, 1936), 44.

Publication of this book was supported by the H. Earle Johnson Fund
of the Society for American Music.

9 8 7 6 5 4 3 2 1

Printed in the United States of America
on acid-free paper

for Harris, always

Who shall speak for the people?
who has the answers?
where is the sure interpreter?
who knows what to say?
Who can write the music jazz-classical
    smokestacks-geraniums hyacinths-biscuits
      now whispering easy
      now boom doom crashing angular
      now tough monotonous tom tom
Who has enough split-seconds and slow sea-tides?

Carl Sandburg, *The People, Yes* (1936)

Acknowledgments

ALTHOUGH IT IS typical to begin by extending professional thanks before moving on to more personal expressions of gratitude, I find it difficult to separate the two, so fortunate am I to have had a host of supportive faculty, institutions, colleagues, and friends. First and foremost, I am grateful to a long list of extraordinary teachers, including Daniel R. Melamed, Robert P. Morgan, and J. Peter Burkholder as well as Rosemary Crawford, Walter Frisch, Cynthia Gessele, Leon Plantinga, Ellen Rosand, Elaine Sisman, and the late Mark Tucker.

My work has been funded by the Dena Epstein Award from the Music Library Association, a yearlong fellowship from the National Endowment for the Humanities, and various awards from the School of Music, Graduate School, College of Fine Arts, Vice President for Research, and Vice President and Provost at the University of Texas at Austin. I thank especially Director B. Glenn Chandler, Associate Dean Doug Dempster, Dean Robert Freeman, and Provost Sheldon Eckland-Olson. Some of these grants enabled me to spend summers working in the Aaron Copland Collection at the Library of Congress, where the librarians, particularly Wilda Heiss and Stephanie Poxon, were unfailingly patient and helpful. At the University of Texas, music librarian David Hunter has been a pleasure to work with, and Dell A. Hollingsworth of the Harry Ransom Humanities Research Center has given generously of her time and expertise.

For permissions to reproduce Copland's words and music, I thank James M. Kendrick of the Aaron Copland Fund for Music; Alexis Hart of Brown Raysman Millstein Felder & Steiner LLP; as well as Jennifer Bilfield, Carolyn Kalett, and Frank Korach of Boosey & Hawkes. Anderson Ferrell kindly granted me access to materials and Jonathan Prude allowed me to quote from sources in the Agnes de Mille Collection at the New York Public Library for the Performing Arts. Passages of this book have previously appeared (in different form) in *The Journal of The American Musicological Society* 2003, vol.

56, no. 2 © 2003 by the American Musicological Society; and *Aaron Copland and His World*, ed. Carol J. Oja and Judith Tick (Princeton, N.J.: Princeton University Press, 2005).

I extend my thanks to the "deans" of Copland scholarship: Vivian Perlis and Howard Pollack, as well as to Joseph H. Auner, Stephen Hinton, Carl Leafstedt, Neil Lerner, Carol J. Oja, Larry Starr, Richard Taruskin, Judith Tick, and especially Beth E. Levy, for their interest in and contributions to my work. James Curtis of the University of Delaware shared his time, enthusiasm, and knowledge of the thirties, and my friends and colleagues at the University of Texas—James Buhler, Andrew Dell'Antonio, Susan Jackson, K. M. Knittel, and Stacy Wolf chief among them—have helped to shape this project from beginning to end. I have benefited from their wit and wisdom in equal measure. Others who have earned my enduring gratitude include Jennifer Reynolds, Forrest Reynolds, William C. Stott, faculty participants in the spring 2004 Humanities Institute seminar at the University of Texas, Rebecca A. Baltzer and Michael C. Tusa. Jeremy Cumbo did an expert job setting the musical examples, and my graduate students (Susan Stroebel and Jennifer Smull) were enormously helpful. I owe a special debt of thanks to Wayne Shirley, a remarkable scholar, collaborator, correspondent, and friend, for offering his invaluable comments on the entire manuscript.

Kimberly Robinson at Oxford University Press has been a most patient and persistent editor; Eve Bachrach and Robert Milks have expertly guided this project through to completion.

My love and thanks go to John and Barbara Bergman, Jeffrey and Gina Bergman, Buckley and Susan Crist, and Alison Crist, all of whom now know more about Aaron Copland than they probably ever wanted to and yet continued to ask how my work was going. And as always, most thankfully, there is my husband, Harris, to whom this work is dedicated—as is my life.

Note on musical examples: For ease of reading, orchestral examples have frequently been reduced, and all have been set at concert pitch. In keeping with Copland's own practice, horn parts have been set without signatures.

Contents

Music for the Common Man

Introduction

DURING THE GREAT DEPRESSION, two of Aaron Copland's close friends, the director Harold Clurman and the playwright Clifford Odets, found themselves frequenting Stewart's Cafeteria on Christopher Street in Greenwich Village. "Though this cafeteria must have represented a high degree of affluence to the really hungry," Clurman recalled, "it struck me as a sort of singing Hooverville. For, strangely enough, this incubator of the depression, with many marks of waste and decay upon it, was in point of fact a place rank with promise."[1] The winter of 1932–33 was "historically cruel," Clurman knew, but even so it seemed to him "a time of renewed faith." In the midst of despair, there was a sense that "something new, not wholly aware of itself . . . was in an early state of gestation."[2]

Change was in the air well before that bleak winter as the economic prosperity and social energy of the Jazz Age began to wane in the late 1920s. The headlong rush toward the future and unrestrained passion for all things modern in the years after World War I had led to the stunning technological achievements of the Holland Tunnel, Lindbergh's transatlantic flight, the Model A, and the first sound film. But postwar American optimism was already yielding to the forces that would create the Great Depression, and 1927 stood as a unique moment of tension between boom and bust, a year in which F. Scott Fitzgerald saw evidence of "a wide-spread neurosis . . . faintly signaled, like a nervous beating of the feet."[3] At the same time, the writer Josephine Herbst recalled "a kind of shuddering premonition of a world to come,"[4] and Clurman recognized "notes of doubt, fear, loneliness" emerging even before the stock market crash in 1929.[5]

The composer Aaron Copland also noted the passing of one age and portent of another. On returning to New York City in 1924 after three years in France, he committed himself to creating music at once unabashedly modern and identifiably American. The "desire to be 'American' was symptomatic of the period," he wrote in a later reminiscence. He recalled being "anxious to write a work that would immediately be recognized as American in character" and so turned to jazz as "an easy way to be American in musical terms."[6] Works like *Music for the Theatre* (1925) and the Piano Concerto (1926) clearly evoke rhythmic and melodic features characteristic of early dance-band jazz and urban blues. These pieces earned Copland praise, scorn, and—most important for a young composer—attention. After the concerto, however, Copland felt that he had exhausted the expressive possibilities of symphonic jazz. "I had done all I could with the idiom," he explained in 1941, "considering its limited emotional scope."[7] Although he never entirely abandoned jazz as a source of rhythmic and melodic invention, he moved away from the overt borrowing of jazz styles.[8]

In the late 1920s the composer entered a self-reflective, transitional phase marked by decreased compositional activity. He produced no major works in 1927, and the lacuna caused him some distress. As he wrote to his former teacher Nadia Boulanger: "When I think that 1927 is coming to a close and that I have produced no work signed 1927, I assure you I have a sinking feeling of the heart. It is as if the entire year were wasted."[9] Despite the notable achievement of the *Piano Variations* (1930), between 1927 and 1933 Copland finished relatively few pieces. He wrestled with the *Symphonic Ode*, for example, missing a competition deadline in 1929, and no new works of his own were programmed for the first Yaddo Festival of Contemporary Music, which Copland organized in May 1932. At the same time he was quite busy during these years, lecturing at the New School for Social Research, directing the Copland-Sessions concert series as well as the Yaddo Festival, and writing articles for *Modern Music*. These activities demanded time and energy that might otherwise have been devoted to composing but, whatever the circumstances, at the tail end of the decade Copland was struggling to move beyond his youthful, jazzy iconoclasm, to translate notoriety into status within the New York contemporary music scene, and to tap a new stylistic vein to mine in future compositions.[10]

While reflecting on his own musical path, Copland also considered the more general trends in American music of his generation. "Where do we go from here?" the composer Emerson Whithorne asked in an article from 1926—a question that might have been posed to the entire culture.[11] Some two years later, Copland gave a most striking answer: "For the present, nowhere." Surveying the state of contemporary music, he advised composers to "be content to rest awhile, to till the ground others have cleared. Soon enough the time will come to set off again for undiscovered territory." After years of frenetic innovation and determined revolution, music seemed to Copland to be "in a summing-up period."[12] In 1933 he again assessed the development of modern music and reiterated his view that young composers had moved beyond an experimental phase. "The day of the 'pathfinder' and the 'experimenter' is over," he declared. "We are in a period of 'cashing in' on their discoveries." The challenge was not to find new styles and techniques to distance contemporary composition from the music of the romantic past, but to find new audiences and modes of expression best suited to the modern present. Copland concluded that contemporary music "should no longer be confined to the sphere of the special society" but should "interest the general public."[13]

Copland's ideas about the future of modern music and its relationship to the audience received their fullest explication in the oft-cited 1939 autobiographical essay "Composer from Brooklyn," first published in the *Magazine of Art*. In the mid-thirties, Copland recalled, he

> began to feel an increasing dissatisfaction with the relations of the music-loving public and the living composer. The old "special" public of the modern-music concerts had fallen away, and the conventional concert public continued apathetic or indifferent to anything but the established classics. It seemed to me that we composers were in danger of working in a vacuum. Moreover, an entirely new public for music had grown up around the radio and phonograph. It made no sense to ignore them and to continue writing as if they did not exist. I felt that it was worth the effort to see if I couldn't say what I had to say in the simplest possible terms.[14]

With the goal of communicating to an expanded "music-loving public," Copland adopted a new approach, which he termed "imposed simplicity."[15]

He did not describe his simplified style in any detail but instead listed those compositions considered to "embody this tendency," among them *El Salón México, The Second Hurricane, Music for Radio, Billy the Kid,* and *Our Town.* Based on this group of works, "imposed simplicity" seems to denote a newly melodic idiom that frequently incorporates folk song—whether borrowed, as in *El Salón México, The Second Hurricane,* and *Billy the Kid,* or imitated, as in *Music for Radio.* In terms of compositional technique, these simplified pieces generally rely on triadic harmonies and diatonic melodies, privileging audible rhetoric over structural logic.[16] *Lincoln Portrait, Rodeo,* the Violin Sonata, and

Appalachian Spring are later works easily added to Copland's own list, as all share these basic musical characteristics.

Yet the ideal of "imposed simplicity" was not merely a matter of compositional procedure. In explaining this new style, Copland stressed not the technique of his musical idiom but the functional nature of his scores, signaling the purposes for which he composed and the audiences that he had in mind.

> *El Salón México* is an orchestral work based on Mexican tunes; *The Second Hurricane* is an opera for school children of high-school age to perform; *Music for Radio* was written on a commission from the Columbia Broadcasting Company especially for performance on the air; *Billy the Kid*, a ballet written for the Ballet Caravan, utilizes simple cowboy songs as melodic material; *The City, Of Mice and Men*, and *Our Town* are scores for the films.

"The reception accorded these works," he reasoned, "encourages me to believe that the American composer is destined to play a more commanding role in the musical future of his own country."[17] Thus the notion of "imposed simplicity" indicated an aesthetic orientation, a compositional attitude that focused on accessibility and conceived of the musical work as a functional as well as artistic creation.

These closing paragraphs of his autobiographical sketch later caused Copland some anxiety. In 1967 he appended a section to his original 1939 essay, lamenting that critics seemed overly "pleased to be able to quote literally" and all too happy to have "pinned the composer down for all time." His own comments had "done me considerable harm," he explained. "Quoted and requoted, these remarks of mine emphasized a point which, although apposite at the time of writing—the end of the '30s—seems to me to constitute an oversimplification of my aims and intentions, especially when applied to a consideration of my subsequent work and of my work as a whole."[18] Copland did not disavow the idea of imposed simplicity but sought to show that he had since gone on to explore other musical idioms. "It is unfortunate that I wrote my little autobiographical sketch . . . just when I was writing these more accessible things," he told Edward Cone in an interview from 1967. "For I gave the false impression that this was the direction I was going to head for in the future. I was just all keyed up by the fact that finally here was a need for our music!"[19]

What he seemed to find most objectionable about the reception of his remarks (and of his music) was the implication that his accessible works were somehow less serious than his more abstract compositions. "For the sake of drawing sharp distinctions you rather overdo the dichotomy between my 'severe' and 'simple' styles," Copland wrote in 1943 to friend and critic Arthur Berger.[20]

> The inference is that only the severe style is really serious. I don't believe that. What I was trying for in the simpler works was only partly a larger audience; they also gave me a chance to try for a home-spun musical idiom, similar to what I was trying for in a more hectic fashion in the earlier jazz works. In other words, it was not only musical functionalism that was in question, but also musical language. I like to think that in Billy and Our Town, and somewhat in Lincoln, I have touched off for myself and others a kind of musical naturalness that we have badly needed—along with "great" works.[21]

"I prefer to think that I write my music from a single vision," Copland concluded in the revised version of his autobiographical essay (1967). "When the results differ it is because I take into account with each new piece the purpose for which it is intended and the nature of the musical materials with which I begin to work."[22]

Yet the functional aspect of Copland's music during these years was not wholly determined by the terms of a particular commission or given genre of composition. Although he emphasized the necessary constraints on music for film or dance—"the music appropriate for the different kinds of cooperative ventures . . . had to be simpler and more direct," he wrote in 1967—even independent concert works now had a purpose: attracting an audience and speaking to the world outside the concert hall.[23] In fact, the first piece to be written in his simplified, folkloric, accessible idiom was *El Salón México*, a purely orchestral fantasy. And although works such as *Statements*, the Piano Sonata, and Third Symphony might seem less "simple" or "simplified" than *Lincoln Portrait* or *Appalachian Spring*, all represent Copland's continuing attempt to establish a relationship between composer and audience, to forge a connection between modern music and contemporary life. Copland sincerely believed "that the two things that seemed always to have been so separate in America—music and the life about me—must be made to touch," and his compositions from the thirties and forties realize that goal.[24] His music between 1932 and 1946 is distinguished by a commitment to aesthetic accessibility and social relevance, expressed within and informed by the cultural and political contexts of the Great Depression and World War II.

It has long been recognized that Copland's accessible manner was, in some measure, a response to the Depression and Second World War; the composer himself said as much in his lectures and writings of the time. When asked at a 1937 concert sponsored by the Works Progress Administration whether "the recent depression and economic upheaval and consequent changes in social thinking had any effect on your music," he answered quite frankly, "Yes! It affected it very much."[25] His influential early biographer, Arthur Berger, considered it "hardly accidental that [Copland's] turn toward simplification and a broader audience should coincide with the later depression years, when artists and intellectuals who had formerly been escapist became aware of politics and economics."[26] Indeed Copland was more than aware: he was involved. In 1941, for example, he acknowledged that the accessible idiom was "no mere opportunism" and was "not without its political implications."[27] Composers could occupy "a first-line position on the cultural front,"[28] Copland recognized, and he was at that time affiliated with a host of radical causes. Particularly in the 1930s, he was aligned with the political Left and associated with Communism as both a cultural movement and a political party. Ultimately his politics are best described as progressive, although this should not obscure his attachment to more radical ideas, especially early in the decade.

These facts—the sense of hope and opportunity Clurman felt within the Depression, Copland's embrace of a simplified style, his involvement in left-wing politics—have thus far seemed no more than a loose set of biographical correlations. How Copland's music relates to its social context and reveals a political alignment are questions that have yet to be fully answered. And until recently it has been difficult to even ask such questions, given the pervasive and distorting influence of Cold War historiography.[29] From the anticommunist perspective, the leftist politics of the 1930s evinced a regrettable loss of faith in America, in the promise of industrial capitalism and power of liberal democracy. What had seemed socially responsive during the Depression was reinterpreted in the postwar political climate as subversive. Politically engaged art came to be viewed with suspicion, even as the U.S. government advanced its own political and artistic program of cultural propaganda under the banner of cultural freedom.[30] Many artists faced the charge of un-Americanism and were called to justify their leftist politics, sometimes before powerful congressional committees. In 1953 Copland testified before the Senate Permanent Subcommittee on Investigations, chaired by Senator Joseph McCarthy, and made sure to distance himself from Communist causes and organizations.[31] Later in life he shrugged off questions about his political activities during the thirties and forties, saying only that "it seemed the thing to do at the time."[32] This guarded comment exemplifies an attitude common among artists, composers, and even scholars who have discussed the radical political and aesthetic alignments with a caution warranted by the enduring institutional and cultural power of McCarthyism in America.

To take Copland at his word, however, and view his work as merely a manifestation of aesthetic commiseration or cultural fashion fuels a serious misunderstanding of his political alignment and its musical expression. The relation of Copland's music to leftist politics has been generally masked by its enduring success, obscured by the legacy of anticommunist historiography, and derided by the resurgence of aesthetic formalism after World War II. But a closer look at the associations between political ideology and aesthetic expression in his music from the era of Depression and war makes clear that Copland's turn toward "imposed simplicity" was not merely a sympathetic or practical reaction to a changed cultural context. Instead, the composer and his music clearly participated in the cultural work of the left-wing social movement known as the Popular Front.

Most familiar as a specific policy of the Communist International, the Popular Front may also be construed as an indigenous, broad-based, left-wing coalition of American labor unions, the Communist movement, and all those who would embrace an American form of social democracy. This is the view advanced by Michael Denning, who describes the Popular Front as "a radical historical bloc uniting industrial unionists, Communists, independent socialists, community activists, and émigré anti-fascists around laborist social democracy, anti-fascism, and anti-lynching."[33] In his monumental study *The Cultural Front*, Denning perhaps fails to explicate fully the relationship between the political struggles of the ethnic, working-class labor movement and New York leftist intellectuals; the intersections between the Communist Party, New Deal, and Popular Front are not systematically mapped, and his obvious (as well as controversial) agenda is to distinguish the cultural history of the thirties and forties from the history of American Communism. Nevertheless, Denning's broad view of left-wing culture during the Depression and war is of particular value in understanding Copland's music.[34] Although this new conception of the Popular Front may resist prescriptive definition, it offers a frame of reference that is at once reasonably distinctive and sufficiently elastic to include a composer who was not committed to a party program but, rather, aligned with a political perspective. As a left-wing movement related to—but independent from—the Communist Party and the New Deal, the Front can be considered an encompassing social movement defined more by its vision than its strategies. So, too, can

Copland's politics be seen as a tangle of left-wing ideas about the aestheticization of politics and politicization of aesthetics.

Denning's central metaphor is that of "labor" and "laboring," referring in part to the expanded role of unions in American politics, the participation of the working class in American popular culture, and the rhetoric of labor as applied to the cultural work of artists and intellectuals. Although Denning does not discuss concert music in *The Cultural Front*, it too experienced a "laboring" during the thirties and forties: these decades witnessed the unionization of composers;[35] the search for a genuinely proletarian music; and the effort to use music education as a means of creating new, more democratic audiences. Copland was involved in all of these activities and thoroughly invested in the project of making contemporary music more responsive to a wide public. This suggests a program of social and cultural uplift, but the goal of writing accessible, modern music also obliged the artist to his audience. That is, the composer interested in affecting his listeners had to hear with their ears such that aesthetic judgment and cultural authority could not rest wholly with the creator. Thus, the ideal of "imposed simplicity" conceives of the artist as a cultural worker, as one who produced music to be consumed as well as appreciated.

As "art" music heard by a decidedly middle- and high-brow public, Copland's compositions might not seem a representative form of Popular Front culture.[36] Yet concert music surely can articulate the aesthetic and ideological positions of the Front. Leftist composers imbued the inherited forms of European and modernist concert music with an emergent social consciousness, adapting traditional, established musical forms to a new cultural context. They wrote symphonies with rhetorical grandeur and real public appeal, arranged folk tunes in orchestral works, and set proletarian texts as art songs. Copland, like many of his colleagues, experimented with genres easily linked to radical politics, including the mass song, *Lehrstück*, and documentary film music—all the while seeking new audiences for his symphonies, sonatas, and ballets, partly through the mass media of the radio and phonograph. Whatever the genre, Copland's works from these decades demonstrate how the cultural politics and aesthetic ideologies of the Popular Front might find their way into the concert hall.

In interpreting Copland as a composer on the cultural front, I do not aver that the political and aesthetic were or are the same. To identify the composer's avowed political beliefs or assess how those beliefs may have influenced his aesthetic choices is not necessarily to define the politics of his music, since political and aesthetic structures are not equivalent. Adopting Denning's terminology, I distinguish between two expressions of political activity: first, the conscious, chosen involvement in such external forms of commitment as party affiliation or political organizing; and, second, the elusive political sensibility that might find expression in a piece of music. The first of these—overt political engagement—is termed *cultural politics*. As Denning explains, cultural politics is "simply the politics of letterheads and petitions, the stances taken by artists and intellectuals, the pledges of allegiance and declarations of dissent" that reveal the "social consciousness" of the individual artist as well as "the politics of the cultural field itself," its organizations and institutions.[37] The conscious display of political involvement may be documented by the facts of history or biography and connected to an aesthetic object quite directly through the model of cause and effect.[38] At the level of cultural politics, Copland's simplified style and interest in writing for amateurs, radio, stage, and screen constitute a considered response to the extrinsic forces of circumstance—forces that cannot, however, wholly explain the material or contextual significance of his music from this era. The second form of political expression—termed *aesthetic ideology*—is the political dimension of artistic form. The notion of aesthetic ideology draws on the concept of the "political unconscious" as defined by the literary critic Fredric Jameson.[39] An analysis of the political unconscious or aesthetic ideology of an artwork attends to the social, historical, and political dimensions of aesthetic expression, regarding artistic production as a symbolic act that may imaginatively reconcile otherwise intractable social oppositions.[40]

The social and political significance of an artwork is interpreted within the model of "structural causality," which establishes connections between distinct structures, whether economic, social, bureaucratic, or aesthetic.[41] The relationship between these separate structures, as between cultural politics and aesthetic ideology, is not homologous but dialectical, because these spheres of human activity intersect only through the process of mediation. Establishing a nexus between "the formal analysis of a work of art and its social ground," in Jameson's theory, mediation respects "the relative autonomy" of these elements.[42] One form of mediation is historical interpretation. An analysis sensitive to the ideological consequence of musical processes reads social and cultural contexts as forces at play within the aesthetic object. Thus to consider Copland's music from the era of depression and war in relation to the Popular Front social movement is not to collapse aesthetics into politics but, rather, to establish ideological affinities that go beyond explanations of authorial intent or mechanical causality.[43] And historical context becomes more than the backdrop for artistic expression: it is a presence within the artwork itself.

The following chapters explore Copland's compositions and their cultural circumstance during the Great Depression and the Second World War. Only a handful of works are discussed; many others could have been included—the Piano Sonata as evocative of World War II; *The North Star* and the imagined Russian collective; *Our Town*, radical theater, and the pastoral. But this is a representative rather than comprehensive survey of Copland's music from the 1930s and 1940s. At its core is the proposition that his work expresses a political perspective. And although Cold War historiography generally relies on Communism as the sole index of radical sentiment, this book considers leftist politics within the flexible and largely complementary categories of progressivism, Communism, and the Popular Front. Ultimately, the goal is to include Copland's music in the cultural history of the Left.

During the 1930s, "the term 'Left movement' in the arts was actually a misnomer," Harold Clurman warned readers in the closing pages of *The Fervent Years*. "It was a form of loose talk that misrepresented the true nature of things. The so-called 'Left movement' in the arts was not 'Left,' 'Right,' or 'Center,' but was for our day the *main* movement of the American consciousness in the process of its growth." For the artists and intellectuals in Clurman's—and Copland's—circle, left-wing politics was mainstream politics. Yet once America had passed through the darkest years of the Great Depression, "a new worry crept into the strong men's hearts." Those in power came to fear the "innocents," those who had protested fascism, "beamed on the Soviet experiment, approved of the CIO, and, after a fashion, entered the vulgar arena of politics." The forces of reaction, Clurman bitterly observes, gave rise to "malevolent allusions to 'Left' writers, 'foreign' ideas, 'un-American' ideals and other spurious epithets that serve to confound everyone so that the world may more easily be set back on the old anarchic path that people of power find normal and pleasant."[44]

Perhaps especially at a time when the term un-American has returned to contemporary political discourse, it is worth examining the cultural values that resonate within music by that most American of American composers, keeping in mind the remarkable irony that Copland's most familiar pieces belong to a culture that would come to be condemned as foreign.[45] To recover Copland's engagement with left-wing politics in his music during the 1930s and 1940s is to hear a different history from the one that has been sanctioned, to reanimate a past that had once hoped to create a less confounding future. Seeking (however unsuccessfully, sincerely, naïvely, or influentially) to balance liberty and equality, individual fulfillment and civic solidarity, to promote social justice and economic equity, the Popular Front tried to imagine a more just world. And this is the ideal that can be heard in Copland's music from the Depression and war, if only we listen.

1 Communism and the Cultural Front

ASKED BY THE MUSICOLOGIST Vivian Perlis in 1979 about his political activities in the 1930s, Copland replied: "Well, I never joined anything. In that sense I wasn't aligned, but I was very sympathetic for the more radical side of things. It was a kind of feeling of the period, one was going to carry it along."[1] While granting his interest in left-wing causes during the 1930s, Perlis maintains that "Copland was not by nature a political person" and describes the composer as a "fellow traveler" during the Depression era, someone associated with but not committed to the Communist Party and its activities.[2] She details "several influences" that "nudged Copland toward the Left," including Harold Clurman and the Group Theatre, Copland's experiences in Mexico, his association with the Composers Collective, and the Marxist aesthetics of Marc Blitzstein and Hanns Eisler, as well as the Depression itself.[3] The composer's most recent biographer, Howard Pollack, credits Copland with greater personal and political agency, arguing that the composer was truly "an engaged citizen."[4] Pollack carefully documents Copland's involvement with socialism in the 1920s, affiliation with Communism in the 1930s, and estrangement from the New Left in the 1960s.[5]

Although Copland later implied that his beliefs could be characterized as "democratic or liberal,"[6] his political stance during the years of depression and war can first be understood in relation to Progressivism. Rooted in turn-of-the-century Republican reform movements, Progressivism in the early decades of the twentieth century was a varied social, economic, and cultural philosophy that generally decried vulgar competitive individualism in hopes of reconciling private desires with public obligations.[7] In *The Promise of American Life* (1909), an important contribution to Progressive thought, Herbert Croly advocates economic centralization and espouses a democratic collectivism that nonetheless preserves opportunities for individual initiative.[8]

Earnest liberals like Croly as well as monied business interests encouraged the government to develop regulatory controls and social programs that would shore up (rather than dismantle or reconfigure) the American economic system. Particularly in addressing the social turmoil of urban industrialization and modernity, the Progressive movement often traversed lines of class and ethnicity, uniting middle- to upper-class white Protestants and ethnic communities (especially Jewish immigrants) in a struggle against unrestrained corporate capitalism.[9]

A Progressive position in the arts and letters was advanced by such notable figures as Van Wyck Brooks, Waldo Frank, and Claire Reis. All believed that the creative energies of modernism needed to be channeled away from an exclusive, elite audience and applied to a more democratic program of cultural uplift.[10] Brooks, for example, famously divided culture into two strains— "highbrow" and "lowbrow"—but advocated a "middle tradition" that "effectively combines theory and action."[11] Claire Reis's passion for modern music was paired with a commitment to social welfare. Perhaps best known for her leadership of the International Composers' Guild and the League of Composers, she also founded the People's Music League, which offered free concerts for immigrants. Like Copland, Reis expressed an interest in the fate of the composer, a sincere concern for the audience, and belief in the political potential of modern music.[12] The avant-garde project to link experimental art and contemporary life intimately relates to the Progressive tradition of social critique.[13]

As a historical phenomenon Progressivism is frequently confined to the years before World War I, but as a general political perspective, it endured through the Great Depression.[14] In the 1930s, many left-leaning intellectuals continued to support a convergence of artistic and social progress. A Progressive philosophy survived in magazines such as the *Dial, Hound and Horn, Seven Arts*, and especially the *New Republic*, whose contributors generally assumed the fact of the capitalist system but advocated a communitarian vision of modern civil society.[15] Copland read the *Dial* while still in Paris and became familiar with some of its contributors during the years immediately after his return to New York in 1924.[16] Through the critic Paul Rosenfeld he met such luminaries as Van Wyck Brooks, Lewis Mumford, Edmund Wilson, and Alfred Stieglitz, forming especially close friendships with Waldo Frank and the photographer Paul Strand.[17] In this circle of artists and intellectuals, Copland discovered a community pursuing socially responsive forms of modernist expression.

The onset of the Depression revivified collectivist energies, encouraged more adventurous economic reform, and invested aesthetic philosophies with greater social urgency. Artists were excited to think that their knowledge and experience might be germane to the world around them. "To the writers and artists of my generation who had grown up in the Big Business era and had always resented its barbarism, its crowding-out of everything they cared about," Edmund Wilson wrote in 1932, the 1930s "were not depressing but stimulating." There was "a new sense of freedom" and "a new sense of power" among intellectuals who were "still carrying on while the bankers, for a change, were taking a beating." Within the crisis appeared opportunity, and "one couldn't help being exhilarated at the sudden unexpected collapse of that stupid gigantic fraud."[18] Decades later, Copland recalled having been energized by the "heady wine" of feeling that the arts had a vital role to play during the Depression.[19] Malcolm Cowley noted that in the early thirties "a new conception of art was replacing the idea that it was something purposeless, useless, wholly individual and forever opposed to a stupid world." The "lost generation" of Americans who had fled to Europe had come home to find that "the artist and his art had once more become a part of the world, produced by and perhaps affecting it." This profound aesthetic shift was a symptom, Cowley continued, "of a vaster change" in American culture and politics. The financial system that had supported and even encouraged a romantic view of artistic isolation "was threshing about in convulsions like those of the dying."[20]

Reflecting on the legacy of Progressive liberalism, Edmund Wilson formulated a more radical response to the Depression in his 1931 essay "An Appeal to Progressives."[21] Wilson argued that those inclined to criticize the incomplete realization of American democracy could no longer believe in the rational, measured reform of capitalist economic and political institutions. "It seems to me impossible at the present time," Wilson wrote, "for people of Croly's general aims and convictions to continue to believe in the salvation of our society by the gradual and natural approximation to socialism which he himself has classed progressivism, but which has generally come to be known as liberalism."[22] He continued:

That benevolent and intelligent capitalism on which liberals have always counted has not merely not materialized to the extent of metamorphosing itself into socialism—it has not even been able to prevent a national disaster of proportions which neither capitalists nor liberals foresaw and which they both profess themselves unable to explain. . . . May we not well fear that what this year has broken down is not simply the machinery of representative government, but the capitalist system itself?—and that, even with the best will in the world, it may be impossible for capitalism to guarantee not merely social justice but even security and order?[23]

Wilson lamented the apparent inability of liberals to prevent disaster or effect change and objected to the conflation of democracy and capitalism. "The truth is that we liberals and progressives have been betting on capitalism," he admitted. "And now in the abyss of bankruptcy and starvation into which the country has fallen and with no sign of any political leadership which will be able to pull us out, liberalism seems to have little to offer."[24]

Wilson was not willing to repudiate the American democratic tradition and so rejected dogmatic Marxism. But he opposed the status quo of liberal capitalism, arguing that progressivism needed to "dissociate its economics completely from what is by this time a purely rhetorical ideal of American democracy." He believed in a form of social democracy that would ensure social justice, regulate the economy, and promote the civic good rather than promise individual prosperity. Supporting a position that would "openly confess that the Declaration of Independence and the Constitution are due to be supplanted by some new manifesto and some new bill of rights," Wilson concluded that "American radicals and progressives . . . must take Communism away from the Communists," issuing a call for socialism without Marxist class revolution.[25]

In a complementary article, George Soule distinguished this more muscular form of progressivism from New Deal liberalism, arguing that progressives "ought not to be satisfied with the recommendation of specific programs or pieces of economic and social machinery, but should also strive to forge the human values which alone can give these devices validity."[26] Yet unlike Wilson, who was willing to consider radical and revolutionary change, Soule held out hope for the possibility of liberal reform. In any event, the progressive drive for substantive social change influenced many of the policies of Roosevelt's New Deal without ever being interchangeable with that governmental initiative.[27] Therefore, progressivism refers to a diffuse but distinct political position to the left of New Deal democratic liberalism and critical of the socioeconomic structures of American capitalism, allied with Communist philosophy but not beholden to Party doctrine.

This is also the terrain occupied in the thirties and forties by the Popular Front, broadly construed as a left-wing social movement. More narrowly, the Popular Front may be defined as an initiative of the Moscow-based Communist International (Comintern) that allowed for the creation of national coalitions to unite liberals, progressives, and Communists in the fight against fascism.[28] Under the previous doctrine of the Third Period, announced in 1928, the Comintern had no tolerance for leftist reform politics, and democracy was considered but a masked form of fascism that ensured bourgeois rule. As a national party subject to the authority of the Comintern, the Communist Party USA (CPUSA) adopted the principles of the Third Period, including a hard-line revolutionary agenda and militant ideal of proletarian culture.

By the summer of 1934, however, the official position of the Comintern had begun to shift, largely in response to the growing threat of Nazi Germany. At the Seventh World Congress of the Comintern in August 1935, the general secretary Georgi Dimitrov articulated a new policy, widely known as the Popular Front, that moved away from the radical proletarianism of the Third Period and toward a more inclusive leftism. National parties were allowed to expand their allegiances to groups outside Communist control and beyond the working class. Under the leadership of Earl Browder, the CPUSA followed this new line, pledging "to bring about the unity of all progressives to the fullest degree possible, for the defeat of reaction." The "People's Front" was to be an alliance of workers, farmers, and the middle classes that would oppose reactionary forces in both mainstream political parties.[29] The American Communist Party also assumed a more accommodating stance toward democratic traditions and developed an interest in folk culture. Whereas the 1932 Party platform had envisioned "the United States of Soviet America," in 1936 the CPUSA tellingly adopted the more inclusive slogan "Communism is twentieth-century Americanism."[30] And although the CPUSA had hoped in the wake of the Seventh Congress to build a Farmer-Labor Party that would challenge Roosevelt, by the end of the decade the Party had thrown its support behind the Democrats and the New Deal.

There is no doubt that Copland was a communist with a lowercase *c* referencing the movement rather than the Party.[31] The composer's politics can generally be described as progressive, and he was drawn to communism as a social movement and political philosophy. His music also may be interpreted with reference to various phases of the Comintern and CPUSA; it is possible to argue that Copland wrote militant proletarian works according to the edicts of the Third Period, turned to folk song at the behest of the Popular Front, and composed nationalistic pieces to celebrate the grand alliance with the Soviet Union at a time when the Party's stock rose in tandem with American goodwill toward Russia. By emphasizing his involvement with Communism, such an account would do much to counter the tendencies either to dismiss his political interests or downplay their presence in his music. But declaring a commitment between Copland and the Party would disregard the composer's hesitation to do so himself. There is no evidence that Copland joined the Party nor that his compositional decisions intentionally followed the dictates of Soviet aesthetic policy. And if Copland's music can be correlated to prevailing Communist aesthetics, such correlations are not necessarily causal.

Even so, it might seem that any attempt to interpret the political perspective of Copland's music would inevitably focus on the Comintern and the CPUSA, because conventional histories of the 1930s place the Communist Party at the center of left-wing politics. On the periphery lay sympathetic yet uncommitted "fellow travelers," as Copland has been described. Likewise, the Popular Front has been considered "an invention and always an instrument of Soviet foreign policy," a convenient if short-lived collaboration between Communists and leftists.[32] Yet a different vantage point exists from which to view these decades. Traditional histories of American Communism have focused on edicts from the Comintern, but others tend to highlight native radical traditions, to consider communism as a movement rather than an institution, and challenge—or even reject—the idea that Moscow controlled events in New York.[33] Such accounts interpret the relationship between the Comintern and CPUSA as a process of negotiation, paying more attention to communist culture and less to Party doctrine while emphasizing the role of people on the ground rather than pronouncements from on high.

The ultimate step in this reinterpretation of the American Left during the 1930s and 1940s is Michael Denning's monumental study *The Cultural Front* (1997). There Denning shifts the focus away from Communism entirely to propose a fairly radical revisionist history that distinguishes between the Communist Party as a particular political alignment and the Popular Front as a larger cultural phenomenon. Denning maintains that the Front was not the mechanism of a foreign ideology nor a sectarian strategy but was instead an autonomous American social movement. The "heart" of the Popular Front, he argues, "lay among those who were non-Communist socialists and independent leftists, working with Communists and with liberals, but marking out a culture that was neither a Party nor a liberal New Deal culture." In other words, the Popular Front comprised Wilson's progressives.[34] This new account of the Front replaces the familiar model of a (red) center and (pink) periphery, each denoting degrees of involvement; as Denning asserts, "the 'fellow travelers' *were* the Popular Front."[35] Although his discussion may risk confusion by retaining the familiar moniker of the Comintern policy, Denning's explanation denies the Communist Party—whether the Comintern or the CPUSA—sole agency in the development of a progressive agenda.[36]

Rejecting the notion that the Popular Front can be understood as but a directive of the Comintern, Denning argues that a group of radical progressives including Lewis Corey (a.k.a. Louis Fraina), V. F. Calverton, Malcolm Cowley, Waldo Frank, and Edmund Wilson "pioneered the major themes of the Popular Front social movement before the Communist Party itself adopted them."[37] The movement took shape in the early years of the Great Depression, and its presence may be traced through World War II, during which time Popular Front culture adopted various forms: a proletarian avant-garde in the early 1930s, a large-scale social movement in the middle of the decade, an aspect of state culture during the height of the Works Progress Administration, and an international antifascist alliance during the war.[38] The "beginning of the end" arrived in 1946 with the onset of the Cold War and hegemony of anticommunism, though the Front ultimately dies only with the natural death of its adherents.[39]

Drawing on the writings of Antonio Gramsci, Denning suggests that the Popular Front be recognized as a historical bloc resting on the material foundation of the American labor movement and working-class culture. Political structures supported by this base include commitments to social democracy, antifascism, and social justice.[40] Likewise Mark Naison has described the "principles and affinities" of the Popular Front as encompassing "unwavering support for the Soviet Union, domestically and internationally; unity of progressive forces, even at the expense of socialist principles; support for racial equality; vigilance against domestic fascism," and a belief in the potential of the New Deal as an instrument of social change.[41] Denning's notion of the "cultural front" speaks to the cultural and aesthetic structures within the social movement, including the artist's individual alignment and its cultural significance.[42] Here alignment (a notion borrowed from Raymond Williams) is considered a form of symbolic enrollment rather than overt display and so supplants commitment as a measure of political engagement. As Denning explains, "alignment shifts the analysis of the artistic career from an individual narrative of commitment to an account of the ways the social and formal alignments that produce artists and intellectuals are reshaped and transformed."[43]

Categories of alignment are defined by such factors as age, education, and class. Copland can be counted among the "radical moderns" along with photographer Paul Strand, critic Kenneth Burke, and director Harold Clurman.[44]

These artists and intellectuals, all born around the turn of the century, represent the first generation of American modernists. Because much of their work in the 1920s lacked obvious political interest, their engagement with radical politics in the 1930s might seem a "conversion" of sorts, an awakening to the social situation and turn away from elitist modernism.[45] But in embracing a more politically explicit or musically accessible style in the 1930s the radical moderns did not necessarily abandon or renounce their oppositional stance; rather, as Denning maintains, they "attempted to reconstruct modernism, to tie their formal experimentation to a new social and historical vision."[46] Thus the familiar historiography of the early twentieth century—which so often contrasts the freewheeling, apolitical modernism of the twenties with the radical politics and conservative style of the thirties—obscures a deeper aesthetic continuity between these two decades.

Considering the Front as an American left-wing movement with politics irreducible to doctrinaire Communism vitiates the need to ask Copland the familiar questions: "Have you ever been a Communist? Have you ever been a Communist sympathizer?"[47] These become less significant not because Copland must be rescued from any association with Communism as a specific party or even a general movement (that would suggest an anticommunist agenda) but because the issue of party membership was not significant in Copland's own circle or to his own politics. In the end, whether or not he could be considered a true believer of the Communist creed, a fellow traveler, or movement sympathizer matters less than the fact that he was politically aligned with left-wing progressivism. Thus, Denning's new paradigm of the Popular Front may be of little use to those interested in the Party as a centralized, disciplined, Marxist-Leninist revolutionary organization, but it has the most interpretive power for understanding Copland's progressive politics. To see the Front as a distinct social and cultural movement allows us to appreciate Copland's political involvements without reducing them to Communist Party dogma and without confusing his leftist perspective with mainstream New Deal liberalism. His music can then be seen as more than an oblique expression of political precept and aligned with American leftist politics during the Depression and war.

This is not to discount Communism entirely. The Communist Party was especially influential in New York City, and Copland, along with most of his friends and colleagues at the time, participated in various Communist groups and causes. Howard Pollack has convincingly demonstrated Copland's interest in Communism beginning around 1932. In that year Copland organized the Young Composers Group, an informal association including Henry

Brant, Israel Citkowitz, Lehman Engel, Vivian Fine, Bernard Herrmann, Jerome Moross, and Elie Siegmeister, which "leaned heavily in the direction of Marx."[48] Modeled to some degree on the "Russian Five" and *Les Six*, the American clique was characterized by a striking stylistic diversity. Had they not been "brought together by Aaron Copland," Arthur Berger observed in an article on the Group written in the wake of its first and only concert, "I dare say they might not today be known to us as a group."[49] Moross was "a disciple of Ives and Varese"; Fine "a veritable musical abstractionist"; and Herrmann owed a stylistic debt to Arnold Schoenberg. "In their relationships one to the other," Berger wrote, these composers "are musical individuals." What they all had in common was a desire to "find the proper footing" in contemporary music and transcend the typical struggle between "the elements of novelty and tradition." Echoing Copland's own published comments about the state of contemporary music, Berger explained that the Group had generally abandoned iconoclastic modernism and eschewed musical revolution in favor of artistic evolution. He noted: "To be traditional is in the very air—to abide longer with its musical forbears, rather than be weaned at birth."[50]

Around the time he was directing the Young Composers Group, Copland also was involved with the Composers Collective. An affiliate of the Workers Music League (later renamed the American Music League) and the Pierre Degeyter Club (named for the composer of the Communist anthem, "The Internationale"), the Collective was an informal association of composers who met on Fridays, at 5:30 P.M., to discuss the theory and practice of proletarian music.[51] Founded in 1932, the organization held meetings, sponsored concerts, and published radical songs.[52] Copland's involvement was purported to be limited in terms of his participation in meetings—a fact that has often led his relation to the Collective to be summarily dismissed. But he certainly moved in the same circles as known members of the Collective: in November 1934, for instance, Copland joined Roy Harris, Elie Siegmeister, and Charles Seeger on a panel titled "The Problems of the Composer in Modern Society," presented by the Degeyter Club. And the musical as well as political agenda of the Collective accorded with Copland's own. His aesthetic position of the 1930s—his rejection of jazz (a music tainted by commercialism), distrust of musical experimentation, and interest in reaching the general public through a newly accessible but plainly modern style (eventually inflected by folk song)—was informed by, and indeed has its origins in, the Communist politics and policies that concerned the Collective.

An article about the Collective in *Unison*, newsletter of the American Music League, clearly mirrors Copland's own assessment of modern music in the midst of the Depression, and describes the gradual political awakening of contemporary composers.

> While artists, writers, and actors have for some time begun to see that the only solution of the crisis now affecting all the arts lies in organized action and closer contact with the masses, composers have for the most part still been clinging to the old shibboleths of rugged individualism and pure expression,—this in spite of the fact that the depression has hit the composer with particular force. Retrenchment by wealthy patrons who have in the past supported modern music concerts, has deprived him of practically the only means of having his music played and of effecting contact with his audience. This isolation has caused the composer of today to write music which is complex, introspective, remote from reality, and understandable to fewer and fewer people.[53]

"If the art of composition is to go forward," the article continues, "composers must abandon their isolated position and address themselves to the broad mass of workers and professional people, for whom music is not a luxury but a thing of immense personal and social concern." The Composers Collective therefore dedicated itself to "writing music in all forms to meet the needs of the growing mass working class movement." Copland's name is mentioned in a subsequent paragraph, where he is characterized as "sympathetic." The Performing Unit served "to bring the music heard on COLLECTIVE programs, as well as that of sympathetic composers and those working in the same field in other countries (Aaron Copland, Henry Cowell, Hanns Eisler, Davidenko, Shostakovich) out of the concert hall and into workers' and professional organizations."

Copland himself wrote about the Collective—if not directly then at least by implication—in a 1935 article for the *Music Vanguard*.[54] First published in the spring of 1935, the *Vanguard* was meant to bridge the gap between music professionals and lay audiences. "Contemporary composers and performers need and desire a wider audience and a sounder economic relationship with it," the editors Amnon Balber, Max Margulis, and Charles Seeger wrote in their introduction to the inaugural issue. Recalling Copland's comments from articles in the early 1930s and anticipating his 1939 autobiographical sketch, they noted that "the masses are the wider audience awaiting contemporary composers. Awakened by the phonograph, the radio and the sound-film to a sense of the cultural deprivation under which they have long existed, they need and demand, among other things, education in music."[55] Thus the *Vanguard* intended to bring together music scholarship, contemporary composition, and "mass music—phonograph, radio, sound-film, amateur chorus, orchestra, band, etc."[56]

In his article, "A Note on Young Composers," Copland argues that the "whole field of modern music no longer carries with it a sense of novelty or even of experimentation."[57] The younger generation had to answer "a question which we older men did not have to face in any so direct a manner, namely: 'Whom are you writing your music for?'" The answer revealed both a stylistic direction and a political perspective. "It is obvious that those young people who just a few years ago were writing pieces filled with the *weltschmerz* of a Schoenberg," Copland observed, "now realize that they were merely picturing their own discontent." He advised young composers to declare "No more Schoenberg. The music I write must have more pertinence than Schoenberg's had even to his own Vienna."[58] Nor could Stravinsky serve as a example after his retreat "into the Elysian fields of his neo-classical manner." Instead, "many of the young composers who had taken one or the other of these two older men as their models have now thrown in their lot with that of the working class" in choosing to write music for the masses. Having answered the question of the intended audience, however, composers still faced "such broad questions as the style and content of their music, practical possibilities (usually limitations) in performance," and they also had to be wary of "sectarian dangers"—a reference, perhaps, to ongoing and often abstract debates about Communist aesthetic policy. Copland concluded that "the young composer who allies himself with the proletarian movement must do so not with the feeling that he has found an easy solution, but with the full realization of what such a step means, if his work is to be of permanent value to the workers and their cause."[59]

These articles in *Unison* and *Music Vanguard* reflect the influence of Communist Party rhetoric, particularly the speeches of Earl Browder, secretary general of the CPUSA from 1930 to 1944. At the first congress of the League of American Writers in April 1935, Browder discussed the relation between Communism and literature in terms that later seem to have been adapted to describe the significance of radical politics in contemporary music. "Writers, moving more and more into contact with and participation in the class struggle, have one and all found this current rejuvenating and enriching their artistic work," Browder claimed. "They have escaped from the corruption that is debasing bourgeois intellectual life. They have found that basic contact with life, for want of which the cultural sphere of capitalist society is rotting and withering away."[60] Denying that the Party had a prescription for revolutionary art, Browder explained that "within the camp of the working class, in the struggle against the camp of capitalism, we find our best atmosphere in the free give and take of a writers' and critics' democracy, which is controlled only by its audience, the masses of its readers, who constitute the final authority."[61] Whatever the truth of such statements (the proper aesthetic expression of political commitment was hotly debated in such forums as the *New Masses*, but, of course, not by the masses themselves), Browder's position surely influenced Copland's own.

Regardless how often he attended meetings of the Composers Collective, by 1934 Copland was, according to Pollack, nothing less than "an active, vocal 'red.'"[62] That summer, while staying on Lake Bemidji, Minnesota, with his companion Victor Kraft, Copland not only attended a campaign meeting of the Communist Party but also ended up delivering his first political speech. He wrote about the experience to his friend Israel Citkowitz. "It began when Victor spied a little wizened woman selling a Daily Worker on the street corners of Bemidji," Copland recounted.

> From that, we learned to know [*sic*] the farmers who were Reds around these parts, attended an all-day election campaign meeting of the C.P. unit, partook of their picnic supper and made my first political speech! If they were a strange sight to me, I was no less of a one to them. It was the first time that many of them had seen an "intellectual." I was being drawn, you see, into the political struggle with the peasantry! I wish you could have seen them—the true Third Estate, the very material that makes revolution. What struck me particularly was the fact that there is no "type-communist" among them, such as we see on 14th St. They look like any other of the farmers around here, all of them individuals, clearly etched in my mind. And desperately poor. None can afford more than a 10¢ pamphlet. (With that in mind I appealed to the Group [Theatre?] for funds and they sent me a collection of $30. which I presented to the unit here for their literature fund.) When S. K. Davis, Communist candidate for Gov. in Minn. came to town and spoke in the public park, the farmers asked me to talk to the crowd. It's one thing to think revolution, or talk about it to one's friends, but to preach it from the streets—OUT LOUD—Well, I made my speech (Victor says it was a good one) and I'll probably never be the same!

"Now, when we go to town," he continued, "there are friendly nods from sympathizers" who "come up and talk as one red to another."[63]

The mention of "type-communists" implies an ambivalence toward the CPUSA and the cultural politics of radicalism that reminds us of the power Denning's model has in interpreting Copland's political alignment even at the very moment the composer seemed most involved in party politics. The area around 14th Street in New York City—Union Square—was the site of frequent labor rallies and weekly demonstrations by both the Communist and Socialist parties, which were headquartered nearby, as were their major publications, the *Daily Worker* and the *Socialist Call*.[64] Copland's sympathy with rural, presumably white Protestant farmers did not, however, entail the erasure of an urban, ethnic community; rather, in the mid-1930s both the cityscape and the landscape became equal parts of his experience.[65] Harold Clurman responded to news of Copland's extraordinary experience in Bemidji with a wry observation: "Some people go east to the U.S.S.R. to become 'radicalized,'" he wrote to Copland, "but you went west to the U.S.A.—away from the nest of red radicalism N.Y.—and are drawn into the 'political struggle' with the peasantry!"[66]

The Proletarian Avant-Garde and "Into the Streets May First"

Although his impromptu address in Bemidji seems to have been Copland's only political stump speech, much of his music from the thirties and forties reflects his involvement in Communist cultural organizations and an alignment with radical left-wing politics. Often the "serious" music that might be connected to Communist causes specifically or the Popular Front more generally—those works written in earnest by trained composers of concert music—has been dismissed by critics as politically misguided and aesthetically unsuccessful. Denning neatly summarizes the standard, reductive account of concert music on the cultural front: "a coterie of dissonant modernist composers" are derided for having written "unsingable 'mass chants' for workers before turning to patriotic cantatas and ballets based on symphonized folk tunes."[67] He offers Charles Seeger as one example of a composer impugned by this caricature, although certainly he has Copland in mind as well. Known first as a young, ambitious, modernist composer with an appropriately iconoclastic streak, Copland responded to the cultural crisis of the Depression by writing a single "mass chant" presumed to disregard the taste and ability of the workers themselves; he later composed more than one ballet that used folk music as a source of melodic inspiration.

Copland's own "unsingable" proletarian song was "Into the Streets May First" (1934), composed for the Communist May Day celebration. Although widely discounted, this was more than a failed attempt at agitprop by a pragmatic modernist eager to express a fashionable political opinion. "Into the Streets" belongs to a group of works from the early 1930s that reflects the development of a "proletarian avant-garde" within the context of the cultural front.[68] The proletarian avant-garde was a brief yet decisive phase of left-wing culture that promoted modernist aesthetics as a challenge to the conventions of American industrial capitalism.[69] Particularly significant in the formation of the proletarian avant-garde were the cultural organizations of the Communist Party and the aesthetic policy of Third Period Communism.

In 1931 the Workers Music League (WML) was founded in New York City as the music division of the Workers Cultural Federation; it became a section of the International Music Buro in Moscow when that organization was formed around 1932.[70] Advancing the ideal of music as "a weapon in the class struggle," the WML recognized "the necessity of strengthening the revolutionary musical forces to meet the growing demand for working class music."[71] The League offered "guidance to all affiliated music units and workers organizations," including the Pierre Degeyter Club, which Charles Seeger described as "an organization of professional musicians having definite Leftist tendencies," and the Composers Collective, whose members represented "every shade of musical opinion" from "conservatism" to "restless radicalism."[72]

Among the priorities listed in the platform of the WML was encouraging "original compositions of American revolutionary composers," most notably four-part choruses and proletarian songs.[73] Examples of both are preserved in two volumes titled *Workers Songbook*, published by the WML in 1934 and 1935. The first includes fourteen works by a variety of composers in the Collective, among them Carl Sands (a pseudonym for Charles Seeger) and L. E. Swift (Elie Siegmeister). The foreword to the collection outlines the cultural policy of Third Party Communism and its ideal of revolutionary proletarian music, describing the new music of the working class as "at once a demand of the new, proletarian culture and an inevitable outgrowth of the old, bourgeois art-music." The "basic elements" of concert music are subjected to "revolutionary scrutiny, with a view of finding which of them we cannot help but use, which must be discarded as unsuitable and which must be given a leftward turn that will yield us a recognizably revolutionary music for recognizably revolutionary words." Composers of these revolutionary mass, choral, and solo songs "take as a basic criterion of their work the following adaptation of the words of Joseph Stalin, viz., that they must cultivate above all things 'a good ear for the voice of the masses, must pay close attention to their revolutionary instinct, must study the actualities of their struggle, must carefully enquire whether their policy is sound—and must, therefore, be ready, not only to teach the masses, *but also to learn from them.*'"[74]

Copland reviewed the 1934 *Songbook* for the *New Masses* and proclaimed it "the first adequate collection of revolutionary songs for American workers." Using language familiar from Communist rhetoric (and seemingly borrowed the collection's preface), he insisted that "every participant in revolutionary activity knows from his own experience that a good mass song is a powerful weapon in the class struggle. It creates solidarity and inspires action. No other form of collective art activity exerts so far-reaching and all-pervading an influence." To write a mass song was to assume "a first-line position on the cultural front," he explained, because "the song the mass itself sings is a cultural symbol which helps to give continuity to the day-to-day struggle of the proletariat." He reprised the foreword to the *Songbook*, noting that musicians might judge the collection "primarily as music" but workers would evaluate the songs by deciding "how they apply to the actualities of the daily struggle." And (now parroting Stalin) Copland concluded that "composers will want to raise the musical level of the masses" but also had to "be ready to learn from them what species of song is most apposite to the revolutionary task."[75]

Copland's own Communist song was published in the second volume of the *Workers Songbook*. "Into the Streets May First" was his entry in a contest sponsored by the Composers Collective for the best setting of a text by Alfred Hayes (ex. 1.1). Like other songs by the Collective's members, "Into the Streets May First" features a homophonic texture, syllabic style, and propulsive rhythms.[76] The texture is clear, prosody natural, and the syncopated rhythms compelling rather than complicated. Simple, rising patterns underpin the diatonic melody. Given its harmonic twists and relatively wide range, however, "Into the Streets" is not easy to sing without some practice, as Charles Seeger observed. Years later, he remembered alternately praising and criticizing the song for its supposed technical difficulties. Although he thought it "splendid" and "magnificent," he was concerned about its "freak modulations" and large leaps in the vocal line. "Everybody here knows that your song is best," Seeger recalled telling Copland as the song was awarded first prize. "But do you think it will ever be sung on the picket line?" "No," Copland reportedly answered, "I don't suppose it ever will be sung in a picket line."[77]

More recently, Arthur Berger has described "Into the Streets May First" as an ill-considered response to the rising tide of left-wing sentiment and an uncharacteristic musical misstep. "Copland felt pressured by leftist sympathies," Berger maintains, expressing surprise "that a composer who, as everyone knows, very soon afterwards developed an approach that was so wide in its appeal and of such fine workmanship at the same time should so miscalcu-

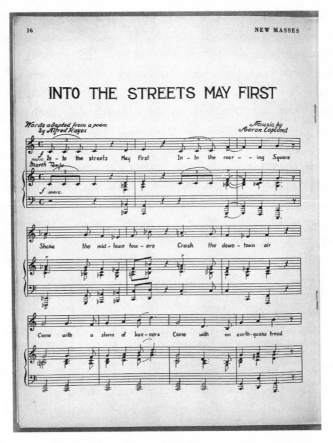

EXAMPLE I.I. "Into the Streets May First," excerpt

late the musical capacities of a worker on the actual picket line." He concludes that "it was not Copland's finest hour (but the good intentions were there)."[78] The suggestion is that Copland was too concerned with writing good music to write a good proletarian song. Yet the song's modest complexities do not preclude its connection to the proletarian aesthetic: music for the masses was not required to be simplistic. The goal of the Collective was to marry left-wing political ideals to an uncompromising musical modernism, not water down the modernist idiom for mass consumption, and artists on the cultural front attempted to make good use of the avant-garde by adopting its oppositional stance to bourgeois conventions, directing its revolutionary energy toward social as well as artistic change.[79] Nor were mass songs always or only to be sung on the picket lines. In fact "Into the Streets May First" was perfectly suited for the types of workers choruses that flourished under the aegis of the Workers Music League. Indeed it was premiered by a well-rehearsed and well-trained chorus at the Second Workers Music Olympiad, although Ashley Pettis lamented that "the excellent Daily Worker Chorus" was "not large enough to produce the volume of tone necessary to an adequate projection of Copland's song." Even so, the performance was still "effective" and even "quite extraordinary."[80]

"Into the Streets May First" was published in the May 1 issue of *New Masses*, in which Pettis described it as "an interesting and practical example of mass song." He explained why the song had been awarded first prize in the competition—without the air of regret Seeger conveyed in his reminiscence.

> Taking everything into consideration, the judges were unanimous in making this selection. It has vigor, directness. Its spirit is identical with that of the poem. The unfamiliar, "experimental" nature of the harmonies which occur occasionally, does not tend to make the unsophisticated singer question. Copland has chosen a musical style of time-honored tradition, but he has imbued it with fresh vitality and meaning. The subtle alteration of harmonies and melodic intervals in progressions of a familiar nature, save it from being relegated to the category of the platitudinous. The harmonic structure, which in less skillful hands would have been mere "Pomp and Circumstance," here possesses freshness and newness! Some of the intervals may be somewhat difficult upon a first hearing or singing, but we believe the ear will very readily accustom itself to their sound.[81]

Given this assessment by the judges of the contest, the perceived difficulties of Copland's song have perhaps been overstated in contemporary discussions. "Into the Streets May First" was not even considered the most challenging piece in the 1935 *Workers Songbook*. An index at the end of the collection grades the repertoire by difficulty: four songs are designated for advanced chorus; Copland's (being in unison) is listed as suitable for beginners.

Along with "Into the Streets May First," one of Copland's most celebrated "modernist" works, the *Piano Variations*, can be placed within the context of the cultural front and the proletarian avant-garde. The work dates from his so-called abstract period and has most often been related to a neoclassical aesthetic, but the *Variations* can also be connected to radical politics. In March 1934, the imposing twelve-minute work for solo piano was featured on an all-Copland program at New York's Pierre Degeyter Club. Reviewing the performance for the Communist periodical the *Daily Worker*, Charles Seeger (writing as Carl Sands) proclaimed the *Variations* "one of the most undeniably revolutionary pieces of music ever produced here." The political content of the piece was discussed by the composer and his audience. "In answer to a question as to what had this music to do with the proletariat," Seeger writes,

> one speaker, announcing himself as a structural steel-worker, answered that it seemed to him to be in keeping not only with the daily job but with the trip to and from it—even with the lunch hour. Copland rejoined that he did not attempt to portray riveters and subways in music, but that he did compose the work in a room on a very noisy New York thoroughfare and had felt that his music must be able to stand up against modern life. For one of the finest definitions of revolutionary musical content yet made, we hail Aaron Copland. "Up against!" And with vigor, too—that is the essence of the Piano Variations.[82]

Here Seeger links the modernist style to a radical politics, suggesting that both are opposed to the hegemony of tradition, whether musical or capitalist. Copland's piece challenges the very nature of a variation set, taking as its subject a decidedly brusque intervallic cell rather than a more traditional melodic theme. In this sense, the work stands up against convention and expectation, while at the same time it draws a connection to the noise, dynamism, and dissociation of life in the modern industrial city. Its thorny dissonances and percussive energy suit the ethos of the proletarian avant-garde.[83] Copland had apparently warned his audience "against viewing his compositions from a revolutionary angle," but Seeger countered that "the class bias of any music can always be distinguished whether or not the composer is aware of it."[84] And Copland's own remarks "brought still one more affirmation of the belief that contemporary art music has lost contact with the vital trends in present-day life and that the only hope for it lies in its frank identification with the great masses of the proletariat."[85]

The *Variations* also can be connected to an international neoclassical style, as Carol Oja has shown by relating the work to a range of models from the European classical tradition and modern repertoire.[86] But it is worth noting that Copland was rather cagey about neoclassicism and distanced himself from the composer who epitomized the idiom, Igor Stravinsky. In a 1928 article for *Modern Music* surveying the music of the 1920s, for example, Copland repeatedly refers to Stravinsky but seems to confine him, with Schoenberg, to an earlier phase of modern music. The "new impersonal approach" is traced to "the essential classicism of Ravel" and even to "the earlier Stravinsky" but not the Russian composer's more recent works. Copland concludes that "for the music of the present it is with men like Hindemith and Milhaud, Honegger and Prokofieff that our faith must rest."[87] In a later review of Paul Rosenfeld's book *Discoveries of a Music Critic*, Copland defended Shostakovich against Rosenfeld's criticism but agreed that Stravinsky was a "great reactionary."[88] And in a lecture delivered at the Toledo Museum of Art in 1940, he wondered why Stravinsky wrote "music which seemed to ape Bach" and relied on historical genres and forms. "I don't understand why it is necessary to write music patterned after 18th-century models," Copland mused. "It seems to me that the true path of music is, in a sense, a return to a more objective kind of music than was characteristic of the 19th century though I don't see why it should depend on forms of the 18th century."[89] Thus he distinguished his particular style of musical objectivity from Stravinsky's neoclassicism, perhaps sensing a reactionary politics at work behind the Russian's aesthetic, an escape to the "Elysian fields" of the past rather than a frank engagement with the present.[90]

Even as an example of Copland's neoclassicism, then, the *Variations* can still be heard to evoke radical reform politics—to face up to rather than retreat from modernity and embrace the cultural context of the Great Depression. It certainly draws on historical models, but it also erects its own modernist edifice; it has the structural integrity of the Brooklyn Bridge, the social energy of New York City, and the political fervor of the Degeyter Club. Although Seeger was perhaps unusual in his politicized reading of the work, he was not the only critic to relate the *Variations* to its contemporary circumstance. A program annotation for a 1940 performance by John Kirkpatrick at Town Hall noted that "the extreme bitterness of this piece may have something to do with the general prevalence during 1930 of similar emotional states resulting from the events of October 1929."[91] This explanatory note may have appeared much earlier in Kirkpatrick's programs; a review from 1936 mentioned a new program annotation that "enabled [listeners] for this first time to associate its bitterness with the economic disaster of 1929."[92]

Thus the divide frequently erected between modernist style and political content was foreign to the composers of the proletarian avant-garde. And despite his apparently critical comments about the inaccessible nature of Copland's mass song, Seeger maintained that modern and proletarian musics were not antithetical. He recalled that composers in the Collective tried "to use ordinary fragments of technique in a unusual way, because we thought *that* was revolutionary . . . [many compositions] had unusual harmonic progressions in them, but usual chords. Or if there were some unusual chords, they put them in conventional patterns."[93] Writing for *Modern Music* in the spring of 1934, just months before Copland's song was published in the *New Masses*, Seeger argued that "the obvious thing to do is to connect the two vital trends—proletarian content and the forward looking technic of contemporary art music. It can be done and is being done."[94]

The Political Statement of Statements

The mass song was not the only accepted medium for expressing leftist political content. As Copland wrote in his review of the first *Workers Songbook*, only four pieces in the collection were "strictly speaking" mass songs.[95] Other genres that fell within the province of the Collective included works for professional or amateur choruses, solo songs, and even instrumental music. "Among the main tasks of the COLLECTIVE so far," an article in *Unison* explained, were

> the writing of (1) Mass Songs, dealing with immediate social issues (United Front, Scottsboro Boys, [Angelo] Herndon, etc.) to be sung at meetings, on parades, and on picket lines; (2) choral music for professional as well as non-professional choruses, dealing in a broader way with the social scene (Song of the Builders, Ballad of Harry Sims, etc.); (3) Solo songs, on social themes to be sung at meetings and concentrate the attention on the subjective, private emotions to the exclusion of the realistic social questions (e.g. "Good-bye Christ," "Death-house Blues," "Strange Funeral"); (4) Instrumental music, to carry on the best musical traditions of the past, now threatened by the collapse of bourgeoise culture, and to create, in the words of Romain Rolland, "A music of the masses, a sort of musical fresco, in broad strokes and sweeps—a music which arouses the people to joy and fury."[96]

Copland began work on—but did not complete—a chorus on the subject of the Scottsboro Boys (the material was later used in *Music for Radio*), and his *Statements for Orchestra* (1935) falls into the last category of Collective compositional activities: instrumental music stirring listeners to experience both "joy and fury."[97] Like the *Variations*, *Statements* is a purely instrumental work that can be related to the cultural politics of the Collective and the musical aesthetic of the proletarian avant-garde.

Statements links a typically modernist, fragmented musical idiom to radical political rhetoric. And even though it is not strictly program music, three of its six individual movements carry politically suggestive titles: "Militant," "Dogmatic," and "Jingo."[98] Copland once considered an even more explicit title for the last of these: a sketch for "Jingo" bears the name "Petty Bourgeois." These titles and the short movements they designate represent a conscious attempt on Copland's part to render his music accessible and his intent audible. "The longer a piece was," he explained of *Statements* many years later, "the more difficulties it would present to the ordinary concert-goer. It occurred to me that if the movements of a work were pithy and compact, the music might seem more understandable. . . . I calculated that by giving each statement a suggestive sub-title, the listening public would have a better idea of what I had in mind when writing these pieces."[99]

One thing that Copland seems to have had in mind was politics. In an interview with Howard Pollack, composer David Diamond suggested that the opening movement of *Statements* ("Militant") was intended to evoke the fervor of such left-wing organizations as the Group Theatre, led by Copland's close friend Harold Clurman. The Group was, according to Arthur Berger, "more than a play-giving unit. Connected with it were discussion meetings that acted as a sounding-board for ideologies of the time that bore some distant relationship to the sort of thing Copland encouraged informally in the Young Composers Group about the same time."[100] Berger's equivocal language reflects his own liberal political perspective and the historical context of his discussion: this passage is from his 1953 biography of Copland, published the same year the composer received a summons to testify before Senator McCarthy. But Copland, Clurman, and the Group were more than vaguely sympathetic to liberal humanism, as Berger suggests.[101] And although Elia Kazan's testimony before the House Un-American Activities Committee (HUAC) has cemented the idea that the Group Theatre was dominated by Communists and slavishly served the interests of the Communist Party, the influence of Communist dogma was never so great.[102] Rather, the Group was aligned with the social democratic, antifascist politics of the cultural front.

Clurman and Copland shared a radical political alignment and corresponded about their political interests. In May 1932—just before Copland began work on *Statements*—Clurman wrote with news that he had been reading (but not relishing) Marx and Lenin. This literature, along with his involvement in the Communist John Reed Clubs, had persuaded Clurman "that people like us are the real revolutionists in America to-day and that we are *revolutionists* in our function of [*sic*, as] artists and leaders." He rejected a doctrinaire view of Communism, however, and believed that the "theoretical communists in America" were "as narrow, as mean, as ignorant, as superficial and as essentially snakelike as all other bodies and institutions in America." Seeming to take up Wilson's call for socialism without revolution, Clurman argued that the path had not yet been paved for a proletarian insurgence and maintained that a change in social structure would first demand a change in cultural attitude. "Any revolution of social order that was not prepared for accompanied by and destined to a corresponding revolution (*conversion*) of men's hearts and mind would be more monstrous than an earthquake and as meaningless," he explained. Thus the artist had a key role to play in transforming American culture and society. "The real revolutionists in America are the Roger Sessions," presumably a reference to Sessions's idiosyncratic style of cosmopolitan modernism and his international interests, "but their revolution is doomed to death without the Aaron Coplands . . . and perhaps the Aaron Coplands—because they are so aware of the *World* as well as their art—are in the final analysis the greater *artists* as well as the greater revolutionaries." Clurman envisioned a revolution through "an art which is personal and *objective*, individual and social, an art for *All*."[103]

This dialectical definition of revolutionary art offers a way to understand *Statements*, which unfolds as a series of coupled movements.[104] The first two, "Militant" and "Cryptic," form a complementary pair, with each alternately evoking public pronouncement and private reflection. "Militant" is an oration for full orchestra. It opens with a rhythmically square marcato theme stated in unison by the winds and strings—a call that is then answered by a sharp one-measure retort in the trombones and tuba before the trumpets, horns, and strings offer their own response. The rhythmic profile of the movement is remarkably declamatory, the texture lean, and the dynamic nearly a constant *forte* or louder. By contrast, "Cryptic" withdraws into private thoughts. Marked *dolce, misterioso* at the outset, the movement is scored only for winds and brass. Any sure sense of meter or pulse is obscured by the slow-moving, unpredictable rhythms with dotted figures now replacing the steady quarter-note cadence of "Militant." The third and fourth movements follow a similar pattern. The full orchestra returns in "Dogmatic," which is loud and brash with a heavy, staccato opening. A rising eighth-note motto recurs almost obsessively throughout; the limited melodic material and stolid rhythmic profile capture the inflexible stance implied by the title. "Subjective," on the other hand, is an introspective essay drawn from material originally written as a chamber piece titled *Elegies* and associated with the American modernist poet Hart Crane.[105] Like "Cryptic," it is scored for partial orchestra—here, just strings.

The fifth movement, "Jingo," pillories a familiar Gilded Age tune and popular carousel melody, "The Sidewalks of New York" (ex. 1.2), which had also been used in Democrat Alfred E. Smith's 1928 presidential campaign.[106] Smith was a product of New York's Tammany Hall, and the ironic setting of "Sidewalks" in *Statements* might be heard to evoke the failed promise of Tammany itself as well as the cultural conflicts surrounding Smith's presidential bid. Founded in 1789 by middle-class New Yorkers to counter the political power of the social elite, by the late nineteenth century Tammany had evolved into a powerful political machine. Its potential as an instrument of social, economic, and political advancement to be achieved through collective organization was ultimately compromised by the individual will to power. While ensuring the immigrant poor and ethnic workingmen some measure of protection and advocacy at a time when the city government could not, Tammany's system of bossism also enabled fraud. In 1932 scandals and investigations culminated in the resignation of New York City's mayor, James J. Walker, a Democrat who had been elected with the help of then-governor Smith.[107] By the time Copland had finished "Jingo" in May or June 1934, Tammany's grip on politics in New York City had finally been broken with the election of Fiorello LaGuardia as mayor on a fusion ticket specifically designed to defeat the Democratic machine.

Born in a tenement district on the lower east side of Manhattan, Smith rose through the Tammany ranks to serve an unprecedented four terms as governor of New York. He was a progressive democrat who fought to improve conditions for working people and ensure the welfare of recent immigrants—especially Jewish émigrés.[108] As a second-generation Irish Catholic, he faced enormous bigotry during his unsuccessful presidential bid. Voters were warned that the pope would move from Rome to Washington, and the Ku Klux Klan burned crosses in the fields for Smith to see as he traveled the country.[109] He and his Republican opponent Herbert Hoover came to embody two conflicting visions of America: Hoover seemed a part of a traditional, Protestant, rural America, whereas Smith belonged to the modern, immigrant, urban world. The race became a contest, Smith's biographer Robert A. Slayton concludes, "over who had the right to be called 'American' and to choose its values."[110]

With this in mind, the appearance of Smith's campaign song in *Statements* might be heard to express some compassion for the beleaguered New York politician. A snippet from the chorus ("East side, west side") is marked *cantabile* and given a comparatively long, lush phrasing. Although distorted, the melody remains an identifiable and perhaps even wistful fragment, whereas nearly all of the other (original) musical material in "Jingo" is presented staccato or marcato. Such articulations lend a sharp, dry edge to the piece and estrange the brief quotation from its musical context. This discrepancy between borrowed tune and newly composed music could be heard to reflect the hostility Smith faced from jingoistic opponents and to capture his own sense of alienation from the American public. The melody is soon displaced by chromatic twists in the trumpet, whose circular motives suggest the other function of "Sidewalks" as a carousel tune.

EXAMPLE 1.2. "Sidewalks of New York" in "Jingo," R 3–4, from *Statements for Orchestra*

Yet Smith proved a disappointment to progressive Democrats—his pro-business platform was nearly indistinguishable from the Republican's—and in between his defeat by Hoover in 1928 and Roosevelt in 1932 (when Smith failed to secure the Democratic nomination), the former governor was primarily occupied with the Empire State Building. "Today, the first of May, the day of the formal opening," Edmund Wilson wrote in the *New Republic*, "Al Smith, in his dark coat and black derby, with his official family around him, looks very compact, decent and well-satisfied." Mayor Walker was on hand for the ceremonies and congratulated Smith for "having provided 'a place higher, further removed than any in the world, where some public official might like to come and hide.'" Before turning to describe life—and death—in a working-class, immigrant community not too far from midtown Manhattan, Wilson recalled "that the Empire State Building is sometimes known

EXAMPLE I.2. (*continued*)

as 'Al Smith's Last Erection.'"[111] Smith soon became a vocal opponent of the New Deal and in the summer of 1934 helped to found the American Liberty League, a reactionary organization formed "to combat radicalism, preserve property rights, uphold and preserve the Constitution," chiefly by pillorying Roosevelt.[112]

The tone of "Jingo" is accordingly disillusioned. Copland's satiric music undermines any potential nostalgia or sympathy that the well-worn tune might hope to elicit. The modernist tendencies toward fragmentation, expressive objectivity, and ironic commentary strip "Sidewalks" of its power as either a sentimental popular song or political rallying cry. Originally in triple meter, the melody begins (six mm. after R5) in duple meter: this does not sound unusual, however, given that the movement itself is also duple. But when the tune returns to its "correct" meter, it is ironically out of synch. The disjuncture between the borrowed melody and its musical context suggests at once a depiction of irrelevance and a frank portrayal of loss, whether of the simple bourgeois pleasure of the carousel ride or of faith in the established political system. "Jingo" offers a dim view of Democratic Party politics at a time when the Communist Party was fiercely opposed to Roosevelt, ultimately making a sardonic statement about belligerent patriotism and narrow-minded political sectarianism.

The quotation returns briefly at the end of the movement but soon fades into silence, and Copland leaves the melody hanging unfinished in mid-air. It is as if a passer-by—watching and hearing a political spectacle from the edge of the crowd—has decided to move on, away from a vibrant but shrill assembly. Tammany Hall itself was located in the Union Square neighborhood where Copland had encountered (even spurned) the "type-communists,"[113] and if he was critical of doctrinaire Communism, so too "Jingo" seems to mock mainstream Democratic politics. In this gap between the radical Left and establishment liberalism lies the politics of the Popular Front.

The sixth and final movement, for full ensemble, completes the symmetrical design of the orchestration and paves the way for a new vision of the future. "Prophetic" begins with a clarion call that introduces clangorous, wrenching dissonances. These rend the sonic fabric and seem to presage conflict, sorrow, or suffering. Yet the movement ends on a note of hope. A return of the opening material leads to a gentle, tonally grounded descent in the solo trumpet, and in the last eight measures the counterpoint of two elegant, diatonic trumpet lines, each marked *dolce, espressivo, nobilmente*, reaches a point of momentary stasis. The shimmer of the tam-tam signals both the end and, possibly, a beginning.

The summer of 1934 was clearly a pivotal time for Copland, as it was for the country. Even though unemployment numbers were down and some economic indicators up, severe storms ravaged the Midwestern "Dust Bowl"; the New Deal seemed incapable of solving the agricultural crisis in the deep south; a wave of strikes swept the country, including a general strike in San Francisco and a particularly bloody conflict in Minneapolis; Hitler was elected führer. "Something is poisoned," Copland apparently wrote to Harold Clurman that

July. "When *I* speak of the unhappiness and maladjustment of a transition period I know I am talking about a reality," Clurman replied,

> but I always suspect that I am exaggerating a bit as far as the rest of the world goes which seems a little less sensitive to world currents, to moral atmosphere. But when you voice the same sense of difficulty I know that it is really universal, since you are not given to generalizations or to the expression of sentiments that you haven't experienced directly. And tho it is a little sad for me to hear you say "something is poisoned" (because I would like for you never to live anywhere but in the most perfect atmosphere) it cheers me a little too—or rather it gives me some sense of exaltation—that what I hope to fight with is so tangible, and the objectives I propose to myself so clear.[114]

Copland's objectives are perhaps less clear, partly because his side of the correspondence no longer exists. But in the early 1930s—under the sway of the proletarian avant-garde—what the composer had to fight with was tangible. Music was a weapon in the class struggle.

The proletarian avant-garde proved to be short-lived, however, and by 1934 the official Communist position on radical aesthetics had begun to shift. The vague stylistic consensus of American leftist composers soon began to change as well, particularly with regard to the use of folk music. The new Soviet policy of socialist realism promoted accessible modes of expression and sanctioned the use of traditional culture.[115] Under the aesthetic doctrine of Third Period proletarianism, folklore had been derided as insufficiently revolutionary in form and content; it was tied to the national circumstances of bourgeois oppression and thus unsuited to convey the international ideal of a socialist future. But with the notion of socialist realism and ascendance of the Popular Front, folk life, art, literature, and music were embraced by the Communist Party as the sincere expression of the people and an appropriate tool in the struggle against fascism.

Evidence of this change in attitude might be found in criticism of Copland's mass song "Into the Streets May First." Whereas in the early 1930s the goal of politicized music was to match revolutionary political content with a relatively simplified but resolutely modernist musical idiom, at mid-decade there was a growing concern with writing more appealing, nativist music invested in the historical imagination of American democracy. Thus the more adventurous style of "Into the Streets May First" and *Statements* fell out of favor almost as soon as they were written.[116] As with the interpretation of the Popular Front more generally, however, it is not necessarily the case that the American communist movement—much less the broader left-wing culture of the Popular Front—was entirely beholden to the dictates of Soviet policy. By 1935, various forces had aligned to promote American folklore as an emblem of progressive politics: the official Comintern policy and Communist Party aesthetics, certainly, but also a rising pan-Americanism, the programs of the New Deal, and the Popular Front as an encompassing left-wing social movement. All encouraged artists and intellectuals to draw on the resources of traditional American culture, such that by the second half of the 1930s, folk music was widely considered by leftist composers to be the authentic expression of the American people and a means of relating their concert works to national culture.[117] Copland, too, moved away from the militant idiom of the proletarian avant-garde and toward an accessible, folkloric style that was to bring his greatest success.

2 Expanding America

ALTHOUGH *Statements for Orchestra* was not finished until the summer of 1935, Copland had started the piece as early as 1932 while living at Yaddo, the estate of Katrina and Spencer Trask. In June he wrote to friend John Kirkpatrick that composition on the *Short Symphony* was "being upset by the fact that I've started still a newer [piece] and am working on the two simultaneously. The newest piece will have 4 or 5 short movements. I have one of these already."[1] Rough sketches for *Statements* dated "Yaddo, June '32" show Copland at work on the shape of the piece and drafting titles for its various movements. He continued to compose both the *Short Symphony* and *Statements* during the fall of 1932 while in Mexico, where he also first conceived *El Salón México*. The *Short Symphony* was eventually finished in 1933, and during the summer of 1934 Copland completed five of the six *Statements for Orchestra* as well as a two-piano version of *El Salón México*.[2]

These three works and their entwined compositional histories document Copland's refinement of a simplified musical idiom that emphasizes aural accessibility and draws on the melodic resources of traditional tunes. The *Short Symphony* follows a path first charted by the *Symphonic Ode* (1929) and *Piano Variations* (1930) leading toward the goal of structural unity. In *Statements* and *El Salón México*, however, Copland began to focus less on the formal structure of his music and more on its rhetorical effect. *Statements* still employs the dissonant, acerbic idiom of the proletarian avant-garde, but Copland hoped that the multimovement design and suggestive titles would make the piece more intelligible.[3] *El Salón México* takes a different tack. Like *Statements*, the form of the piece is episodic, but *El Salón México* accentuates melody. As the first of Copland's works to make extensive use of borrowed tunes, this one-movement orchestral fantasy captures the spirit of the eponymous dance hall by quoting Mexican songs and musical idioms. Notwithstanding the advanced compositional techniques applied to the basic source tunes, *El Salón México* retains an engaging melodic and rhythmic vitality that garnered immediate popular approbation. By 1938, only a year after its orchestral premiere, twenty-one American and foreign orchestras had performed the piece—a striking contrast to the performance histories of the *Short Symphony* and *Statements*.[4] In his memoirs, Copland proudly recalled that *El Salón México* had "started the ball rolling toward the popular success and wide audience I had only just begun to think about."[5] The piece was but the first in a series of vibrant, folkloric, accessible scores to achieve immediate acceptance and lasting renown.

It might seem surprising that Copland turned to the songs of Mexico before those of the United States, but he had long been aware that another America existed to the south. One introduction to the music of Latin America came through meeting the Brazilian composer Heitor Villa-Lobos during the early 1920s when both men were in Paris. Back in New York, Copland made the acquaintance of the Mexican composer and conductor Carlos Chávez in 1926, inaugurating an enduring friendship between the two.[6] Even though Copland remained always a tourist, easily enchanted by the exotic, the cultural and musical traditions of Latin America profoundly influenced his sense of musical nationalism. Through his personal friendships and institutional affiliations as much as through his musical borrowings, Copland encouraged the Americas to unite in the never-ending effort to find a musical identity apart from Europe. Thus his lifelong preoccupation with expressing an American identity in music was not limited to an interest in the United States and can be described as an engagement with musical pan-Americanism.

As a composer, conductor, and listener, Copland's experience with the music of the Americas can be considered as a network of individual affiliations leading to creative cultural exchange and as a manifestation of sociopolitical interests in Mexico and South America. These interests were heightened during the Great Depression and World War II in the United States thanks to the ideology of the Popular Front social movement and policies of the Roosevelt administration. First and foremost, Copland forged personal relationships and professional contacts with numerous composers. He visited Chávez in Mexico several times during the 1930s and 1940s. Touring South America on behalf of the United States government in the summer of 1941 and the fall of 1947, Copland met with leading musical figures in each country visited: he spent time with composers, conductors, journalists, and scholars, seeking to learn about local musics. Through such personal contacts and travels, Copland came to hear Latin American popular, folk, and concert musics—all of which influenced his style in terms of specific melodic material (more than one work quotes preexisting tunes) as well as characteristic rhythmic figures and timbral effects.

Moreover, the veneration of the Hispanic new world in the American progressive consciousness imbues those works connected to Latin American culture with greater cultural and ideological significance. In particular, *El Salón México* embraces the class-based politics of the Popular Front and the ideal of ethnic pluralism. *Danzón Cubano* (1942) emerges during the war years from the cultural politics of strategic relations between the Americas. These two works speak to a sense of shared destiny in times of crisis, to the vision of a panethnic American community united against the continuing cultural hegemony of the Old World and opposed to the destructive legacy of industrial modernism in the New.[7]

Copland, Chávez, and New World Nationalism

One of Copland's longest and most important musical friendships was with Carlos Chávez. The two met during Chávez's stay in New York City between the fall of 1926 and the spring of 1928; they seem to have quickly recognized in each other similar compositional and professional goals.[8] Copland and Chávez both aspired to write music that was recognizably American, and each assimilated distinct musical characteristics from his respective culture into concert compositions. The jazzy rhythms and harmonies in *Music for the Theatre* (1925) and the Piano Concerto (1926) reveal Copland's interest in the popular music of New York City, whereas Chávez drew on Aztec subjects and indigenous Mexican music in such works as *Los Cuatro Soles* (1924) and *Caballos de Vapor [H.P.]* (1926–32). Active in New York's contemporary music scene, the two composers also displayed remarkable professional acumen even in their youth and quickly focused on the problem of institutional support for new music. They gradually assumed positions of leadership within the musical establishment, using consequent opportunities to promote each other's work. Chávez performed his Third Piano Sonata, dedicated to Copland, in a concert organized by Copland in April 1928, for example; the next month Copland published an article in the *New Republic* hailing Chávez as "as one of the few American musicians" who was "more than a reflection of Europe."[9]

When Chávez left New York in 1928 to become director of two leading musical institutions in his native country, the Orquesta Sinfónica de México (OSM) and the Conservatorio Nacional de México, he began to champion Copland's music in Mexico. Chávez immediately invited Copland to visit, promising a performance by the OSM of Copland's Piano Concerto with the composer as soloist. Although Copland acknowledged "that heaven and earth were being moved to bring me to Mexico City," he declined to visit in 1928, claiming that work on the *Symphonic Ode* prevented the trip. "I am like a woman who is pregnant," he wrote, who "dares not travel for fear it would endanger the life of her child."[10] (Instead of the Piano Concerto, Chávez conducted Copland's *Music for the Theatre* with the Orquesta Sinfónica.) For his part, Copland continued to program pieces by Chávez, as well as works by other Latin American composers. In 1932, Copland did travel to Mexico, where Chávez led the first-ever program devoted solely to Copland's music.

The composers kept abreast of each other's latest works, sending scores and records through the mail, and a copious correspondence documents their life-long friendship. "I can't tell you how happy it made me to receive your very affectionate letter," Copland wrote to Chávez in August 1930. "Sometimes I could not help feeling that you had become so absorbed in your work in Mexico that you forgot me and all the friends you have here. But now I see it is not true—now I see you do miss me and the rest, which makes me very glad. Your letter made me feel very close to you, as if all the time we were separated was very little." That such sentiment is exceedingly rare in Copland's letters reveals just how close Copland and Chávez felt to one another. "I have a great desire to see you again," Copland continued, "and letters are such poor substitutes."[11]

Copland regarded Chávez's music from the 1920s as a prime example of modern nationalist composition. He admired the ways in which Chávez integrated folk music and a contemporary compositional idiom, melding techniques associated with musical modernism and Mexican Indian music. There was a natural overlap between these apparently disparate musics insofar as Chávez credited his apparently modernist modal melodies, rhythmic ostinati, irregular meters, and complex cross-rhythms to indigenous Mexican sources. Writing about his friend in the *New Republic*, Copland noted that "no other composer who has used folk material has more successfully solved the problem of its complete amalgamation into an art form." He lauded Chávez's ability to evoke indigenous music without overt quotation and "rethink the [Indian] material so that only its essence remained."[12] Thus Chávez seemed to have satisfied Copland's own desire to write modern music that was identifiably American. Chávez's music, Copland continued, "exemplifies the complete overthrow of nineteenth-century Germanic ideals which tyrannized over music for more than a hundred years," offering "the first authentic signs of a new world with its own new music."[13]

Copland also respected the influence Chávez wielded in Mexico and envied his opportunities to connect with an audience. Forecasting the stance of his 1939 autobiographical sketch and even foreshadowing its language, Copland lamented in a 1933 letter to Chávez that "when I was in Mexico I was a little envious of the opportunity you had to serve your country in a musical way. Here in the U.S.A. we composers have no possibility of directing the musical affairs of the nation—on the contrary, since my return, I have the impression that more and more we are writing in a vacuum. There seems to me less than ever a real rapport between the public and the composers and of course that is a very unhealthy state of affairs."[14] Copland suggested that Chávez's role as head of the department of fine arts in the Mexican government could have a salutary effect on his composing. "For me your work as *Jefe de Bellas Artes* is a very important way of creating an audience, and being in contact with an audience. When one has done that," Copland concluded, "one can compose with real joy."[15] Both Copland and Chávez wrote passionately about the need for music to be a part of life and for the composer to have contact through music with his community. In a 1938 article for *Modern Music*, for example, Chávez explained that "the composer should be integrated into the musical life of the present, and should have in himself a full sense of reality about his work and about the meaning it will have for the public at whom it is directed."[16] Copland's own success in the later 1930s with scores such as *El Salón México* and *Billy the Kid* led him "to believe that the American composer is destined to play a more commanding role in the musical future of his own country."[17] This desire for a connection between composer and audience—a connection Copland felt that Chávez had successfully established in Mexico—undoubtedly informed Copland's development of a folk-based, accessible style, appropriately realized first in *El Salón México*.

If Copland's view of the relationship between composer and audience was influenced by Chávez, his conscious appropriation of Latin American folk and popular music owed much to the example of another Mexican composer, Silvestre Revueltas. Copland first met Revueltas in Mexico when the latter was assistant conductor of the Orquesta Sinfónica de México. Chávez and Revueltas had an uneasy friendship that apparently dissolved around 1935, but Copland did not choose sides, writing enthusiastically about both composers' music in a 1937 article for the *New York Times*. Chávez was musically in touch with Mexico's pre-Columbian Indian culture, Copland explained, whereas Revueltas's style was based "more directly on actual tunes that originated from popular Mexican music." Copland further noted that "the music of Chávez is strong, stark and lacking in any exterior colorfulness; Revueltas's music, by comparison, is derived from the more usual everyday side of Mexican life. It is often highly spiced, like Mexican food itself. It is full of whims and sudden quirks of fancy and leaves one with a sense of the abundance and vitality of life."[18]

At a 1944 concert in Mexico City, Copland heard Chávez and the Orquesta in a performance of Revueltas's *Ventanas*. It was "very amusing to listen to—chock full of orchestral color—but the form isn't very good," Copland observed. Revueltas "was like a modern painter who throws marvelous daubs of color on canvas that practically takes your eye out," but the effect "doesn't add up."[19] Despite this critique, in *El Salón México* and successive pieces Copland, like Revueltas, drew inspiration from contemporary Mexican folk music and opted himself for a patchwork, sectional form delineated by the tunes themselves. Thus in the nature of melodic materials and formal structures, Copland's accessible music sounds reminiscent of—and influenced by—Reveultas's compositional style.[20]

The Communitarian Vision of El Salón México

Copland's friendships with Chávez and Reveultas were not his only point of contact with Mexican music and culture during this period. In the midst of the Great Depression, many artists and intellectuals in Copland's circle responded to the economic and cultural crisis by mounting a critique of industrial capitalism and envisioning a holistic modern community grounded in folk culture. Latin America, and especially Mexico, was widely seen as unspoiled terrain spiritually bound through its pre-Columbian history to an aboriginal American character. To many progressives, including Waldo Frank, who had long decried the cultural dependence of the United States on Europe, Mexico represented a uniquely American sensibility and so provided a means to appraise the cultural effects of liberal capitalism. Prominent progressive authors like Carleton Beals and Stuart Chase construed Mexican folk life as an alternative to contemporary industrial society, suggesting that in Mexico, people enjoyed the kind of aesthetic existence described by John Dewey in his influential treatise, *Art as Experience* (1934). In keeping with the progressive tradition, Dewey directed his philosophy toward the restoration of "continuity between the refined and intensified forms of experience that are works of art and the everyday events, doings, and sufferings that are universally recognized to constitute experience."[21] He envisaged the union of person and place, art and life, individual and community. For Frank, Chase, and Dewey, the simple beauty they found in Mexican culture seemed the fulfillment of this organicist vision.

Explicit in the idealization of Mexican culture was the censure of capitalist, industrial society. Stuart Chase's 1931 best-selling study, *Mexico: A Study of Two Americas*, advanced this strain of progressive social criticism.[22] Focusing on the rural village of Tepoztlán, Chase celebrates Mexican folk culture and, in the process, enumerates the shortcomings of life in the United States.[23] He concludes with advice to the people of Middletown, U.S.A. (the community at the center of Robert and Helen Lynd's seminal sociological study of 1929), that points out the aesthetic limitations of capitalist, bourgeois life.[24] Whereas bourgeois culture in the United States prized efficiency, mass production, and endless consumption, the Mexican way of life was seen as valuing leisure, handicrafts, and self-sufficiency. As a result, Chase believed that Mexico did not suffer the psychic toll of modernism. "In Tepoztlán," he asserted, "a Freudian complex is unthinkable."[25]

Many writers portrayed life in Mexico as a study in social harmony and individual fulfillment, a stark contrast to the alienation perceived as endemic to modern American life. Reporting in *Modern Music*, for instance, Luis Sandi characterized Mexican life as "rather art than industry, rather the expression of emotions than the satisfaction of needs." He described a symbiotic relationship among the individual, his environment, and society. "The landscape lives in each man," Sandi wrote, "the landscape in all its complexity: mountains lonely on a strangely beautiful sky, cacti and ferns, rocks and plateaus, the gleaming altars in churches of beautifully worked rose-colored stone, slavery, and a modern socialist organization of workers."[26] Waldo Frank envied Mexican culture as having "a deep sense of destiny and the persistent strain of the mystic tradition." Urging closer contact between North and South America, he maintained that "if we knew these Americans, we should know more of ourselves; for they have the heart of the matter—the creating of an American world that shall be more than the grave of Europe. This is the essence of our wholeness with them."[27]

This romantic view of Mexican or Indian culture owes to a basic stereotype of the primitive, of native peoples connected to nature by a numinous bond and free from the corrupting knowledge of modernity.[28] In the nineteenth century, this stereotype was used to rationalize the displacement of indigenous communities and the destruction of their supposedly crude cultures. But in the 1930s and 1940s, Chase and other like-minded intellectuals no longer criticized Native Americans as hopelessly naïve or dangerously uncivilized; rather, rural peoples were valorized as "machineless men," free from the tyranny of clocks, the market economy, and mechanized civiliza-tion.[29] The presence of a vital, rural Indian culture was an essential part of Mexico's appeal and of its American identity. Noting that "no more than fifty Spaniards ever settled in Tepoztlán," Chase suggests that "Tepoztlán is far more American than Middletown, when all is said and done, but it is alien to everything we regard as typically 'American.'" And advocating a renewed appreciation of "the art of living," Chase advises busy, middle-class Middle-towners that "there are certain features of the early American way of life as typified in Mexico which, if you could acquire them, would make you more human and more happy."[30]

Waldo Frank celebrated the aesthetic quality of Mexican life as inherently musical. "Music is so deep in Mexico," he wrote in *America Hispana*, "that even the builded and carved stones of the churches flow from their plastic bonds into the waves of song."[31] He found in Mexico a "tragic mood" that music both captured and transcended. Like Chase and Sandi, Frank admired Mexican culture as having a mystical connection between past and present, nature and civilization. "In a world of unwieldy earth like Mexico, whose his-tory for many hundred years has been bondage and body-betrayal, the breath of music is the release of spirit," an unburdening of the soul. "To understand the music of Mexico's folk," he concluded, "one must first know the essential element that makes it: the will of Mexico to be free of its death and of beauty that flowers in death: the will of Mexico to enjoy its earth, and to *breathe*."[32] In rural Mexican culture, Frank thought he had discovered an aesthetic com-munity in which art forged cross-cultural and transhistorical continuities that then mitigated the alienating effects of life in the modern world.

Given the glorification of Mexico in the American progressive conscious-ness, it is not surprising that Copland was eager to visit and, once he had, was repeatedly drawn back. His first trip in 1932 was prompted most imme-diately by an invitation from Carlos Chávez, but was also representative of pilgrimages made in the 1930s by so many progressive intellectuals, including Dewey, Frank, and Chase.[33] Copland's 1932 sojourn lasted four months, split equally between Mexico City and Tlalpam.[34] He was especially enamored of such rural towns as Xochimilco, which he described as "an Indian village in exactly the same state it was before Columbus," and Cuernavaca, "a sort of week-end place like Atlantic City is for Americans" that was still "extremely Mexican."[35]

Copland found himself sympathetic to Mexican culture and profoundly moved by his experiences, writing in 1932 to Virgil Thomson with a mixture of sincere admiration and unmistakable condescension.

Mexico has turned out even grander than I expected—and I expected pretty grand things. The best is the people—there's nothing remotely like them in Europe. They are really the "people"—nothing in them is striving to be bourgeois. In their overalls and bare feet they are not only poetic but positively "émouvant" [moving].[36]

He was also fascinated by the contrasts in Mexico between rural and urban, ancient and modern, economic poverty and cultural wealth. As he wrote to his parents about Chapultepec: "It's the first city I've ever been in where it seems quite the regular thing for the poorer classes to go around bare-footed, and this on the busiest streets where there are the most modern office buildings."[37] And to Mary Lescaze, Copland described his stay in Mexico as "a rich time."

Outwardly nothing happened and inwardly all was calm. Yet I'm left with the impression of having had an enriching experience. It comes, no doubt, from the nature of the country and the people. Europe now seems conventional to me by comparison. Mexico offers something fresh and pure and wholesome—a quality which is deeply unconventionalized.[38]

Crediting such freshness to Mexico's "Indian background," Copland concluded that "I must be something of an Indian myself or how else explain the sympathetic chord" struck within him. What Copland seemed to find in Mexico and credit to its Indian heritage was his ideal of America itself as a world apart from the oppressive influence of European culture and an alternative to the fragmented reality of industrial modernism.

His 1932 visit prompted a musical response, namely the orchestral tone poem *El Salón México*. The piece was inspired by a dance hall in Mexico City of the same name, known to locals as "El Marro"—a policeman's nightstick. "As with a hit of such a stick," writes one historian of Mexican dance, so "one was hit with a strong smell of sweat at the entrance" to the *Salón*. The club was popular with foreign visitors, who "would be seen at 'El Marro' to experiment in the flesh with how the 'chusma' [the lower class] sought entertainment," and patrons danced the waltz, fox trot, and the *paso doble*, as well as the traditional *danzón* until the early morning hours.[39] A mix of people frequented the hall, "from fruit vendors and merchants . . . renowned mobsters and occasional petty thieves" to politicians and artists, "the former to certify their 'bread-and-circus' policies, the latter to see . . . murals celebrating folk dance purportedly executed by Diego Rivera."[40]

Copland's 1939 published description of *El Salón México* echoes the private sentiments expressed in his correspondence with Thomson and Lescaze.

Recalling his visit to the actual dance hall in Mexico City, Copland detailed a colorful scene.

> A sign on the wall of the dance hall read: "Please don't throw lighted cigarette butts on the floor so the ladies don't burn their feet." A guard, stationed at the bottom of the steps leading to the three halls, would nonchalantly frisk you as you started up the stairs to be sure you had checked all your "artillery" at the door and to collect the 1 peso charged for admittance. . . . When the dance hall closed at 5 a.m., it hardly seemed worthwhile to some of the overalled patrons to travel all the way home, so they curled themselves up on chairs around the walls for a quick two-hour snooze before going to a seven o'clock job in the morning.[41]

He seemed genuinely captivated by the lack of pretension he felt in Mexico, though he could not entirely lose the mien of an urban sophisticate (hence the telling slip into French when writing to Thomson). Moreover, his curious romanticization of poverty reveals a somewhat awkward attempt to align himself with the antibourgeois perspective of the landless farmers in rural villages and working-class clientele of the urban dance hall. He further explained that his *El Salón México* was intended to capture the sense of "a really live contact with the Mexican *peuple*—the electric sense one sometimes gets in far-off places, of suddenly knowing the essence of a people—their humanity, their separate shyness, their dignity and unique charm."[42]

Copland's insistent reference to "the people" as the inspiration and audience for his music resonates with Kenneth Burke's 1935 suggestion that the proletarian figure of the worker be subsumed by the more inclusive symbol of the people in the aesthetic philosophy of politically aligned artists.[43] A leading literary theorist engaged in Marxist criticism during the 1930s, Burke was a part of the Popular Front social movement but not the Communist Party. His controversial and influential address before the first American Writers' Congress in April of 1935 (an assembly that succeeded the John Reed Clubs) anticipated the coming rhetorical and political shift in Communist Party rhetoric away from militant proletarianism and toward the more inclusive cultural front. "The symbol I should plead for," Burke explained, "as more basic, more of an ideal incentive, than that of the worker, is that of the 'the people.'"[44] This would be more in keeping with an American democratic tradition, he argued, and claim "the tactical advantage of pointing more definitely in the direction of unity."[45]

Burke was not interested in the formation of party doctrine but in the political alignment of the artist and its aesthetic expression. Explicit propaganda was "the work of the pamphleteer and political organizer," whereas the writer's contribution was "implicit" yet no less political. "If [the writer] shows a keen interest in every manifestation of our cultural development," Burke argued,

> and at the same time gives a clear indication as to where his sympathies lie, this seems to me the most effective long-pull contribution to propaganda he can make. For he thus indirectly links his cause with the kinds of intellectual and emotional engrossment that are generally admired. . . . Reduced to a precept, the formula would run: Let one encompass as many desirable features of our cultural heritage as possible—and let him make sure that his political alignment figures prominently among them. . . . And I am suggesting that an approach based upon the positive symbol of "the people," rather than upon the negative symbol of "the worker," makes more naturally for this kind of identification whereby one's political alignment is fused with broader cultural elements.[46]

As a symbol, the people could be used to "borrow the advantages of nationalist conditioning," meaning an Americanist, democratic sentiment, and "combat the forces that hide their class prerogatives behind a communal ideology." Burke's rhetorical sleight of hand does not so much discard the worker in favor of the people as elide these two symbols to infuse populist rhetoric with leftist political content.[47] Articulating a form of radical populism, Burke claimed that nationalism, Americanism, and cultural myths all had the potential to serve the revolutionary goals of social democracy. Therefore the American cultural heritage (both north and south of the Rio Grande) could be productively appropriated by a left-wing political ideology committed to "the ultimate *classless* feature which the revolution would bring about."[48]

The people become a presence in *El Salón México* through the use of traditional songs that Copland found in two published collections: *Cancionero Mexicano*, compiled by American Frances Toor, and the more scholarly *El Folklore y la Musica Mexicana*, edited by Ruben M. Campos.[49] Regardless of whether the songs in these volumes and in *El Salón México* might reasonably be considered examples of Mexican folk music, Copland certainly felt that they were representative of the people; he described his borrowed tunes as both "popular Mexican melodies" and "folk material."[50] Through the use of Mexican songs as well as popular dance-hall idioms, *El Salón México* musically enacts a progressive vision of community, evoking the grit and grime of an urban metropolis while drawing melodic material from traditional tunes, thereby linking the proletariat to the people. And so the Mexican people, encompassing both a mythical folk culture and modern proletariat, served for Copland as an idol in the veneration of a precapitalist naïveté, constructed in opposition to the modern industrial social order.[51] His imaginative association with and determined invocation of the people—and particularly of an identifiably ethnic, working-class population—offered a creative solution to the social fragmentation of modernism and a musical realization of the Popular Front agenda, with its focus on ethnic pluralism and cross-class solidarity.[52]

The fusion of disparate elements in *El Salón México*—of borrowed tunes and popular idioms, rural and urban experiences, and even of the distinct melodies themselves—is accomplished in part through the Popular Front trope of the grotesque. Drawing on Burke's literary theory, Michael Denning interprets the grotesque as the aesthetic mode best suited to expressing the contradictions of Depression-era culture.[53] Burke describes the grotesque as "planned incongruity . . . wherein the perception of discordancies is cultivated without smile or laughter."[54] He finds in Marx's realignment of class identification through international solidarity just such a "gargoyle element," a challenge to established values.[55] The disturbing juxtaposition of the grotesque is exemplified by one of Diego Rivera's illustrations from *Mexico: A Study of Two Americas* (see fig. 2.1). Rivera's drawing contrasts rural and urban while offering little hope for reconciliation. In the wake of the speeding motorcar, with its well dressed, amorous passengers, the faceless men walking on the side of the road appear no different from the beasts of burden in the distance; the hunched figures in the other car are simply cargo, and all of the men travel with goods—the products that mark the people as commodities themselves. The image offers a radical critique that parallels the argument of Chase's book, which details the ravages of industrialization on the Mexican people and their way of life. A humorless discordance between cityscape and landscape, civilization and desolation, human and natural is also apparent in a striking photograph of Copland walking along a Mexican road, nattily dressed in coat and tie (see fig. 2.2).

Such striking juxtapositions also characterize *El Salón México*. The apparent humor in the piece—distracted trumpet fanfares, drunken harmonies, and pervasive distortions of the tunes—exemplifies a proletarian grotesque that wrenches social realism into the more compelling world of cultural revolution. "Humor tends to be conservative," Burke observed, whereas "the grotesque tends to be revolutionary."[56] Were the borrowed tunes quoted in a more straightforward, uninflected manner, *El Salón México* might evoke a sentimental, reactionary longing for what the working-class, dance-hall audience had lost in the cultural transition from rural communities to urban industrialism. But, as Raymond Williams has noted, "the 'folk' emphasis, when offered as evidence of a repressed popular tradition, could move read-

FIGURE 2.1. Diego Rivera, line drawing from Stuart Chase, *Mexico: A Study of Two Americas* (1931)

ily towards socialist and other radical and revolutionary tendencies." *El Salón México* captures the "vitality of the naïve" as evidence not of a reactionary tendency or projected return to an imagined past, but "as witness of the new kinds of art which a popular revolution would release."[57] The fragmentation and deformation of these tunes mirror the distortion of the modern, capitalist social order, but *El Salón México* simultaneously projects a vision of utopian solidarity. The heterogeneous surface of the music suggests a discontinuity between pre-capitalist folk culture and industrial modernism while anticipating a symbolic reconciliation of that disconnect within the musical whole.

Within the first few minutes of *El Salón México*, various affective modes emerge one after another without preparation or transition. Frequent shifts

FIGURE 2.2. Copland walking along a Mexican road, c. 1930s

in mood highlight the discontinuous musical surface and bring to the fore a more fundamental distinction between the genres of traditional song and orchestral music. At the same time, however, the piece never fails to cohere. *El Salón México* begins with a brash, *tutti* opening based on the initial ascent of "El Palo Verde" that drives toward a *sforzando* flourish. The texture then abruptly thins to an unruly accompaniment figure composed of errant dissonances in the bassoons and trombone (ex. 2.1). Staggering, syncopated rhythms belie an underlying tonic to dominant motion and vacate any sense of forward momentum created by the introductory flourish. The bare accompaniment is interrupted by an improvisatory sounding trumpet solo based on the triadic, arching melody of "La Jesusita," a love song associated with supporters of the Mexican revolution.[58] A showy clarinet cadenza closes the melodic paraphrase before the entire sequence—bassoons, followed by solo trumpet, then clarinet cadenza—is repeated.

The timpani then manage to straighten out the tonic-dominant oscillation, and a new melody, "El Mosco," enters three measures before R 5. The rhythm remains somewhat unsettled, featuring unexpected rests and a sporadic accompaniment. Although the tune in its original source is marked *appassionato* and

EXAMPLE 2.1. *El Salón México*, opening trumpet fanfare (based on "La Jesusita") and clarinet cadenza, R 2–3

Copland himself indicates *espressivo*, the uneven groups of two and three beats coupled with the wry orchestration for bass clarinet and bassoon annul the sentimental and imbue "El Mosco" with a sense of urbane irony.[59]

Two more tunes follow on the heels of "El Mosco." At R 7 a variant of "El Palo Verde," combining the arpeggiated ascent of the first strain with the tune of the second, acquires gentle lilt thanks to alternating meters of 6/8 and 3/4, a metric play characteristic of the Mexican *son*. Next Copland gives "El Mosquito" a lush, romantic setting in the violins above a subtle, pulsing rhythmic accompaniment that vacillates between groups of two and three (ex. 2.2).[60] The subtle chromatic turns in the melody evoke a sense of wistful longing and the

EXAMPLE 2.2. *El Salón México*, "El Mosquito," R 8

"desperate hope" Waldo Frank considered characteristic of Mexican folk song. "Even when it is gay," he wrote of Mexican music, "it has a falling cadence: and its sensual sweetness is like the ebb of blood."[61] Before the tune is allowed to fade away, however, it is interrupted by the insistent pounding of the timpani, with hard sticks, and brass. A quick crescendo leads to a recall of the exuberant opening fanfare (R 11), now scored more delicately for oboes. Dissonant clusters and a kinetic energy push toward an aggressive statement of "El Palo Verde" at R 15, the once jaunty, staccato tune now transformed by heavy accents.

Throughout, the Mexican songs are never presented as complete unto themselves. Instead, they are refracted through a kaleidoscopic lens that distorts the traditional melodies. Copland abstracts his borrowed tunes so thoroughly that some passages sound more akin to the *Short Symphony* than other folk-based works from the late 1930s and 1940s. Perhaps such moments inspired the critic Warren Storey Smith to hear in *El Salón México* the "atmosphere of tenseness and unrest that is to be found in Mexico as in so many other places on this unhappy planet."[62] In the middle section of *El Salón México* the languorous "Corrido de Rivera" and "Corrido de Lucio" as well as the syncopated "El Malacate" are never given the opportunity to establish discrete melodic profiles, and their primary interest remains rhythmic. The persistent cross-phrasing and shifting between groups of two and three create a rhythmic vitality that eventually propels the disjointed melodic texture through a return of earlier material and on to a stunning *tutti* finish.

The aesthetic contradictions showcased by the grotesque reveal the social tensions of industrial capitalism as the traditional tunes are exploited and distorted, while at the same time a utopian ideal imaginatively restores the cultural continuity of rural and urban communities, of folk music and the urban dance hall, within the musical whole. *El Salón México* reflects the ideology of the Popular Front in its symbolic allegiance to a "pan-ethnic Americanism,"[63] sympathy with working-class ethnic culture, and radically inflected populism. As a symbolic act, the music forges an identification between otherwise distant cultures: traditional and modern, rural peasants and the urban proletariat, Americans of all nationalities and ethnicities. Hardly an example of agitprop, *El Salón México* nonetheless demonstrates that Copland's bid for popular acceptance owes in part to the tradition of progressive social reform and the class-based labor politics of the Popular Front. But, like agitprop, it loses its critical edge when released from its ideological context, when the revolutionary vision of solidarity fades into a sentimental embrace of the exotic.

Inter-Americanism and Danzón Cubano

In the context of World War II, the informal relationships that progressive artists and intellectuals in the United States established with their Latin American colleagues acquired greater political significance as cultural exchange found governmental support in the name of hemispheric unity and security. Henry A. Wallace, then secretary of agriculture, explained in 1939 that "the events of Europe and Asia have waked us up." The challenge, as he saw it, was "to build here in this hemisphere a new culture which is neither Latin American nor North American but genuinely inter-American."[64] In accepting the nomination for vice president, Wallace again articulated the sense of a shared destiny. The world war seemed in part a struggle "to prevent the people of North and South America from developing their resources without paying tribute to Europe and without being victims of European secret police serving a self-appointed master race."[65] As Axis and Allied nations fought for the economic, political, and cultural allegiance of the Americas, inter-American relations were intended to counteract German and Italian propaganda as well as to prevent the Nazis from establishing a commercial stronghold on this side of the Atlantic.

Copland was a natural choice to participate in government programs for cultural exchange, as he had already established himself as a leading figure in

American musical life and had ties to Mexico. In 1940 he was appointed to the Advisory Committee on Music within the Department of State Division of Cultural Relations.[66] The Division worked in conjunction with another, separate organization headed by Nelson Rockefeller, originally formed in August 1940 by President Roosevelt as the Office for Coordination of Commercial and Cultural Relations between the American Republics (OCCCRBAR). This office, which fell under the aegis of the Council of National Defense, was renamed in July 1941 as the Office of the Coordinator of Inter-American Affairs (OCIAA) in the office of the president; it was later renamed again (in 1945) as the Office of Inter-American Affairs (OIAA) and was dissolved in 1946. In every guise, Rockefeller's organization was responsible for ensuring strong political and economic ties to Latin America and using cultural diplomacy to create political alliances. The Office for Coordination of Commercial and Cultural Relations was funded directly by the Executive Branch; consequently, it enjoyed far greater support than the State Department's Division of Cultural Relations, which relied on congressional funding.[67] Within the OCIAA Copland was appointed to the Committee for Inter-American Artistic and Intellectual Relations, headed by Henry Allen Moe, and chaired the U.S. group for Latin American music.

Whereas both the State Department Division of Cultural Relations and Rockefeller's agency served to foster inter-American relations, the Division of Cultural Relations was to focus on long-term programs, Rockefeller's office on more immediate initiatives. The acting chief of the Division of Cultural Relations, Edward G. Trueblood, attempted to distinguish these two entities and their programs in a letter to Copland relaying news of the composer's appointment to the State Department's Advisory Committee on Music. "The functions of this committee will supplement those of the music committee appointed by Mr. Nelson Rockefeller," Trueblood explained.

> Mr. Rockefeller's committee, it is planned, will give attention to specific and concrete problems of immediate concern while it is envisaged that the Advisory Committee on Music will devote its activities to research and long term development of musical relations with the other nations of the hemisphere. Constant consultation on matters relating to the work of these committees will be maintained between Mr. Rockefeller's office and the Department of State to avoid any overlapping.[68]

As confusing as these various administrative structures may have been (or still be), the result was that Copland served on committees under the dominion of two powerful government entities—the Department of State and the Executive Office.

In 1941 both the State Department and the OCCCRBAR cooperated to send Copland on a mission to explore the musical life of the Americas, introduce Latin American audiences to contemporary North American music, and investigate opportunities for further musical exchange. The Music Advisory Committee of the Division proposed the visit in November of 1940, then contacted Henry Allen Moe of the Committee for Inter-American Artistic and Intellectual Relations, in Rockefeller's office, about financing the trip.[69] Moe supported the proposal and wrote to Copland in June 1941. "As grantee of this Committee," Moe explained, Copland was "in no sense . . . a government employee" nor "a representative of the United States Government," although Moe noted "it is inevitable that you will be regarded in Latin America as representative of the United States and of your profession; and this is what we desire."[70] The visit was obviously meant to have ramifications beyond the purely musical, and more than once Copland used letterhead reading "Council of National Defense" in making arrangements for his lectures and concerts, foregrounding the serious nature of programs for cultural exchange. The distinctions between education and propaganda, between cultural exchange and strategic alliance, began to blur as the United States pursued the project of hemispheric unity.

Copland toured Latin and South America from August 19 to December 13, 1941.[71] In sum, he visited nine countries, made twenty-five public appearances, including three concert performances as a pianist, met sixty-five composers, eight musicologists, and as many conductors. His experiences are documented in a travel diary that details encounters with various composers, students, and scholars, impressions of concert programs and orchestras, reactions of audiences to his lectures, and general thoughts about the state of musical life in the countries he visited. His observations served as the basis for a required report to Moe's Committee and an article published in *Modern Music* titled "The Composers of South America."[72]

According to these accounts, Copland found that only Mexico and Brazil possessed "a distinctive school of creative musicians."[73] Brazilian composers were particularly successful in writing music "easily distinguishable from the European model" thanks to the use of folk song in their concert works. "This rich source material," he explained, "in combination with the Brazilian temperament—highly romantic, abundant, uncritical, uninhibited—gives their music more 'face' than that of any other group of composers in South America."[74] The most notable composer in Brazil, with whom Copland had been specifically directed to meet, was Heitor Villa-Lobos. Copland and Villa-Lobos had first met in 1923 but became acquainted only during this 1941 visit. The Committee sponsoring Copland's trip hoped that Villa-Lobos could be convinced to visit the United States. In his official report, however, Copland questioned "whether it would be wise to attempt to bring him here in any official capacity. . . . At best he would be a difficult fellow to manage. He seems to be a rare combination of worldly-wise and naïve outlook—can easily become *entêté* [stubborn]—likes to shock by sudden flat statements contrary to what you would expect him to say."[75] Copland found Villa-Lobos to be "extremely cordial" as well as "brutally frank" but was seemingly unnerved by the Brazilian's unpredictable temperament.[76]

Moreover, Copland was generally unimpressed by Villa-Lobos's music, which he dismissed as having "one outstanding quality—abundance."[77] This biting comment speaks to not only the number of compositions but also the music's formal and melodic largess. Villa-Lobos's style was "enormously picturesque at times," Copland thought, "free of prejudices, full of rhythmic vitality" but "sometimes cheap and vulgar . . . loosely thrown together in a inextricable mélange." The music was "full to the brim of temperament—a temperament that is profoundly Brazilian, I imagine—a temperament that is show-offish and not without some bluff thrown in."[78] Of course such criticisms reveal as much about Copland's compositional aesthetic as about Villa-Lobos's style and technique. Copland generally distrusted any composer who seemed an instinctive melodist, and even after he himself began to focus more on melody in such works as *El Salón México*, he still prized formal lucidity. Criticizing Villa-Lobos for a perceived lack of critical distance and aesthetic objectivity, Copland continued to prefer the taut lines and sparse textures of music by Chávez.

Despite his apparent interest in Brazilian folk music, Copland returned from his trip inspired to use not the music of Brazil but of Cuba. He had first visited the island in the spring of 1941—a short visit spent writing *Our New Music* and the Piano Sonata. At the end of his South American journey in December 1941, Copland returned to Cuba for ten days. Then as now, the United States had a particularly difficult relationship with Cuba that involved questions of economic and political sovereignty. The United States had helped Cuba win independence from Spain in 1899, then insisted that the new constitution adopt the Platt Amendment, which guaranteed the United States rights to intervene in Cuban affairs and to station military forces on Cuban soil. According to the progressive author Carleton Beals, this arrangement had forced Cuba into perpetual debt and allowed the United States to secure the dominion of a fascist government, led by the dictator Gerardo Machado.

Beals pointed out the apparent hypocrisy of the U.S. position in his popular Depression-era study, *The Crime of Cuba* (1933), which featured illustrations by well-known photographer Walker Evans. Referring to the despotic government under Machado, Beals demanded: "What right have we to get excised about Hitler, when we helped to maintain in Cuba, a protectorate at our very doorstep, a government which has committed far greater crimes than those which have occurred in Germany?"[79]

Machado was overthrown in the Revolution of 1933 and replaced by Carlos Manuel de Céspedes, whose rule was undermined by the impression that he had been handpicked by the United States. Eventually military leader Fulgencio Batista claimed power, then chose a succession of presidents to serve under his direction before assuming the presidency himself in 1940. In the midst of the political turmoil, progressive critics voiced opposition to the Platt Amendment (abrogated by Roosevelt in May 1934 as part of the "Good Neighbor" policy) and support for Cuban sovereignty. Beals himself, reacting to the governmental upheaval and the succession of leaders in Cuba, concluded that whatever government might be installed, its legitimacy could be won only through tackling the issues "of absentee ownership by American capital, the reinstating of the rural population on land and the re-creating of decent living standards for the Cuban people."[80] These reforms were similar to the goals of the Mexican Revolution, which Beals had applauded in previous writings.[81] In 1940, under Batista's rule, a new constitution was adopted and some of these progressive reforms instituted. Such basic rights as that of speech and assembly were guaranteed, as were a standard forty-hour work week, minimum wage, and social security.[82]

With the election of Batista as president, the Communist Party acquired a measure of institutional power, particularly in the ministry of labor, because the Communists had been part of the victorious coalition.[83] Despite continued criticism from the left-leaning American press (most notably the *New Republic*), who saw Batista as a virtual dictator, the Batista government seemed to many to be Cuba's best hope for secure self-rule and stable relations with the United States. Batista also showed unwavering support for the United States during World War II, allowing new military installations to be built on Cuban soil and fighting against Axis influence. Given the uneasy relations between the two nations as well as the island's unique strategic position, programs for cultural exchange between the United States and Cuba acquired special significance during the war years.

As a composer and a cultural ambassador to Cuba, Copland was primarily interested in Cuban musical life. He had made an effort to listen to local music during his first visit in April 1941, and wrote to Leonard Bernstein with an exuberant report of his musical activities.

Dear L

Naturally, I missed your broadcast because I was out at the Beach getting sun tan. Isn't that a good excuse? One works in the morning, beaches in the afternoon, and listens to Cuban music at night. Perfect program, no? Oh, yes, and I mustn't forget my Spanish lessons—excellent teacher, still not out of high-school!

I wish you were here to share the music with me. I have a slightly frustrated feeling in not being able to discuss it with anyone, and a sinking feeling that no one but you and I would think it so much fun. Anyway, I'm bringing back a few records, but they are only analogous to Guy Lombardo versions of the real thing. I've sat for hours on end in 5¢ a dance joints, listening. Finally the band in one place got the idea, and invited me up to the band platform. "Usted musico?" *Yes*, says I. What a music factory it is! Thirteen black men and me—quite a piquant scene. The thing I like most is the quality of voice when the Negroes sing down here. It does things to me—it's so sweet and moving. And just think, no serious Cuban composer is using any of this. It's awful tempting, but I'll try to control myself.[84]

During his second visit in December 1941, Copland became acquainted with two young Cuban composers, José Ardévol and Gilberto Valdés. Both showed promise, according to Copland's report, in which he also noted that Valdés was "the only example of a Cuban composer working with Cuban folk material that I know. He ought to be the Gershwin of Cuba, but he lacks the technical equipment and a sufficient self-critical faculty."[85] Copland spent time studying scores by contemporary composers and listening to Cuban popular music, even visiting a local dance hall in Havana as he had done in Mexico City some years earlier.[86] And, as before, he returned from his visit with ideas for a musical portrait. Finally giving in to the temptation of Cuban dance music, Copland completed the two-piano work *Danzón Cubano* in December 1942, a year after his second visit to Cuba and return from South America.

He explained the nature of the *danzón* in a preface to his score, clarifying the character of the actual dance.

The Cuban Danzon is not a fast dance. It should not be confused with the rhumba, the conga, or the son. It fulfills a function rather similar to that of the waltz in our own dance emporiums, providing contrast for the more animated forms. Its special charm is a certain naïve sophistication, alternating in mood between passages of rhythmic precision and a kind of non-sentimental sweetness. Under a nonchalant guise, the danzon is meant to be executed with precise rhythmic articulation.[87]

Markings in the score reinforce this particular interpretation of the dance and reveal Copland's general attitude toward the expressive qualities of Latin American culture. The opening of the *Danzón Cubano* is to be "nonchalant, but precise," and another melody is labeled "dolce (naïve and non-sentimental)." Such indications echo the directions in *El Salón México* and in their objective, unsentimental stance suggest that Copland hoped to avoid a romantic, nostalgic exoticism in favor of neoclassical objectivity.

Beyond these apparent similarities in tone and attitude, however, lie significant differences between Copland's two Latin American–inspired scores in terms of compositional processes and use of borrowed materials. Copland found the traditional melodies for *El Salón México* in published collections and resituated those tunes in the modern context of an urban dance hall. In contrast, the rhythms of *Danzón Cubano*—and the score's interest is truly rhythmic rather than melodic—were taken from music that Copland actually heard during his visits. "Unlike *El Salón México*," a note in the 1949 orchestral score explains, "*Danzón Cubano* is derived from melodic and rhythmic fragments heard and recorded by the composer during several visits to Cuba." These fragments, which Copland might have transcribed while enjoying an evening of musical entertainment, are perhaps the same sketches as preserved among the manuscripts for the *Danzón*. On a loose page of hotel stationery, Copland jotted down three musical ideas (ex. 2.3). The rhythm and contour of example 2.3b serve as the basis for a percussive episode that opens the second half.

From the beginning, *Danzón Cubano* is all about rhythm. The opening is purely percussive, with a syncopation characteristic of Latin American rhythms as well as African American ragtime (ex. 2.4). The second half of

EXAMPLE 2.3. Rhythmic motives written in Copland's hand on "Hotel Royal Palm, Havana Cuba" note paper

EXAMPLE 2.4. Opening of *Danzón Cubano*, arr. for piano solo

the piece features two especially distinctive figures: the *tresillo*, which divides a duple measure into asymmetrical groups of 3 + 3 + 2; and the *cinquillo*, with a tie across the third beat of the 4/4 bar. These patterns are typical of Cuban dance music—one scholar of Cuban music describes the *cinquillo* as "the most characteristic rhythmical expression of Cuba."[88] In example 2.5, the accompaniment figure and top line present the *tresillo*, while the inner voice in the pianist's right hand is based on the *cinquillo*. These rhythms recur in various guises throughout the second half of the *Danzón*.

If these rhythmic ideas do indeed preserve what Copland himself heard in a local dance hall, *Danzón Cubano* would then stand as one of very few works to appropriate folk or popular material from direct observation or firsthand musical knowledge. Generally Copland found his tunes in books: this was true of *El Salón México* and such later folkloric scores as *Billy the Kid*, *Rodeo*, *Appalachian Spring*, and *Lincoln Portrait*. In a sense, then, *Danzón Cubano* is a memento, an object brought back as a memory of lived experience, and Copland himself described the piece as "a genuine tourist souvenir."[89]

He also considered *Danzón Cubano* to have "a touch of unconscious grotesquerie, as if it were an impression of 'high-life' as seen through the eyes of the populace—elegance perceived by the inelegant."[90] In *El Salón México* the grotesque is achieved through the juxtaposition of folk tunes (or at least tunes that Copland himself associated with a rural, folk sensibility) and the urban dance hall. But *Danzón Cubano* uses a different means to accomplish the

EXAMPLE 2.5. Opening of the second half of *Danzón Cubano*, arr. for piano solo

grotesque: caricature, which "pursues the course of planned incongruity by a technique of abstraction."[91] The process of abstraction highlights the strange and unusual, magnifying the minor ("One should study one's dog for his *Napoleonic* qualities," Burke wrote, "or observe mosquitoes for signs of wisdom to which we are forever closed") and trivializing the grand ("converting mastodons into microbes, or human being into vermin upon the face of the earth").[92] According to Burke, "in caricature, certain aspects of the object are deliberately omitted, while certain other aspects are over-stressed (*caricare* 'to overload')."[93] *Danzón Cubano* is just such a caricature, an abstraction of the Cuban *danzón* that overemphasizes the rhythmic profile of the dance and so sacrifices all other musical elements, whether melody, structure, or timbre, to rhythm. Those few interesting melodic lines that do emerge are less distinct and memorable than the rhythms. The highly sectional form voids a notion of organic structure or temporal narrative, fragmenting the musical whole. And as a work for two pianos (though it was later orchestrated), *Danzón Cubano* eschews the colorful timbres of *El Salón México*, of the music Copland likely heard in the Cuban clubs, and of the Cuban-inflected dance music popular in the United States during the 1930s and 1940s.

If Cuban music was typically perceived by audiences in the United States as a sensuous, popular dance idiom for jazz orchestra, then the grotesque form of *Danzón Cubano*—a rhythmically overloaded, melodically vacant, structurally simple, and timbrally monochromatic concert work for piano— suggests a radical revision, or rehearing, of those qualities considered typically Cuban. By honing in on characteristic Afro-Cuban rhythmic patterns stripped of orchestral color or melodic interest, Copland presents the North American listener with a new perspective on Cuban music. The grotesque musical caricature opens a space between the realm of Cuban music as Copland experienced it and the highly commercialized forms of Latin American music familiar to American audiences from records and radio broadcasts. Clearly Copland was interested in moving away from these commercial musics and in capturing something more affecting. As he wrote to Bernstein, the records he found—even in Cuba—were "only analogous to Guy Lombardo versions of the real thing," whereas his lived experience with the music was a "piquant scene" of musical, cultural, and racial miscegenation. Like *El Salón México*, *Danzón Cubano* presents another example of a productive incongruity with the power to reshape established classifications and encourage critical awareness.

And although caricature might be assumed to mock that which is depicted, in fact the subject is not ridiculed; rather, the established categories of perception are held up for contempt. Burke notes that "caricature usually reclassifies in accordance with clearly indicated interests."[94] In *Danzón Cubano*, Copland hints at the interests that might lie beneath his abstract musical portrait. He regards the *danzón* with "the eyes of the populace" and sees "elegance perceived by the inelegant." But herein lies the reclassification, the twist, the aesthetic challenge at the heart of the piece: the elegant is, in fact, inelegant. The dance is grotesque, the music of the supposedly sophisticated *danzón* naïve and unrefined. Its form is simple—a highly sectional binary form with a great deal of repetition; the melodic material is unexceptional; the timbres unvaried, articulation dry and, as Copland himself writes in the score, "nonsentimental." As a caricature of the "high-life," *Danzón Cubano* implicitly questions how elegance is defined and revels in the "unconscious grotesquerie" that seeks to bridge the divides between high and low, naïf and sophisticate, an American tourist and the Cuban people.

Copland made two more government-sponsored trips to Latin America in 1947 and 1963, each time giving lectures, making radio appearances, conducting local orchestras, and meeting various composers and musicians in every country he visited. By 1963, however, he felt less connected to the contemporary music in and cultural life of Latin America, which in his opinion had failed to live up to their initial promise. Writing in his travel diary, he noted during his stay in Buenos Aires that "it was a lonely week. It has been a long time since I felt so little needed." The poor acoustics in concert halls, lack of rehearsal time, and quality of the orchestras also grated on his nerves. "Sometimes," he wrote, "I think I've 'had it' in these parts, as far as orchestras go." Even his social interactions seemed unhappy. Reflecting on a dinner with the composers Alberto Ginastera and Jacabo Ficher, Copland felt that the evening "didn't come off too well. They all knew each other for too long and too well."[95] The insular quality Copland noted in the dinner conversation seemed to him to pervade American musical life south of the U.S. border. Although Chávez had certainly succeeded in becoming an international figure in modern music, few composers of the younger generation had found comparable fame.

Copland came to know younger Latin American composers through his activities at Tanglewood, summer home of the Boston Symphony Orchestra. Chávez and Copland taught there together for a season, and over the years a host of students from a range of countries filled Copland's courses. Among those who studied with Copland were Blas Galindo (Mexico), Antonio Esteves (Venezuela), Alberto Ginastera (Argentina), Mario Davidovsky

(Argentina), Julian Orbón (Cuba), Héctor Tosar (Uruguay), Roque Cordero (Panama), and Juan Orrego-Salas (Chile).[96] Voluminous correspondence testifies to the continuing exchange between Copland and the younger generation of Latin American musicians, and Orrego-Salas spoke respectfully of Copland's pan-American connections as evidence of "deep interest, not just a Good Neighbor policy."[97]

On his own initiative Copland frequently returned to Mexico to compose, conduct, and vacation. In 1944, for example, he and his companion Victor Kraft spent a few months in Tepoztlán, the same village studied by Robert Redfield in 1930 and Stuart Chase in 1931. Copland described the town to Leonard Bernstein as "pure Aztec," with "no paved streets—therefore no traffic, except the pitter-patter of bare feet. There's no electricity—therefore no radios. There *is* one telephone—but it doesn't work—it's *decompuesto*. The only sign of civilization as we know it is the afternoon rugby game that takes place in the courtyard of the church."[98] He enjoyed the solitude immensely: "Just think," he wrote to Bernstein, "not a single soul in all this town has ever heard of you or me." Occasionally, when such tranquility became "too boring," Copland went to Mexico City to see Chávez and hear the Orquesta. But "the orchestra has changed," he lamented in another letter to Bernstein. "It plays more correctly and better in tune—but with a certain student-like carefulness that spoils half the fun. (*Don't* quote me.) In the old days (1932) they made a mess—but it was such a pretty mess."[99]

It was indeed the mess that Copland enjoyed, the sense of possibility, the potential for transgression, of cultural and musical mixing. Like so many other leftist artists and intellectuals during the era of depression and war, Copland looked south for inspiration and found a new ideal of Americanness. In Latin American culture, he discovered the potential for the integration of self and community so central to the Depression-era critique of industrial modernism and the continuing search for a vital (pan)American culture.

3 Creating Community

TOWARD THE END of the 1930s, Copland became involved in a number of collaborative projects and composed several works for stage and screen. Among them were *The Second Hurricane* (1936), a "play opera" for performance by high-school students with a libretto by Edwin Denby, and *The City* (1939), Copland's first film score, composed for a documentary directed by Ralph Steiner with commentary written by Lewis Mumford. In their very nature as well as in their particular subjects, these works raise questions relevant to the cultural and political turmoil of the Depression era: questions of self-sufficiency and cooperation, of the relation between the individual and the group, self and society, liberty and equality. Perhaps of paramount importance to Copland, at once a very private and eminently sociable artist, was the issue of community.

As essentially collaborative works, *The Second Hurricane* and *The City* produce their own cultural communities by creating networks of alliances and allegiances among the artists, performers, listeners, and characters, such that the artistic sum is necessarily greater than any individual contribution. *The Second Hurricane* is authored not only by its composer but also by its librettist, the writer Edwin Denby. The two friends worked closely together, discussing nearly every detail of the drama, and of course the director, conductor, musicians, and singers also participated in the realization of the dramatic whole; members of the audience were in their own way participants, since many in attendance had helped to finance the production. *The City* was likewise the result of creative collaboration: among the participants were multiple writers and directors. Moreover, the very narratives of these two pieces enact the formation of communities. *The Second Hurricane* concerns a group of schoolchildren who fight among themselves but are later reconciled, and *The City* portrays the greenbelt town as the locus of civic cooperation. Finally, as works related at least tangentially to the idea of *Gebrauchsmusik*, or "music for use," *The Second Hurricane* and *The City* reach out to an audience beyond the concert hall, establishing new communities of listeners in an attempt to ameliorate the alienating effects of modernism as an aesthetic practice and modernity as a social system.

Copland's sense of community was informed by the immediate cultural and ideological context of the Popular Front, but his leftist political engagement and its musical expression also reflect the communitarian ideals of an earlier generation of intellectuals, including Randolph Bourne, Van Wyck Brooks, Waldo Frank, and Lewis Mumford. Known as the "Young Americans," these cultural critics held often vague and sometimes contradictory positions, but Casey Nelson Blake has identified the core tenet of their social thought as "a communitarian vision of self-realization through participation in a democratic culture."[1] They offered trenchant critiques of American industrial society and imagined an organic community that vitalized both the private individual and the public citizen.

In the 1930s, the Young Americans were brought into the sphere of Popular Front politics, although they never quite realized the full radical potential of their own cultural critique. As Blake notes, their "generous vision of a democratic culture" too often "gave way to a rhetoric of mystical wholeness, prophetic leadership, and organic mutuality that dissolved politics in silent communion and emptied their ideal of community of the voices and aspirations of real people in real communities."[2] Their failure was that of liberal Progressivism more generally, which proposed to reform democratic structures but basically preserved a system of social stratification. At worst, the Young Americans seemed to espouse an essentially antidemocratic position that invested cultural authority in the creative individual and political power in the benevolent state. For example, Frank's commentary on the ills of contemporary society often projected a blurry image of a mystical union of the self and society engendered by the enlightened individual at its center. And although Mumford offered a damning appraisal of the dehumanizing forces of industrialism, he argued that solutions lay in urban planning and social organization, not in the radical reconception of capitalism. Even at best, the political program of the Young Americans remained ambiguous. Nonetheless, Blake explains, "by making the realization of personality the goal of cultural renewal, the Young Americans gave legitimacy to longings for moral meaning and personal identity that liberals and Marxists alike would have banished to private life or dismissed as false consciousness. Frank and Mumford placed at the center of their cultural criticism the emotional, symbolic, and value-laden aspects of social experience in which most people understand themselves and their surroundings."[3] Ultimately, the Young Americans struggled to define and realize "the good life of personality lived in the environment of the Beloved Community."[4]

Copland, too, embraced the ideal of community and its possibilities for personal fulfillment, cultural cohesion, and political action, but he was more firmly aligned with the cultural politics and ideologies of the Popular Front. His notion of community, as expressed in his music, embraces Mumford's philosophy of urban planning as well as the ideals of social justice and multi-ethnic tolerance characteristic of the Front. These alignments—the romantic and republican anticapitalism of the Young Americans along with the more radical social leftism of the Front—inform both *The Second Hurricane* and *The City*. In presenting symbolic forms of self-realization and communal attachment, these works envision an organic community with the capacity to mend the fractures of contemporary life. They may lack a honed political edge—this is especially true of *The Second Hurricane*—and move too quickly from a statement of the problem to a celebration of the solution. But if they are not radical expressions of militant leftism, neither are they examples of liberal populism. Instead, they fall within the compass of the cultural front.

The Second Hurricane *as "Gebrauchsmusik with a Difference"*

Even as the energies of the Composers Collective and proletarian avant-garde began to dissipate, Copland continued to adapt the techniques of modernism for unconventional performers and audiences in a pair of piano works that he wrote in 1935. *The Young Pioneers* and *Sunday Afternoon Music* were composed specifically for children and appeared in a series ("Contemporary Piano Music by Distinguished Composers") edited by Isadore Freed and Lazare Saminsky. In *The Young Pioneers*, the connection between radical politics and modern music is implicit in the title. The Young Pioneers was a Communist youth club, akin to the Boy Scouts, and children who played the piece were likely exploring for the first time—pioneering—the realm of contemporary composition.[5] A note to the performers (written not by Copland but by the series editors) explains that the work features "especial rhythmic interest" in its use of uneven groupings of three and four eighth notes within a 7/8 meter. "It would be wise to practice a rhythmic exercise based on these two figures," the editors advise, providing two simple, eighth-note patterns of 3 + 4 and 4 + 3 for study. *Sunday Afternoon Music* is described as a "sensitively tinted piece" that "is built around a single harmonic progression." The progression is fairly simple, but the harmonies are greatly enriched through chromatic inflections, and the piece includes an ostinato in the pianist's left hand.[6]

As works that place the style and technique of musical modernism in the hands of amateur performers, *The Young Pioneers* and *Sunday Afternoon Music* relate to the musical agenda of the Composers Collective and the proletarian avant-garde as well as to the ideals of *Gebrauchsmusik*. Copland had witnessed first-hand the rise of *Gebrauchsmusik* as a new musical style and aesthetic perspective emphasizing the functional relevance of music over the ideal of aesthetic autonomy.[7] In 1927 he attended the *Deutsche Kammermusik* festival in Baden-Baden, which featured two concerts of chamber music, a program of music for mechanical instruments, an evening of film music, and a concert of four one-act operas, including Weill's *Mahagonny-Songspiel* and Paul Hindemith's *Hin und Zurück*. He and fellow American Marc Blitzstein returned to Germany in 1929, and during a tour of German opera houses, the two heard Weill's *Dreigroschenoper* and Hindemith's *Neues vom Tages*.[8] All of these pieces may be productively related to *neue Sachlichkeit* ("new objectivity"), and *Hin und Zurück* epitomizes the genre of *Gebrauchsmusik*.

Much like the vaunted "new spirit" in France with which Copland was already familiar, *neue Sachlichkeit* in Germany rejected artistic expressionism in favor of aesthetic detachment, formal clarity, and a more accessible musical language. Generally translated as the "new objectivity," *neue Sachlichkeit* literally means "new thingness." Thus, the term in the original German has a sense of materiality lost in translation: in English, "objectivity" seems to indicate a composer's perspective rather than a concretizing of artistic expression into an object. But utilitarianism lies at the heart of the matter. *Neue Sachlichkeit* dismantles the romantic notion of autonomy, of the composer as an isolated imaginative force and the artwork as a transcendent aesthetic creation. The musical object, or *Sache*, is then put to use in works of *Gebrauchsmusik*.[9]

Although Copland stood in uncertain relation to the ideological, aesthetic, and political debates surrounding *neue Sachlichkeit* and *Gebrauchsmusik* in Weimar Germany, the broad principles and musical exemplars of these new aesthetic modes accorded with Copland's own stylistic turn in the late 1920s and early 1930s toward a simplified, accessible musical idiom addressed to a broad musical public and often suitable for amateur performance. In addition to *The Young Pioneers* and *Sunday Afternoon Music*, in 1935 Copland wrote *What Do We Plant?* for the girls' glee club of the Henry Street Settlement Music School. Later in the decade he wrote an orchestral piece for the

High School of Music and Art, *An Outdoor Overture*, which Paul Rosenfeld described as "Three Cheers for the Red, White and Sickle!"[10] None are mere trifles. In keeping with his goal to write functional music of aesthetic substance, Copland employed sophisticated musical techniques and adopted a serious tone in these seemingly lighter works. And he did not shy from engaging with the issues that formed the cultural context of his newly simplified musical style: some of these works for children directly invoke the cultural politics of the era in their descriptive titles and the musical agenda of the proletarian avant-garde in their compositional idiom. As noted, the *Young Pioneers* was the name of a Communist youth organization, and Howard Pollack has observed that the lyrics of *What Do We Plant?* ("What do we plant when we plant the tree?") recall the mission of the Civilian Conservation Corps (CCC), one of President Roosevelt's most successful and popular work programs (although one particularly reviled by the CPUSA as a fascist boot camp).[11] Inaugurated within his first hundred days as president, the CCC engaged in a variety of conservation activities, most notably the planting of innumerable trees across the United States. The style of Copland's short piece also recalls the homophonic, declamatory idiom of his earlier work for chorus, "Into the Streets May First."[12] Moreover, the celebration of communal effort and slow but steady transformation of objects into ideology—the tree is a ship's mast, paper ballots, a house, a flagpole, and a symbol of freedom—evokes the Popular Front and its goal to transform American democracy.

Copland was enamored with the concept of a more useful, relevant form of serious music, but he seemed slightly disappointed with its realization in the works of Hindemith and Weill. Hindemith's *Hin und Zurück* was merely "highly diverting," Copland wrote in his review of the festival in Baden-Baden. Weill's *Mahagonny* was but "a series of pseudo-popular songs in the jazz manner," and Copland dismissed the score as the product of "a composer trying too hard to be revolutionary."[13] Blitzstein expressed a similar dissatisfaction with *Gebrauchsmusik* in a 1934 article for *Modern Music*. Although its aesthetic and social goals were admirable, he explained, the resulting musical style depended too heavily on the imitation of popular music. "Look at the style of music it brought forth!" Blitzstein exclaimed. "Music which abjectly copied what the mob had *already learned* to like. Instead of educating, it pandered."[14] (He later recanted: "Weill hasn't changed," Blitzstein wrote in praise of *Johnny Johnson*, "I have.")[15] He recognized that any form of functional music aimed at a large audience would by necessity engage with the burgeoning entertainment industry, including the world of radio and sound films, but he suggests that the progressive potential of *Gebrauchsmusik* had been compromised by its unqualified embrace of commercialized popular culture. The genre had failed to realize its potential as a challenge to the existing bourgeois order. "*Gebrauchsmusik* is apparently doomed," Blitzstein lamented.[16]

Copland's own criticism of *Gebrauchsmusik* as a "contaminated" musical style can also be read as a rebuke of its ties to musical styles associated with the culture industry.[17] In his 1941 book *Our New Music*, he recounts a prosaic history of the genre: the newly simplified style had been "encouraged by the German music publishers, who saw in it the possibility of opening new sales in a hitherto untouched market" of amateur musicians. Moreover, Copland felt that "the actual musical content of most *Gebrauchsmusik* was weak," because "composers continued to reserve their best thoughts for their 'serious' music."[18] And in correspondence with his friend Henry Cowell, he was apparently critical of *Gebrauchsmusik*, taking issue not with its intent but with its realization. Copland's letter is no longer extant, but Cowell's response preserves a sense of the conversation.[19] In the context of an exchange about *The Second Hurricane*, Cowell wrote:

> Am glad to hear about the High School Opera. It is a very good idea. There is a genuine need for our best composers to devote attention to works of this sort. Your phrase "gebrauchsmusik with a difference" seems to hit the nail on the head. If music isn't of use, it is useless! The only thing about gebrauchsmusik that has gotten it, as a term applying to the music written under that name, in disrepute, is a sort of smartalekyness, coupled often with lack of workmanship and idea. Then these things are certainly not essential to the term, nor the sort of music it COULD represent.[20]

Copland himself described *The Second Hurricane* as "'Gebrauchsmusik' with a difference." In a handwritten account presumably prepared as program notes, Copland explained that "most music 'written for use' generally attempts no more than that, while this music was written as a labor of love and somewhat more ambitiously as to musical quality than an ordinary 'Gebrauchsmusik' opera would be."[21]

Thus he approached the task of writing music for amateurs in all earnestness and with a clear sense of purpose. Weighing heavily on his mind in the mid-thirties was the public apathy toward contemporary music, a state of affairs he aimed to improve by writing functional works addressed to the largest possible audience. He was especially interested in amateur performers and inexperienced listeners—new groups he had first come into contact with through the activities of the Composers Collective and musical organizations of the Communist Party—who might bring fresh ears to contemporary music. His self-described "high-school play opera," *The Second Hurricane*, was thus a form of musical recruitment. Copland explained that he was

> attracted to the idea of writing a work for school performance for many reasons, not least of which was the sense that in addressing their music to the usual run of symphony audiences modern American composers had, to a degree, come up against a stone wall. Such audiences submit to new music when it is played at them, but they never show any signs of really wanting it. The atmosphere, therefore, is a deadening one, and anything but conducive to the creation of new works. Yet the composer *must* compose!

"If modern composers can reach the youth of the country," Copland concluded, "their future is assured!"[22]

Copland's interest in writing for amateur forces reached its apex with *The Second Hurricane*. In the wake of a successful production of Kurt Weill's *Der Jasager* and Paul Hindemith's *Wir bauen eine Stadt* at the Henry Street Settlement music school, the director Grace Spofford suggested that Copland also compose a musical theater piece for use in the school—a *Schuloper*. Copland chose Denby to write the libretto and began composing the score while in Mexico during the summer of 1936. Back in New York that fall, work progressed quickly, and the premiere of *The Second Hurricane* took place at the Neighborhood Playhouse, a stone's throw from the Henry Street Settlement, on April 21, 1937. Lehman Engel conducted (he directed the Henry Street children's chorus and had led the performance of *Der Jasager*). The young Orson Welles was brought in to direct, and Hiram Sherman served as assistant director. All three men also were busy working on Marc Blitzstein's *The Cradle Will Rock* (1937), which was in rehearsal at the time.[23]

The Henry Street Settlement music school was a most appropriate sponsor, given the institution's commitment to social welfare and educational opportunity. Settlements represented a response to the pressures of immigration and industrialization during the Progressive Era, and the Henry Street Settlement was one of the oldest such institutions in New York City.[24] Founded by Lillian Wald in 1893 on the lower east side of Manhattan, the Settlement provided basic health services as well as language instruction and job training for new immigrants, many of whom were of Russian-Jewish extraction. Indeed, Henry Street was once described as "the American home of the Russian revolution."[25] Educational initiatives were strongly influenced by the work of John Dewey, whose pragmatic epistemology supported the active application of knowledge rather than its passive reception. Dewey believed that children were to learn the skills of cultural citizenship in a self-directed learning environment that emphasized the value of cooperation and collaboration; education was to foster an awareness of private agency and public responsibility, preparing children for participation in a communitarian democracy. Coupled with social and educational programs was a legislative agenda to improve housing and promote responsible urban development.

Wald served as the director of Henry Street until 1935, when she was succeeded by Helen Hall. That same year Hall brought in Grace Spofford as the new head of the music school. Arts education and musical instruction at the settlement were promoted as a means of social uplift, a way to bring beauty to the lives of the urban poor and create new audiences for "good" music. Often, settlement schools struggled to define the role of music in their mission and balance a traditional program of conservatory-style instruction with more socially oriented activities (including choirs and bands) that emphasized participation over practice and required little private study. The Henry Street music school remained committed to the aesthetic and moral value of music within the European classical tradition, and neither popular music nor jazz was ever included in the curriculum.[26] Whatever the conflicting views on music within the settlement agenda, school operas for young performers like *Wir bauen eine Stadt* and *The Second Hurricane* were perfectly suited to programs in social music and theater.[27] At the same time, such works represented serious efforts by leading contemporary composers, thus satisfying the desire for music of high quality and great beauty.

Copland's own contribution to the genre of school opera was influenced by his experience with the Henry Street music school—he was on the faculty from 1935 to 1939—as well as by German exemplars of the genre.[28] In particular, the open textures and pared-down neoclassical orchestration of Hindemith's *Wir bauen eine Stadt* and *Lehrstück* are echoed in the wind-based instrumentation of *The Second Hurricane*. Certain superficial features of *Der Jasager*, with a libretto by leftist playwright Bertolt Brecht, also resound in Denby's story. Both Brecht and Denby foreground the didactic intent of their respective libretti by featuring schoolchildren and teachers as characters. Each of their plots involves a journey: in *Der Jasager*, a young boy leaves his sick mother to accompany his teacher and other students on a perilous trip that ends in his death; *The Second Hurricane* concerns a group of children who travel with supplies to a flood-stricken rural town. Yet the pessimistic core of Brecht's tale and its emphasis on *Einverständnis*, or assent to the common good, stand in stark contrast to the joyous affirmation of Denby's story, in which the individual achieves self-fulfillment (rather than self-abnegation) through the engagement with others.[29]

Denby, who had lived and worked in Germany during the 1920s, greatly admired Brecht, particularly the libretto for *Mahagonny*. Brecht was "a good poet," Denby explained in a 1936 article for *Modern Music*, in part because he "uses the contrast between the informative part of a show *(der Lehrwert)* and the theatric effect *(das Artistische)*, and the contrast of stage personality in relaxed moments against technical proficiency at others—in other words the Mozart *Singspiel* tradition." Denby felt that the *Singspiel* resolved an inherent conflict between singing and storytelling by eliminating recitative and thereby freeing the dramatist to write more natural prose. "It is in the informative, the recitative parts where the librettist gets confused," he noted, "but it is quite possible to tell the story of an opera without subterfuge, if you will interrupt the music for awhile and let some words be spoken."[30] In *The Second Hurricane*, he and Copland chose to follow their understanding of the Mozartean *Singspiel* as a historical model as well as contemporary examples of Brecht and Weill in *Mahagonny*, or Paul Green and Weill in *Johnny Johnson* (premiered by the Group Theatre in November 1936), by incorporating spoken dialogue as a means to tell their story.

The Second Hurricane concerns six schoolchildren, specified as between the ages of fourteen and seventeen, who assist in relief operations during a flood "in the southern Middle West." Children play all of the lead roles: the six chosen to help, plus a younger child who has been displaced by the floods. There are a handful of adult characters, including the pilot charged with transporting the children and their supplies to the devastated areas, as well as choruses of adults and pupils who comment on the action. The pilot and six would-be rescuers fly to the flooded area, but the plane suffers mechanical trouble. After briefly touching down, the pilot takes off again to get his plane repaired in the nearest town. The children are left behind with the supplies on a patch of dry land dubbed "Two Willow Hill." Nervous and frightened, they squabble among themselves. Unexpectedly, they are joined by Jefferson, a black farm boy who has also been left alone to wait while his parents travel into town to buy food. As floodwaters rise (on account of an improbable "second hurricane"), the seven children reconcile in the face of shared adversity and are eventually rescued.

That hurricanes never reached the Midwest was an incongruity Denby later acknowledged. "I added hurricanes for excitement," he explained, "not realizing that hurricanes do not go inland." But the floods were real. The spring of 1936 and winter of 1937 saw devastating storms sweep across the Ohio River valley. In March 1936, floodwaters swelled in fourteen states from Maine to Georgia, including West Virginia, Pennsylvania, and Ohio. Nearly two hundred people were killed and more than 400,000 left homeless. Again in January 1937 the Ohio River overran its banks, as did the Mississippi. A dozen states were flooded, among them Missouri, which was later specified as the location for *The Second Hurricane*. Newspapers reports placed the total number of people killed at over two hundred and those left homeless at nearly one million. Coverage of these natural disasters was extensive, and Denby recalled reading "daily newspaper accounts of floods and airplane rescues in the Midwest" as he worked on his libretto.[31] The fictionalized—but not entirely fictitious—events in the drama, including the delivery of relief supplies by plane, thus suggest the real hunger suffered by flood victims as agencies ran low on food and the courageous flights by rescue pilots documented in newspaper articles at the time.

Stories of the 1937 floods in the *New York Times* struggled to capture the magnitude of the crisis by comparing the natural disaster to war. Kentucky experienced "devastation like war," and the government was mobilized on a "wartime" basis.[32] A similarly violent, martial simile appears in Denby's lyrics for the climactic chorus of the opera, "Like a Giant Bomb," which closes act 2. The choruses of parents and children describe the hurricane as "like a giant bomb that strikes to kill. / With the force of a dynamite blast." Repeated strikes of the gong in the orchestral accompaniment represent the concussions. Such military references were all the more striking given that the European conflict occupied other headlines in the same papers as news of the floods and promotional articles for *The Second Hurricane*. Moreover, the connection between the natural disasters and the play opera was solidified in advance stories. A piece in the *New York Times* noted that the libretto made "use of current news events as subject-matter," for example, and the *Herald Tribune* explained that "the libretto is on a contemporary subject, dealing with the problems faced by some children attempting rescue work during the recent floods in the Ohio and Mississippi valleys."[33]

This relationship between reported and dramatized events reflects the emergence of documentary as a modernist vehicle for social commentary as well as the development of radical theater in Germany and the United States. Denby, like Copland, was familiar with German *Zeitoper*, or works "of the time." These musical theater pieces possessed an obvious immediacy and relevance as they explicitly referenced contemporary events. In the United States, the documentary impulse was characteristic of Depression-era culture, as evidenced by the photography of Walker Evans and Dorothea Lange, the travel guides compiled by the WPA, and the multitude of documentary films, fiction, and nonfiction prose produced during the thirties. Such works have often been contrasted with modernism and interpreted as evidence of an aesthetic retreat to realism in the 1930s. But whereas the discourse of the documentary may rely on the notion of unmediated representation, the documents themselves are aesthetic and ideological constructions.[34] The "realistic" photographs of sharecroppers produced under the auspices of the Farm Security Administration Photography Unit manipulate reality as much as, if not more than, they reflect it. Lange's "Migrant Mother"—arguably the central, iconic image of the Depression—was purposefully, artistically, and knowingly framed in keeping with Lange's aesthetic sensibility and the ideological perspective of the middle-class Americans who were the primary audience for the picture.[35]

In the realm of radical theater, the documentary impulse was epitomized by the Living Newspaper, a dramatic genre that fused formal experimentation, news reportage, and leftist politics. First produced in the Soviet Union, Living Newspapers dramatized current events and disseminated information (or propaganda) to a broad public. In 1927 the Blue Blouse group brought the genre from Moscow to Germany, where proletarian theater groups staged their own productions with scenes by Brecht and the American Communist author Mike Gold, among others.[36] In the United States, Living Newspapers were sponsored by the Federal Theater Project; the first public American production was *Triple-A Plowed Under*, performed in March 1936 at the Biltmore Theater in New York City. In a series of twenty-six scenes, *Triple-A Plowed Under* details the impetus behind the Agricultural Adjustment Act (AAA), a 1933 program intended to match the supply of agricultural products with demand. The Act mandated that overproduction of any given crop result in plowing under the excess. In 1936 the Supreme Court invalidated the AAA, along with numerous other ambitious programs launched under the rubric of the New Deal by President Franklin D. Roosevelt during his first hundred days in office. From a leftist point of view, the court's decision served largely to protect the mechanisms of liberal capitalism from legislative reform.[37]

Triple-A Plowed Under explores the effects of the agricultural crisis and the AAA on four distinct groups of people: (1) labor, represented by the farmers and the unemployed; (2) capital, embodied by an upper-class couple dining on the profits of agricultural inflation; (3) consumers, depicted as Detroit housewives facing higher meat prices; and (4) government, in the person of Henry A. Wallace, then secretary of agriculture. These four groups are opposed and juxtaposed throughout the play as their interests appear to conflict. Resolution is achieved in the climactic final scene as a farmer cries out the moral of the story. Turning to his fellow farmers, the housewives, and the legions of unemployed, he shouts: "All our problems are the same!" News flashes read over a loudspeaker detail the development of the Farmer-Labor Party as an alliance of rural and urban interests in states such as Minnesota (where Copland had witnessed the radical movement first hand during his visit to Bemidji in 1934), and *Triple-A Plowed Under* ends with everyone on stage. The spotlight fades on the apparently unrepentant well-dressed capitalist and on Secretary Wallace, but the housewives, farmers, and unemployed are left standing together in the light—a testament to their shared interests and commitment to collective action. The goal of the production was thus to enact the alliance between farmers and labor, rural and urban workers, and to demonstrate the pervasive and pernicious role of capitalism in lives of the people—government leaders, the rich, middle-class consumers, the working poor, and the jobless alike. Its message recalls the conclusion to Lillian Wald's autobiographical account of the Henry Street Settlement, where she explains that the lesson of the settlement experience was "that people rise and fall together, that no one group or nation dare be an economic or a social law unto itself."[38]

Like *Triple-A Plowed Under*, *The Second Hurricane* dramatizes a current crisis (albeit a decidedly less political one) and offers a communitarian moral embracing a diverse collective. A typed scenario for the production even suggested projecting one newspaper heading per scene in the manner of the Living Newspaper.[39] Likewise, it is the fate of the group in *The Second Hurricane* and not of the individual characters that motivates the drama. The children are not greatly differentiated through either musical or dramatic characterization except for Jeff, whose race is made clear in words and music. His presence is typical of communist children's literature, which often included an African-American boy or girl as a means to critique racism and capitalist oppression while highlighting the importance of racial diversity in American culture.[40] In the original version of *The Second Hurricane,* the sense of racial inequity is heightened through the use of derogatory language and dialect. Jefferson Brown, as he is now known in the published score, is there Jefferson Black, and his initial encounter with the schoolchildren on Two Willow Hill draws on some familiar stereotypes.

> JEFF: I'se seen you takin a bag o' taters out of that airyplane. It's down there.
>
> BUTCH: So that's what you're after. Well, you steer clear of them, nigger. They're not for you.
>
> GWEN: They're not ours. We're taking them to some starving people in the flood area.

JEFF: Yes ma'am, but I'se starvin.

LOURIE: You don't look it, you can't make us believe that your parents didn't leave you enough food to last you till they came back.

JEFF: No they didn't sir. I'se starvin.

GWEN: Do you think he really is?

GIP: He's lying like the devil. I bet he's got some swell corn pone in there.

JEFF: No sir, I'se starvin, ma'am.

FAT: Oh cut it, nigger. I'm starving myself.[41]

All of the dialect was later excised, as were the racial slurs, but their presence here is significant, because attitudes toward race are shown to be chief among the challenges to cooperation.

Jeff continues to plead for food from the other children, asking "Isn't anybody goin' to give me somethin' to eat 'cause I'se starvin'?" The most physically powerful of the children, Butch, is also the most domineering, and he snaps back at Jeff, "Somebody's going to wring your neck if you don't shut up, and crawl back where you came from." Moved to act by Butch's cruel retort, Queenie offers Jeff a chocolate bar. "This child's starving just as much as anybody," she argues. "I won't sit by and see him die of starvation, just because you're too mean to let him have something." Queenie is the only one to recognize and respond to the present need rather than to the abstract ideal of flood relief; much like the women in the Settlement House tradition, she reaches out to the poor child before her. Perhaps this dramatic display of charity prompted a sense of self-gratification among the bevy of wealthy women patrons in the audience for the premiere at the Settlement playhouse, and Queenie's display of bourgeois beneficence also might recall Lionel Trilling's condemnation of the literature of social consciousness. "The 'social consciousness' of the Thirties," Trilling wrote in a 1942 review of James Agee and Walker Evans's documentary volume *Let Us Now Praise Famous Men*, was "abstract and without fibre of resistance," suited for "the drawing-room," and "essentially . . . a pity which wonderfully served the needs of the pitier."[42] That Queenie herself unapologetically eats some of the candy—gratifying her own selfish desire—suggests that her actions are not entirely motivated by compassion, and her generosity cannot of course compensate for the children's racism.

A second hurricane then hits Two Willow Hill "like a giant bomb." The children scatter but are later reunited as the floodwaters rise again. Seeking comfort, the white principal characters come together to form a sextet. "Well, we're safe together here for a while," they sing. Jeff is also with the group but

EXAMPLE 3.1. From *The Second Hurricane*, act 2, "Jeff's Song"

stands apart and has his own jazzy song that comes on the heels of the dance-band music the children imagine hearing on their broken radio (see ex. 3.1). "You was all mighty mean," he sings above syncopated ostinato. "I'se mighty scared of you all. / Now you'se all mighty nice and I'se not scared at all." Reassured by Queenie's kindness and strengthened by the presence of the group, Jeff no longer fears the rising river nor the other children. "I'se not scared that we can drown, / Come on, river, / Show what you can do," he challenges. Characterized by the bluesy altered third scale degree, triads built on the flatted sixth degree, and syncopated rhythms, his music is nearly as racially marked as the words themselves. The six other children soon join in, and all sing the final lines together in dialect. By virtue of this musical and linguistic identification, the group is integrated. In contrast to a conservative view of assimilation, however, and in keeping with a leftist ideal of cultural pluralism, unity does not demand the denial of difference for the sake of social harmony. Instead the white children assume the voice of the black character to validate, rather than negate, the presence of difference.

In her song that follows, Queenie encapsulates the ideological core of the story, celebrating a progressive vision of personal fulfillment through communal solidarity. "I never know [*sic*] that I could feel the way I do and have it real," she sings, her ascending vocal line reflecting her aspirations. "In the dream we meet we're side by side, / It's so strange and sweet the way we glide." She concludes by reasserting a spirit of collectivism: "You dream along the sky with others too." Coming on the heels of her musical and linguistic identification with Jeff, her vision bespeaks a Popular Front commitment to creating an integrated community of black and white, rural and urban, impoverished and middle class.

This brief, delicate song is asked to bear the weight of the drama. Denby had trouble deciding how best to express a didactic moral based on his leftist ideal of community without resorting to Marxist dogma. He wrote to Copland with his thoughts as he drafted and redrafted the lyrics for Queenie's song.

> I feel too that Queenie's song is weak, but anything obvious would be social democratic "Marx is in his heaven, & the dew is on the Brotherhood of Man" wish wash. So I'll have to think hard of that again. It must express the job of being united, which I think is the root of society—it's post-revolutionary ideology (like Bach)—it's not "Forward" it's "We *are* together and we like it." At the same time it has to be represented as Future in Queenie's mind. Do you see?[43]

In another letter, Denby concluded that her song was meant to capture "the moment of peace that makes a revolution worth doing."[44] Thus the song is intended to prefigure the nature of world after the struggle for social democracy. The mood is anticipatory, and Copland's ethereal music reinforces the inescapable fact that this is still a dream, suggesting that it may not be time for postrevolutionary contentment. Queenie's song has a decidedly otherworldly—even utopian—musical mood. The orchestral accompaniment floats along with languid running scales and a pulsing bass that underscores the supple, rising melody. The pervasive *rubato* (phrases are marked *ritard* and *poco accelerando*) generates a rhythmic ebb and flow, lending an organic naturalness to her vocal line, and the even, undifferentiated rhythms obscure the meter to add a sense of weightlessness or suspension that echoes the lyrics. "It's like a dream of floating in the sky,/ A lovely dream when you seem to fly," she muses. And indeed it is a dream that she sings about—a goal to be attained, not a reality to be celebrated.

After Queenie's song, she, Butch, Fat, Gyp, Gwen, and Lowry sing "The Capture of Burgoyne," a folk tune about the Revolutionary War. This marks the first time that Copland borrows an Anglo-American folk song. He found

"The Capture of Burgoyne" in a collection edited by S. Foster Damon, an authority on poet Robert Blake, friend of Virgil Thomson, and director of the Harris Collection of American music and literature at Brown University.[45] Copland owned a copy of the publication, which later provided material for the two sets of *Old American Songs* he wrote in 1950 and 1952. Unlike his later borrowings, however, in *The Second Hurricane* the preexisting melody is not assimilated into the overall musical language of the work, nor even associated with the songs immediately surrounding it; rather, it stands apart as a set piece.

Folk songs occupied pride of place in children's musical education—in the social music programs of the Settlement School, for instance, and by mid-decade traditional music was also integral to the music of the cultural front. Copland's appropriation of a traditional tune is indicative of a growing interest in folk song among leftist composers in the mid-thirties and can be correlated to changes in Soviet aesthetic policy.[46] With the formulation and promulgation of socialist realism beginning in 1934 and announcement of the Popular Front in 1935, the Communist Party assumed an attitude of accommodation toward cultural nationalism and the use of folklore. Whereas folklore had previously seemed the product of repressive social structures and was thus considered inherently reactionary, it was now regarded as the authentic expression of the people. A similar and related aesthetic shift occurred in American left-wing culture. The demise of Third Period proletarianism in the United States is exemplified by the renaming of the Workers Music League as the American Music League (AML) in 1936. Hoping to challenge the "big financial and banking interests which now dominate our leading opera, orchestra, conservatories, publishing houses and radio stations," the AML issued "the call to musicians and music-lovers everywhere FOR THE DEVELOPMENT OF MUSIC AS A PEOPLE'S ART IN AMERICA." Its mission was

1) to encourage the development of the highest type of amateur musical activities among wide numbers of people; and to draw into active participation in these activities those who have been denied the benefits of musical education and culture.

2) to encourage the presentation of, and to create organized audiences for, concerts presenting the best music of the past and present at prices within reach of everyone.

3) to bring composers and other professional musicians into closer contact with amateur musicians and with working people who form the bulk of the potential American music audience.

4) to guide and further the development of an American music addressed to the people, reflecting their lives, interests and problems.

5) to collect, study and popularize American folk music and its traditions.

6) to defend musical culture against fascism, censorship and war.[47]

As a work written in an accessible yet modern style for performance by amateurs, incorporating American folk song, and presenting a theme entirely relevant to contemporary circumstance, *The Second Hurricane* fulfills the mission of the American Music League.

By the mid-thirties, interest in American traditional culture was also being supported by programs of the New Deal. In 1935 Charles Seeger went to Washington, D.C., to work for the Special Skills Division of the Resettlement Administration. Two years later he took the post of deputy director of the Federal Music Project.[48] In both positions, Seeger promoted research in and recording of folk songs. In addition to those recorded by the Resettlement Administration and Federal Music Project, folk songs were collected by the Farm Security Administration of the Department of Agriculture, the Writers' Project, the Folk Arts Committee, and the Library of Congress Folk Archive. By 1939, the Archive of American Folksong at the Library of Congress contained over twenty thousand items.[49]

Also in the mid-thirties (1935 to be exact) Kenneth Burke implored radical writers to adopt the symbol of the people, which would inspire the allegiance of more Americans than that of the worker, and left-wing composers began to consider the possibilities of folk song—particular Anglo-American song—as a means to create an accessible and identifiably American music. This turn toward folk song does not necessarily indicate the demise of radical sentiment, nor a purely romantic view of the American past. The search for community—especially a community figured as an idyllic rural republic—could still contain a critique of American industrial society. As Robert Cantwell has argued,

> To restore the old artisanship and the close community of the small town, and the sense of direct connection to a traditional collective culture, was a form of nostalgia at least as old as the work of Washington Irving and the Fireside Poets, but one to which the Great Depression added a powerful new economic intensity and a sharp political edge: a dream of social justice that would repair the dreadful racial, economic, and cultural rifts tearing the social fabric apart.[50]

This, of course, is Queenie's dream, and that of *The Second Hurricane*.

Yet Jefferson Black does not sing "The Capture of Burgoyne" with the others; the implication from the dialogue is that he simply doesn't know it. "By Virtue's tongue," the white children sing in unison, "like colors of even sweet praises to Freedom were sung"—the final word then divided in antiphonal repetitions.[51] Jeff remains silent. His exclusion reveals a need less obvious than hunger, but perhaps no less urgent, for his instruction in American history. Despite a given name that evokes the era of the Revolutionary War, he lacks awareness of the American tradition, and it seems likely enough that such knowledge has been denied to him on the basis of his race and class. The revolution that will create true freedom is yet undone. In the context of the *Lehrstück*, his inability to join in recalls the core of the Settlement House agenda to educate disadvantaged children and thereby enable their full participation in democratic society.

After the children are rescued, the concluding chorus brings everyone together for a happy ending. Like Queenie's song, the finale celebrates community and solidarity, though now from the perspective of the group rather than the individual. The choruses of students and parents begin the final musical sequence by explaining what has happened since the children were rescued from Two Willow Hill: "Later on they got a chance to work for the flood relief/ And they did it together and did it well." With a light syncopation that matches natural speech rhythms, the melody of the chorus descends disjunctly above a similarly disjointed harmony. The children have "drifted apart again," the lyrics note. But the principals then appear to reassure everyone that "even if we six drift apart," they will still recall the feeling of belonging. "We got an idea of what life could be like," they sing, "With ev'rybody pulling together, / If each wasn't trying to get ahead of all the rest." They revel in "a sort of love . . . making you feel easy . . . a happy, easy feeling, / Like freedom, like freedom, like real freedom."

But freedom is not the only virtue to be celebrated, and following their brief ensemble, the six run off only to return with Jeff, who joins in the final, climactic chorus. Everyone celebrates their hard-won camaraderie, singing "sweet praises" to freedom and equality. "That's the idea of freedom," the entire corps proclaims, "it's feeling equality."

> All feeling free and equal,
> All feeling joined together,
> All feeling free and equal,
> feeling join'd together,
> feeling free and equal,

feeling join'd together,
Feeling good that way.
Ev'rybody as good as ev'rybody else.
Feeling good that way.

The simple, diatonic melody and antiphonal repetitions lead to an unaccompanied, unison outburst, and *The Second Hurricane* ends with a climactic chord on "free!" held for over twenty beats. As the principal characters and chorus of children sing of unity and equality, the individualistic sense of fulfillment expressed in Queenie's solo song gives way to a civic communalism. As the critic Paul Rosenfeld recognized, the story projects "a desire for companionship that has pure sociality at its base and is fulfilled by the experience of solidarity. Sociality—that definitely is the kernel of the nut; and for this truth, we have to thank the librettist and, to an even greater degree, the composer."[52]

The emphasis in this final chorus on feeling as a source of meaning—everyone *feels* free and equal—reflects a tendency in the 1930s to locate authenticity in experience and emotion. "Feeling comes first" in the documentary expression of the 1930s, William Stott argues in his classic study *Documentary Expression and Thirties America*, because the emotional force of documentary was to be found in its presentation of lived experience.[53] Although the "cult of experience" was derided by the anticommunist intellectual Philip Rahv, he nonetheless offered a perceptive description of the Depression-era approach to "the real . . . as a vast phenomenology swept by waves of sensation and feeling."[54] The final chorus of *The Second Hurricane* is swept along by just such waves to an ecstatic, communal release, which Copland himself compared to the finale of Beethoven's Ninth. "When I first heard the chorus and orchestra together," he wrote to Carlos Chávez, "I said 'My God, it sounds like the Ninth Symphony'! By that I meant it had a surprisingly *big* sound, and a highly dramatic one. Also, the end has something of the same 'Freude, Freude' feeling, tho in completely different terms."[55] These terms—Copland's terms—reflect an awareness of the contemporary American political, social, and cultural context and the influence of the Popular Front.

This reliance on feeling may seem to indicate a turn to sentiment and away from radical action. Certainly the sentimental vein runs true in many forms of leftist art from the 1930s; the films of Frank Capra and fiction of John Steinbeck exemplify an innocuous liberal leftism that might best be considered in relation to the New Deal rather than the Popular Front, for instance. *The Second Hurricane* may share some aspects of the sentimental tradition insofar as it emphasizes culture over class, raises the issue of race without really grappling with it, and skips over the period of struggle to envision a postrevolutionary, postideological world. But the play-opera hinges not on a paralyzing empathy but on action: the six children choose to help the relief effort; Queenie offers Jeff a chocolate bar; all seven come together for comfort and security; they adopt the voice of the Other to express their resolve and courage; the white children invite Jeff into the finale; his presence inserts equality into the definition of freedom; everyone sings together. Emotion never wholly cedes to sentimentality such that *The Second Hurricane* remains attached to a more radical critique of American society.

Finally, the drama resists becoming merely a sentimental, self-reflexive celebration of middle-class liberal values if only because its very form—a high-school play opera—retains a critical edge honed by the tradition of modernist musical theater. In writing a "play opera," Copland and Denby avoided the conventions of both musical theater and opera to offer a work that fits into neither genre nor its attendant cultural hierarchies. *The Second Hurricane* flouts the conventions of opera by relying heavily on spoken dialogue (though clearly Copland and Denby had the *Singspiel* in mind) and subverts the expectations of its elite audience by featuring a bare stage peopled by teenage singers. At the same time, Copland wanted to write "serious" music, presumably of a higher caliber than the commercial entertainment on Broadway, and recruit new audiences for modern American music. Copland and Denby sought a new form of musical theater, one that could wear its didactic premise lightly but earnestly. "Of course the kids had everyone completely interested," Copland wrote to Chávez after the premiere. "Kids are like Negroes, you can't go wrong if they are on the stage."[56] Despite the jarring remark, Copland uses the children not simply as a way to ensure success but as an essential part of the work's conception. Their naïveté is a necessary counterbalance to the moralistic story line. As the production notes explain, "the director should sacrifice his knowledge of adult professional theatricality to his feeling for what young students are really like on a stage. Their general atmosphere is the main thing about the play; it will give conviction to the story and bridge the jump to the conclusion at the end."[57]

Though ostensibly a work to be enjoyed by children as well as performed by them, *The Second Hurricane* was premiered before a distinguished audience that likely included some of the notable figures listed in the program as members of the Committee on Arrangements or under the title of Sponsor. Chaired by Mary Lescaze, the committee included Mrs. R. Kirk Askew and

Mrs. Bernard Reis (Claire) among others. These women promoted the performance and sold tickets. On the list of sponsors were composers (Carlos Chávez, George Gershwin), artists and intellectuals (Lincoln Kirstein, Carleton Sprague Smith, Paul Rosenfeld, Carl Van Vechten), as well as women patrons married to prominent men (Mrs. Alfred Knopf, Mrs. Rita W. Morgenthau, Mrs. Leopold Stokowski). Perhaps the audience for *The Second Hurricane* was akin to that for *The Cradle Will Rock*. "It is roughly the leftist front," Thomson wrote in a 1938 review of Blitzstein's show. "That is to say, the right-wing socialists, the communists, some Park Avenue, a good deal of the Bronx, and all those intellectual or worker groups that the Federal Theater in general and the Living Newspapers in particular have welded into about the most formidable army of ticket buyers in the world."[58] As much as Copland (and Denby) may have sincerely hoped to create new, young audiences for contemporary music, it seems likely that the values espoused in *The Second Hurricane*—the values of charity, tolerance, compassion, and equality—were purposefully directed to this elite assemblage.

Although the audience at the premiere was composed of well-heeled members of "the carriage trade," in Copland's words, subsequent performances ensured a wider public for the work. It was broadcast over CBS radio (May 9, 1937) during National Music Week, and excerpts were later performed on a *New Masses* concert (February 6, 1938). In the winter of 1939, *The Second Hurricane* received its first performance by public school children, at East High School in Akron, Ohio.

The work found renewed import during the war years. In prefatory comments for a 1942 broadcast performance, Copland pointed out the inherent significance of internal unity as the true motivating force of the story. "On the surface the libretto tells the story of six ordinary high school kids who think they are going off in a plane to be heroic," he observed. "Instead they find out that until they know something about working together for a common cause, practically nothing can be accomplished."[59] Although the moral of the story seemed obviously applicable to present circumstance, as the "entire war effort is based on a spirit of cooperation," Copland was already looking ahead to the world after the war. "There will be even more need for cooperating after the war is won," Copland concluded, "for then we shall lack the powerful incentive of a ruthless enemy." The struggle for cooperation and sociability would thus remain, even after external obstacles had been conquered.[60] Despite such universal themes, however, *The Second Hurricane* eventually fell into obscurity. In January 1961 Copland narrated a concert performance at the Museum of Modern Art and wistfully recalled the original context: "The action of the story was set in the Middle West and in the present. It is still set in the Middle West, but now takes place in a nearly forgotten period called 'The Thirties.'"[61]

"The Thirties" indeed define the political and cultural circumstance of *The Second Hurricane*, which draws on the influences of the Composers Collective, ideals of *Gebrauchsmusik*, and radical theater of the Living Newspapers as well as the values of the Settlement house movement, progressivism, and the Popular Front. It constructs a community that transcends the divides of race and class to offer both personal fulfillment and social cohesion. Although the work avoids sentimental populism, the sociality achieved through shared emotional reactions to lived and observed experience perhaps begs important questions of representation in the context of middle-class participation in the Popular Front. Queenie's song expresses a postrevolutionary ideology, as Denby explicitly desired, but the terms of revolution are obscured, and the final chorus exults in a freedom easily imagined but difficult to effect. As in the cultural criticism of the Young Americans and broad spectrum of leftist sentiment in America during the 1930s, *The Second Hurricane* presents the possibilities of social solidarity and cultural renewal. Yet its communitarian vision remains but a dream.

The Eutopic Flow of The City

Soon after the premiere of *The Second Hurricane*, Copland's first foray into musical drama, the composer set his sights on another new genre, film music. Many of Copland's musical acquaintances, including Silvestre Revueltas, Virgil Thomson, and George Antheil, had already written music for films, and other artists in his New York circle had found creative opportunities and financial success in the movie business during the 1930s. In 1936 Harold Clurman went to Hollywood. "If you really would like a job in Hollywood sometime," he wrote optimistically to Copland, "I think it could be arranged. I got connections!!"[62] The following summer Copland went west with the hope of being hired to compose the score for a major motion picture. Because he planned to be in Mexico by mid-July for the First Festival of Pan American Chamber Music, he apprised Carlos Chávez of his summer plans. "Harold convinced me that if I come to Hollywood now it would surely end up by getting me a job sometime before October," Copland explained in a letter to Chávez. "The money arrangements are O.K. It is just a question of finding a feature film which needs my kind of music. So I said I would come to 'look over the ground' until July 1st. Then to Mexico."[63] But the ground was less than fertile for Copland, whose lack of experience perhaps precluded him from finding work, and he traveled on to Mexico without a contract.

His first opportunity to compose for film came two years later through photographer and director Ralph Steiner, who hired Copland to write music for *The City*. This forty-four minute documentary film was commissioned by the American Institute of Planners, with financial support from the Carnegie Foundation, for the 1939 World's Fair in New York. From the beginning it was a collaborative effort. Writer and director Pare Lorentz developed the initial outline; the scenario itself was written by Henwar Rodakiewicz, who also directed parts of the film. Lewis Mumford wrote the final commentary, and Steiner worked with Willard Van Dyke on the direction and cinematography.[64] Copland composed the score, which Henry Brant helped to orchestrate.[65] This was an experienced group of artists and intellectuals with connections to each other and to the Popular Front. Both Steiner and Van Dyke had worked with Lorentz on his previous films: Steiner as a cameraman for *The Plow That Broke the Plains* (1936), Van Dyke in the same capacity on *The River* (1937). Brant had previously orchestrated Virgil Thomson's music for these two Lorentz documentaries. Rodakeiwicz had worked with Paul Strand, a photographer well known to Steiner, Van Dyke, and Copland, on the radical Mexican film *Redes*, released in the United States as *The Waves* (1935). Morris Carnovsky, who read Mumford's narration in the film, was a leading actor in the Group Theatre. Copland was the relative newcomer, though he had known Steiner since the late 1920s and had even helped the director edit three short films, *Mechanical Principles, H₂O,* and *Surf and Seaweed,* shown at a 1931 Copland-Sessions concert.[66]

Steiner and Van Dyke had worked together before as members of Nykino, an association of radical photographers and filmmakers dedicated to "making documentary-dramatic revolutionary films—short propaganda films that will serve as flaming film-slogans, satiric films, and films exposing the brutalities of capitalist society."[67] In 1937 this informal association was officially incorporated as Frontier Films, an independent, nonprofit production company.[68] Copland's friend Mary Lescaze served as an associate director of the new organization, and Copland himself was listed as a member of the "advisory board," which included such luminaries as Waldo Frank; Clifford Odets, dedicatee of Copland's Piano Sonata (1941); Genevieve Taggard, author of "The Lark," a poem Copland set as a choral work in 1938; and Lewis Milestone, the director who would later hire Copland to write the score for *Of Mice and Men* (1939), the composer's first Hollywood credit. The name "Frontier" was meant to evoke the American West and associate the progress of westward expansion with progressive politics. The filmmakers were themselves pioneers, as the film historian William Alexander has noted, because "left independent production had never before succeeded in America."[69]

Success proved elusive for Frontier as well. The organization was troubled by internal conflict, and in 1938 Steiner and Van Dyke left to form their own corporation, American Documentary Films, which then produced *The City*. Their split from Frontier may have been partly political—a fracture along Communist lines. Van Dyke was particularly hostile to Communism, although he may have overestimated the degree to which Frontier's productions were influenced by the American Communist Party and its members. More significant than any political disputes, however, were the creative differences among the leading members of Frontier: Steiner and Van Dyke grew tired of working in the shadows of fellow directors Leo Hurwitz and Paul Strand. In leaving Frontier and forming American Documentary Films, Steiner and Van Dyke secured greater artistic freedom and expanded directorial opportunities for themselves.[70]

When they left Frontier, *The City* went with them, because Steiner had already been hired by the American Institute of Planners. Filming began in July. More than 100,000 feet of film (the final film uses 4,000) were shot in numerous locations, including Deerfield, Massachusetts; Center Sandwich, New Hampshire; Pittsburgh, Pennsylvania; Chicago; Los Angeles; New York City; Greenbelt, Maryland; and Green Hills, Ohio. Although some members of the Carnegie Foundation were not entirely pleased with the documentary—Steiner recalls one particularly irate gentleman who had to be escorted to a taxi after an advance screening—*The City* became one of the most successful films at the 1939 World's Fair, where it was shown twice a day in the Science and Education Building.[71]

The film can be divided into three main sections that document four different locales: the New England town (part 1), the industrial center (part 2a), the modern metropolis (parts 2b and 2c), and, finally, the green city (part 3). Although Mumford wrote only the final commentary for the film, his published writings, especially *The Story of Utopias* (1922), *Sticks and Stones* (1924), *Technics and Civilization* (1934), and *The Culture of Cities* (1938), constitute the determinant influence on *The City*.[72] Mumford was a leading figure in American urban planning and a founding member of the Regional Planning Association of America, which also included the economist Stuart Chase, forester Benton MacKaye, and architects Clarence Stein and Frederick Ackerman. (Stein and Ackerman were later named to the board of Civic Films, the production arm of the American Institute of Planners and producer of

The City.) The association promoted urban and rural renewal beyond the cosmetic beautification of cities and electrification of rural towns. Their philosophy of "planned decentralization" relied on technological advances such as automobiles, hydroelectric power, and electric transmission lines to facilitate the development of distinct, productive regions.[73]

The region was a geographic, economic, and social unit built around, but not dominated by, an urban core. According to Mumford, the city and region were to exist in a "working partnership" defined by "apportioned distribution." He rejected the typical hierarchical relationship between the urban center and its surrounding suburbs in favor of a flexible symbiosis.[74] This notion of the region as a distinct unit may seem similar to, but is in fact distinct from, the regionalism of those writers and intellectuals known as the Southern Agrarians. Mumford attacked their racially exclusive notion of community and reactionary drive toward the lost Arcadia of the South. "The self-sufficient life of a crude agricultural regime is no longer possible," he argued, "except in terms of gross cultural indulgence."[75] The imagined rural past could not serve as a model of future reform. "No effective change can be worked in the regional unit on the basis of past historic situations," Mumford explained. "What one seeks is not the ancient structure, but the emerging one."[76] In a debate between those who sought escape from the cultural turmoil of industrial modernism by romanticizing an agrarian ideal and those who unequivocally embraced the machine aesthetic, Mumford sought to find an alternative, to define an organic modern culture that revivified the individual and his community.[77] This regional agenda had its political implications. "The re-animation and rebuilding of regions as deliberate works of collective art," he wrote in 1938, "is the grand task of politics for the opening generation."[78]

Mumford's analysis of urbanization and his vision for reform establish the narrative trajectory of *The City*. Although the film may seem to fall within the logical pattern of "problem-solution," a model closely associated with documentaries by Pare Lorentz, a dialectical analysis underlies the tripartite form of the film as well as Mumford's own thought about urban development.[79] Mumford's writings (like Copland's music) defy a simple opposition between rural and urban. Instead, Mumford explained, the technological and cultural advances of the contemporary city were to join "the life-sustaining environment and life-directed interests of the countryside."[80] Thus the green city and its surrounding region synthesized rural and urban, bringing together technological development and cultural diversity while overcoming the social division of labor. The city provided the possibility of "humanizing the natural environment and of naturalizing the human heritage."[81]

Progress toward this ideal is charted through a series of utopian spaces. *The City* opens in an idyllic New England village, described in the typescript scenario as "set among rolling fields and woodlots, with its tree-lined dirt road, its church and common, its town hall and blacksmith shop."[82] A "spirit of friendliness and freedom" animates the scenes of a town meeting, people working at home and in the fields, a young boy with his dog, and an old man in a garden. In *Sticks and Stones*, Mumford had specifically described the New England village as a utopia. "In the organization of our New England villages, one sees a greater resemblance to the medieval Utopia of Sir Thomas More," Mumford had claimed, extolling the virtues of communitarianism, common land ownership, and corporate governance.[83] But More's neologism contains the truth of utopia within it: the word combines *outopia*, meaning no place, and *eutopia*, the good place. In *The City*, the New England utopia stands for that lost world—or, rather, a world that never really existed but is construed as a place where "the self-sufficient life" and its "life-directed interests" once were nurtured. As the camera pans across a series of gravestones in a sequence from part 1 of the film, the voice-over commentary speaks directly of death and rebirth: "The seed was ready for the earth again, ready to die, ready once more to grow." The film exploits nostalgia as an impetus for reform, and its images of rural life evoke the decidedly contemporary cultural context of the film. "One can hardly imagine a more pointed rendering of the period's slogan 'Communism is Twentieth-Century Americanism,'" Howard Pollack observes, "than its images of New England farmers with scythes and blacksmiths with hammers."[84] Mumford himself described the communitarianism of the New England town as "Yankee Communism," crediting the phrase to an unnamed friend.[85] Like the fictional island More described, the New England utopia is *no* place, an imagined world invoked not as a consolatory memory but a portentous oracle.

The new world is, however, born deformed. In parts 2a and 2b, the film portrays the factory town and urban metropolis as the dystopias of modernity, the negation of the rural village. The factory town, which Mumford associated with the fictional Coketown from Charles Dickens's *Hard Times* (1854), was not simply a grotesque form arising from the industrial age but a distorted projection of the New England village, the unforeseen but inevitable consequence of progress. Whereas technology had once been under man's control, in the industrial setting it controls man. The water-powered wheel was extolled by the commentary in part 1 as "better fit to do the work than human hands," quickly and easily providing sustenance in the form of grain for "hominy grits and Johnny cake." Yet the steel mill does not spare man from hard labor but necessitates it. Man now feeds the machine, and together they defile the natural world in the relentless pursuit of production. "Men and machines are pictured tearing wealth from the earth," the scenario explains. Filmed in Pittsburgh, the industrial sequence vividly depicts Mumford's notion of *Abbau*, or "un-building," a process characterized by the deliberate and imprudent exploitation of resources.[86]

The products mined from the earth are then used to build the modern metropolis of "Megalopolis," as Mumford terms it. The urban leviathan, epitomized by New York City, is ruled not by the natural cycle of rural life nor even the mechanical order of the factory but by the endless obligations of consumerism. Citizens of Megalopolis worship the unholy trinity of finance, insurance, and advertising.[87] Part 2b shows scenes of "crowds squirming to work, of traffic snarled, of children dodging trucks as they play ball, of lunch-hour mobs gulping food at drugstore counters, of ambulances and firetrucks stalled in traffic jams, of crowds pushing, hurrying, running." As a church bell rings out across an empty street, the scene shifts to a line of cars along a highway in part 2c. Urbanites take to the road in search of a pleasant day in the country but find only the congestion that they had hoped to escape. Families confront "maddening Sunday traffic jams, the hazards of unprotected two-way traffic, the defacement of the landscape by ugly billboard signs, the strain of stop-and-go traffic, and the danger of roads crossing at the same level."[88] The episode ends with a car crash.

Part 3, the last and longest section of the documentary, presents an alternative way of life in the "green city." Here traffic moves smoothly; the workplace is clean and cheerful; children and adults enjoy the parklike setting outside their efficient, orderly town-homes. "This is not a visionary city of some distant future," the typescript scenario explains, "but parts of actual planned communities as they now exist." Indeed, these scenes were filmed in Greenbelt, Maryland, and Green Hills, Ohio, two model communities designed and built under the direction of the federal government.[89] This concluding segment celebrates "the healthful, orderly life that is possible in a community designed with forethought, and points out the objectives to be sought not only in the building of new communities but in the remoulding of our present cities."[90] The green city is the new eutopia, an archaic term (meaning "the good place") that Mumford revived in *The Story of Utopias*. According to Mumford, the "choice is not between eutopia and the world as it is, but between eutopia and nothing—or rather, nothingness." The "fundamental problem of eutopian reconstruction," he argues, was "the problem of realizing the potential powers of the community." The project of realizing "the good place" demanded the refutation of the "fake utopias" like Coketown and Megalopolis "and all the other partial and inadequate myths to which we have given allegiance."[91]

The City explores these utopian, dystopian, and eutopian worlds through the mode of "expository documentary," a form that presents an apparently objective account through the use of spoken commentary. Words advance the argument; the film as a series of images and sounds is subordinate to the text.[92] But this structure—commonly identified with Lorentz's work—troubled the filmmakers. "How do you overcome the problem of that voice from on high?" Van Dyke wondered.[93] The answer came in confining the commentary and binding various elements together through negotiation rather than hierarchy. Contrary to the conventions of its genre, *The City* does not rely solely nor even primarily on the spoken word for its rhetorical effect but uses the manner of its presentation to develop the dialectical argument. The presence or absence of the voice, as well as its structural integration with the visuals and Copland's music, is as much a part of the film's argument as the words themselves. At times, the nondiegetic voice seems to dictate and order events on the screen, at others simply to follow the visual cues. Throughout *The City*, these shifts in the character and presentation of the commentary diminish the role of the narrator as an omniscient authority. The very form of the film thus accords with Mumford's philosophy of urban planning: no one element (the commentary, the city) dominates the others (the images, the region).

The visual rhetoric of *The City* preserves a measure of autonomy from the commentary through the use of recurring images that establish a structure not wholly dependent on the spoken voice.[94] Scenes of work, technology, transportation, and children pervade the New England village, industrial city, and modern metropolis, as well as the green city. These visual motifs generate a filmic logic that counteracts the semantic force of the voice-over, so that the persuasive rhetoric lies as much in the images as in the spoken word.[95] And of course the film does not only comprise commentary and images: Copland's musical score participates in the construction of meaning beyond the ken of the commentary. The significant differences among manifestations of these visual tropes and their varying musical presentations structure the film while also establishing the terms of comparison for the eutopic vision of *The City*. The New England village is shown to possess an inherent musicality and natural order; it is an enchanted, if unreal, place, the agrarian myth made manifest.[96] In the industrial town and modern metropolis, however, the narrative of experience is fragmented, the music disconnected. Finally a newly flexible sense of coherence is created in the green city, which is characterized by melody and motion. In each of these three main sections, the relationships among commentary, music, and image are constructed to advance the basic argument of the film and demonstrate the value of the eutopic city.

Throughout part 1, the spoken commentary and visual story are carefully integrated. Because the disembodied voice is tied to diegetic sounds, it acquires a substantive presence in the film. Writer and director Henwar Rodakiewicz described the natural correlation of spoken text to visual images in his production notes, drafted before *The City* was shot and scored. The entrance of the voice was to arise as naturally as possible, according to Rodakiewicz, whose notes match the finished film in this instance. "The sound of the bell fades" in the New England town, "or perhaps merely recedes and continues as a curtain-like background, and the narrator's voice begins. It is the first spoken word in the picture and arises quite logically from the fact that a town meeting is in progress."[97] The commentary is connected to the visual presentation of speech, as the narration seems to substitute for the unspoken words of characters on screen.

As the camera moves inside the church, the voice enters to explain that the gathering is a town meeting. The commentary is essential here: without its explanation, it would be difficult to understand events on screen. The same is true of the next sequence, which presents a series of distinct, disconnected shots of a woman at a loom, a man weaving a basket, and a miller at his grinder. Again the voice-over explains these disparate images, tying them together as a collective portrait of the town at work. "We work from sun 'til dark," the narrator intones, "if you can call just work a job that makes a body feel at peace while doing it. . . . Art isn't something foreign that we look at in a showcase; it's in the blankets that we've spun and woven right at home, it's in the patchwork quilts sewn by our daughters . . . the locks and hinges that the blacksmith shapes."

This passage recalls Mumford's description of the Thames Valley in *The Story of Utopias* as well as Stuart Chase's account of life in Mexico, and John Dewey's philosophy in *Art as Experience*. All three authors present leisure in the small town as not idleness but labor invested with aesthetic pleasure, art as socially useful. "In this utopia," Mumford wrote in *The Story of Utopias*, "the instinct of workmanship, the creative impulse, has free play; and since the majority of people are neither scholars nor scientists, as Sir Thomas More would have had them, they find their fulfillment in adding beauty to all the necessities of their daily toil."[98] At the end of this sequence of images the church bell tolls again, dismissing the voice from the soundtrack. "This whole

EXAMPLE 3.2. From *The City*, part I

episode is very definitely bounded and treated as an interlude," Rodakiewicz explains of the montage of the townspeople at work.[99]

Just as the voice has a natural relationship to the visuals in this section of the film, so too Copland's music matches the images. Part 1 introduces the tropes of transportation and technology, forces that are depicted as natural and easily harnessed, like the horse that pulls the wagon or the water spilling down the wheel. Copland underscores these images with music that closely mimics natural motion. A falling triplet motive complements the cascade of water, and the gentle trot of the horse is captured by a jaunty but unsyncopated rhythmic pattern (ex. 3.2). The irregular phrasing and simple *pizzicato* ostinato effectively mirror the uneven ride along a rutted path.[100]

When the wagon arrives at a blacksmith's shop, the smithy begins to work with a hand crank. His manual labor is accompanied by a languid melody that manages at once to preserve a preindustrial rural sensibility and project a nascent awareness of modernity. The static, nonfunctional harmonies of open fourths and fifths and pentatonic patterns suggest the pastoral, but the melody is scored for saxophone—an unusual choice for Copland.[101] Here it serves as a sonic marker of modernism. A musical hybrid (a wind instrument made of brass) closely associated with jazz, the saxophone connotes modernity itself. Its striking timbre gives the rural theme an urban edge, and thus the agrarian scene is shown to contain the seeds of modernity. Toward the end of part 1, the camera moves inside the blacksmith's shop, revealing his hammer and forge. This visual shift marks the passage to industrialization, and the pulsing chords behind the saxophone line that had previously been but a gentle accompaniment suddenly become searing dissonances that underscore images of an industrial foundry in part 2a.

The foundry represents the perversion of the blacksmith's labor. In the utopian village, the blacksmith himself wielded the hammer and bellows, but in the coal town, machines control the men who feed them fuel and choke on the pollution of mechanized labor. "Smoke makes prosperity, they tell ya here," the commentary explains, but the horror of the *Abbau* gives lie to the platitude. Men are dwarfed by their technology, literally and figuratively, as the smoke engulfs the figures in the factory. Beneath the montage of scenes from the foundry is an ominous syncopated bass line that works against the rhythm of rising, dissonant chords in the strings and trumpets. The natural, mimetic relation of music to image established in part 1 is undone, and the conflict escalates until a climactic release. Dissonant chords come crashing down as slag pours down a hill in a distorted recall of the New England water wheel and its flowing accompaniment.

The striking, prolonged absence of commentary in all three segments of part 2 suggests a godforsaken world in which no unseen force supplies a logical continuity or totalizing framework to make sense of the experiences shown on screen. This sequence of the film was originally intended to have no commentary at all, according to Rodakiewicz.[102] In fact there is commentary in parts 2a and 2b, but the character of the voice is greatly altered in both form and function. The narration is no longer related to diegetic sound but appears unprompted and unbidden, barking out short imperative phrases. A hurried cadence corresponds to the quick cuts between scenes in a steel factory: "Black out the past, forget the quiet cities. Bring in the steam and steel, the iron men, the giants." No words accompany the wide, distant shots of a landscape denuded by the manufacture of coal and covered by row upon row of flimsy houses.

As the scene shifts to show individual men, women, and children, the commentary returns with an uncertain, questioning tone. The narrator now speaks for the people in the industrial town, the slow deliberate cadence of his voice matching their resigned expressions. "We got to face life in these shacks and alleys. We got to let our children take their chances here." A new melody of sorts enters underneath the line, "There's prisons where a guy sent up for a crime can get a better place to live in than we can give our children." Unlike the graceful triplet motive that had accompanied both the water wheel and the little boy running across the field in part 1, however, this new theme is a solemn plaint that obsessively circles a minor third, recalling nothing so much as an animal pacing around its cage. The melodic range is restricted, its growth stunted like the children's. The bassoon and English horn—instruments frequently associated with the pastoral—are used ironically to underscore these images of industrial squalor, and the music reveals no hint of Copland's pastoral style. As the melody continues, technology and people are shown to be at odds in work and in leisure. Young boys try to play ball, for instance, but they must quickly cross the railroad tracks to avoid a passing train. In stark contrast to the grassy fields shown in part 1, children in the industrial town play on dirt and live in danger. A series of questions are posed, but no answers offered. "Who built this place? What put us here, and how do we get out again? . . . Does this mean there's no way out for us?" Copland's music suggests that there is no escape.

The rushed, clipped cadence of the voice returns in part 2b to indicate a further loss of discursive control and authority while effectively illustrating the chaotic rush of people on screen. This is the loudest section of the film, not because Copland's music is especially prominent but because diegetic noises fill the soundtrack. The cacophony of Megalopolis includes ambulance sirens, police whistles, and ticking meters in an endless line of taxicabs. Disembodied voices say the words that ranks of women are seen to type. The narrator speaks only at the opening of the section, his words and cadence echoing the choppy rhythms of advertising copy.

> Follow the crowd! Get the big money! You make a pile and raise a pile that makes another pile for you. Follow the crowd! We've reached a million, two million, five million, watch us grow! Going up! It's new, it's automatic, it dictates, records, seals, sterilizes, stamps and delivers in one operation, without human hands. What am I bid, what am I offered? Sold! Who's next? The people, yes. Follow the crowd, to the empire city, the wonder city, the windy city, the fashion city.

The very brief passage ends with a reminiscence of Carl Sandburg's iconic poem *The People, Yes* (1936). "The people, yes!" the narrator proclaims, quickly reconsidering. "The people. . . perhaps." As in the industrial sequence, the voice projects a haunting uncertainty, and the commentary implicitly questions the grandiose claims of commerce to be building a better life.

Like the children in Coketown, the people in Megalopolis face a multitude of dangers. Pedestrians dodge one other and weave through thickets of traffic. Perhaps inevitably a man is hit by a car, and the voice-over—which is now not the omniscient narrator but the conversation of spectral nurses in a hospital—explains that he will lose the leg just above the knee. This image (not shown on screen) subtly recalls an earlier shot in the factory town of a black man with a wooden leg. Likewise the plaintive melody first introduced in part 2b returns to accompany the accident scene and various shots of children playing amid cars. The repetitive theme, with its minor mode and narrow range, suggests the narrow confines of the cityscape and limited possibilities for growth. The children's play is corrupted by their environment, and there is even a suggestion of incipient juvenile delinquency in the aggressive interaction of the boys. One pair uses wooden swords and shields to battle on the street; elsewhere, a policeman watches suspiciously over a group of kids. Adolescents are seen throwing rocks, and a stickball game ends with a line drive through a residential window. The melody does not mimic these actions but provides an ostinato lament.

These shots of children on the city streets serve as an interlude between two sequences focused on the congestion of cars and people. No melodic material emerges as a distinct theme to accompany the traffic and crowds; instead, the musical interest is purely rhythmic. Copland's score imitates the quick cuts between images and the unnatural rhythm of the city in its use of ragged syncopations and short contrasting phrases. Thus the Megalopolis seems bereft of melody and of humanity. Even one of the most basic and natural acts—that of eating—is perverted in the modern city. In a sequence of part 2b, people are shown eating at a lunch counter, a scene no doubt familiar enough to New Yorkers watching the film at the World's Fair. But the extreme camera angles, closely cropped shots, and repetitive, syncopated rhythms of the musical accompaniment alienate the images from any lived experience. The specialized machines for flipping pancakes or making toast are shown in tight close-up, and the camera dissects the patrons at the counter, focusing only on severed hands or faceless mouths. The music is similarly fragmented, jumping between a rhythmic pattern in the bass and a short run in the winds to mirror the disjointed images. The distinctive camera placement and musical accompaniment estrange the viewer, preventing sympathetic identification with the people and experience shown on screen.

Parts 2b and 2c are divided by a church bell ringing out across a deserted street—an echo of the bell in part 1 and reminder that, unlike the rural village, Megalopolis lacks an omniscient presence that might order the world and imbue it with meaning. There is no commentary at all in part 2c, the "form and pattern" of which, according to Rodakiewicz, "rest very definitely on the musical framework." He notes that "though the arrangement of shots does follow a rough continuity, the reason for their placement, relation to each other, and duration on the screen arises from the meaning and logic of the music."[103] The music does indeed have a clear internal logic. Perhaps the most conventional melody in the entire film (in terms of phrase structure and harmonic progression) enters in part 2c to accompany a fleet of cars and families trying to make their way to the country (ex. 3.3). This tune, beguiling in its simplicity, sounds like the melody of a child's nursery rhyme, but its function here is clearly ironic—even grotesque—given the orchestration and accompanying visual track. The melody is carried by a shrill piccolo and solo trumpet, while the piano and low strings offer a dot-

EXAMPLE 3.3. From *The City*, part 2c

ted, scalar accompaniment. In its second iteration, the tune is harmonized with simple triads, filled out by the winds and strings, and the jaunty tune that at first might have sounded playful and innocent begins to project a mocking, insistent sarcasm.

In the absence of narration, the images and the music alone depict the frustrated attempt by people to flee the city and find respite in the country. Shots of fathers sitting behind the wheel in stoic silence, of a family picnicking by the side of the highway, traffic signs warning of dangerous roads and potential injury are accompanied by sharply syncopated chords in the muted brass that alternate with a staccato melody in the clarinets and off-beat bass. The dotted melody returns at the end of the sequence, gradually becoming louder and faster as the sequence builds to a visual and musical climax. A car plunges down a hillside, its descent recalling both the falling water and slag in parts 1 and 2a. Dissonant chords follow the vehicle, and part 2c ends with a fade to black as a filmic depiction of death.

The opening of part 3 suggests resurrection and redemption as triumphal chords in the brass accompany an impressive array of technological achievements, including a streamlined train, imposing dam, and an airplane. Aerial shots of greenbelt towns offer a bird's-eye (or perhaps a God's-eye) view, while the narration extolls the remarkable fit between man and machine in the new eutopia. "Science takes flight at last for human goals. This new age builds a better kind of city, close to the soil once more, as molded to our human wants as planes are shaped for speed. New cities take form, green cities." The view of the city dissolves to an aerial shot of a highway cloverleaf and a medium-shot, back at ground level, of a streamlined bus moving along an exit ramp of the highway. The narrator commends its progress in a mellifluous timbre: "The traffic really *flows* along, and forty miles an hour is faster here than seventy when it's stop and go, stop and go and stop." Copland's music really flows along as well, with a tonally grounded circular motif in the winds and high strings.[104]

As in part 1, the commentary in part 3 "arises as definitely and structurally from the filmic construction as did its absence in other sequences," Rodakiewicz explains, adding that "it is essential that the narrator be chosen for a certain special quality of fluidness, clarity, and resonance of voice," because he represents "the 'good.'"[105] And the voice of good is the voice of God. "As the plane flies through a cloud," Rodakiewicz writes, "the drone of the engine fades, then the ship emerges again and the narrator's voice begins—the voice of the 'good' speaking from the sky."[106] But in the eutopic world of the "new city," the voice does not reclaim sole power to generate meaning; rather, the spoken commentary enters a partnership with the visual narrative and musical score. Although Rodakiewicz suggests that the New England sequence has a clear visual storyline that follows a young boy and his father on a trip into town, these events in part 1 are not at all clear. The relationship between the boy and the man is not established. Nor is it obvious that the gathering is a town meeting, and the montage of work requires commentary to explain its significance. Only the narration orders an otherwise fragmented succession of images. By contrast, part 3 has a definite narrative trajectory. Events shown on screen—a baseball game, young boy fixing a bicycle, children at play—have a logic all their own that requires no ancillary explanation. The score of the baseball game is tied; the winning run crosses home plate; a boy comes home for a snack and rushes off again on his bicycle. The montage of children at play and adults at work features shots that are long enough to establish a sense of visual continuity.

In contrast to the alienating effects of the lunch-counter scene, the viewer is made to feel at home in the green city. The camera often lingers in long, middle-ground shots that present a realistic viewpoint and so encourage a sense of identification between viewer and film. Hovering at the eye level of a young mother watching over her charges, for example, the camera becomes the viewer's eye. Other images of children solidify the relationship between the camera position and the parental gaze. We seem to sit on a bench watching children at play, to kneel next to a toddler, to bend down and pick up an infant. Likewise, the audience of the film is identified with the crowd at the baseball game; both parties are spectators to the action on screen.[107]

Copland's music is just as ingratiating. After a passage of unaccompanied narration, a solo flute introduces a lyrical new theme very similar to the music

EXAMPLE 3.4. From *The City*, part 3, "flowing" flute melody

of the bus (ex. 3.4). The well-defined E-major harmonies of this melody establish a sonic stability that the themes in parts 1 and 2 had lacked. Emphasizing the submediant, the harmony evokes the pastoral, and the gapped qualities of previous themes give way to a long melodic line that touches on all notes of the major scale. The measure of the difference between earlier melodic moments—including the saxophone melody in part 1, children's theme in parts 2a and 2b, and the ironic tune in part 2c—and this new, flowing melody is the measure of the eutopian city.

The flowing flute theme pervades part 3, accompanying images of buses, cars, children riding bicycles and at play. The extremely repetitive quality of the music in this section, which owes in part to the aural similarity between the bus theme and flute melody, also may be attributed to changes in the structure of film itself and indeed to Copland's general approach to writing music for film.[108] Nevertheless such repetition serves an important function here. The melodic continuity knits together the human and the machine, healing the fractured relationship between man and his technology. "Who shall be the master," the narrator asks, "things or men?" Even before the commentary itself responds—"at last, men take command"—Copland's music has provided the answer. The melody accompanies images of work and play, of both machines and men, and so creates the organic wholeness that Mumford desired for the new city. "Here science serves the worker and the work together," the commentary continues, echoing Mumford's own words in *The Culture of Cities*, "making machines more automatic and the men who govern them more human."

As in the New England town, work in the green city is invested with pleasure. "You can't tell where the playing ends and where the work begins. We mix them here; we learn by living," the narration explains. This summary of Dewey's heuristic philosophy of progressive education is enacted on screen: children are shown at school, taking art classes and pretending to run a post office. Dewey emphasized the need for aesthetic education and for children to participate, through imaginative play, in the processes of democracy. And so the children learn to be good citizens in the green city. "Here the boys and girls live and relive the life around them, getting the measure of our bigger world and shaping it anew. . . . Here boys and girls achieve a balanced personality, ready to build and meet a many-sided world, facing the good and bad and choosing the best."

The film ends with a juxtaposition of images. "You take your choice," the narrator bluntly says, as scenes from Coketown and Megalopolis are recalled with appropriately dissonant music accompanying the dystopic images. "Each one is real, each one is possible." The narration concludes: "It's here, the new city, ready to serve a better age. You and your children: the choice is yours." But of course the film has already decided for the viewer. The choice between contemporary urban life and the eutopian city is made by the filmic logic and musical rhetoric before the question is ever posed in the commentary.

The issue of choice is central to the interpretation of *The City* as a radical film. In his thoughtful review, the critic Richard Griffith bitterly observed:

> *The City* proceeds as though everyone could [make a choice], as though it had only to convince us of the *value* of the future town. But people do not live in slums by choice. They need to be shown not only what they ought to have but how they can get it. And this the film does not mention.[109]

The filmmakers themselves struggled with the degree to which they wanted or even were able to offer a more direct critique of social and economic injustice. William Alexander suggests that in part 2a, Rodakiewicz might have preferred to use the text first drafted in his notes for the film. There he offered "a cold, matter-of-fact account of the development of the Monongahela Valley and the growing demand for steel"—words sure to offend the members of the Carnegie Corporation, as robber-baron Andrew Carnegie was responsible for much of the development in Pittsburgh and the surrounding Monongahela Valley.[110] Mumford's commentary for the industrial sequence leaves the crucial questions of responsibility hanging in the air, which, according to Alexander, "denied the sequence some of the impact that Lorentz and Rodakiewicz would have liked to give it."[111]

But Rodakiewicz preferred no commentary at all. "Any words that could be said," he explained, "would surely distort the purpose of this sequence." He concluded that "the pictures will speak for themselves and tell their story far more vividly and honestly."[112] He did propose adding more pointed commentary at the conclusion of part 3 to strengthen the ending. As Alexander notes, Rodakiewicz "planned that contentious voices would argue the merits of the planners' vision of the model city. . . . The carping, abusive, cynical voices of a 'slick realtor,' a demagogue, and a city tough would be combated by the unruffled voice of the Green City itself."[113] But Mumford's narration won out. His more measured language in both the industrial sequence and the closing section of the film ensured that *The City* would not antagonize its corporate sponsors, particularly the Carnegie Foundation.

Thus *The City* is not a fully developed radical film. It does not offer any explanation for the circumstances it would wish to change nor point to a guilty party. Yet it is not simply a celebration of the New Deal.[114] Its very existence stands as a rebuke of the Resettlement Administration and its failure to fulfill the mission of civic planning as defined by the Regional Planning Association. The three greenbelt towns in Maryland, Ohio, and Wisconsin built in 1935 might have begun to realize the goals of the Association, but when the Resettlement Administration was dissolved in 1937, the greenbelt program was abandoned. *The City* decries this loss. In turning away from the communitarian ideal of the greenbelt towns, the New Deal had seemingly made its choice, and so the urgency of the commentary at the end of the film seems a call to action. "We've got the skill, we've found a way. We've built the cities. All that we know about machines and raw materials and human ways of living is waiting. We can reproduce the pattern and better it a thousand times. It's here, the new city, ready to serve a better age." Yet people could not opt to live in eutopian cities that were not built.

Mumford publicly criticized Franklin Roosevelt and the New Deal in the pages of the *New Republic*, pointing out that many government programs lacked a comprehensive agenda for urban renewal and reform.[115] As Mumford explained in *The Culture of Cities*, the challenge of constructing civic spaces called for decisive action.

> Our whole program of re-urbanization and housing demands a definite choice. That choice may not be revolutionary in the sense of implying a complete break and an overpowering catastrophe: but it is revolutionary in the sense that when, by steady pressure and day-to-day movement, it has achieved its end, the metropolis and the insidious pecuniary values of metropolitan life will be obliterated, and a new set of working institutions, more consonant with a human scheme of values, will have taken its place. Planners who are not aware of these implications are sociologically too unsophisticated to be trusted with important functions: instead of helping to define an adequate public policy, they can only obfuscate the issues and sabotage a sound social program.[116]

Such is the choice outlined in *The City* and the political agenda of left-wing progresssivism. Beyond this particular negative assessment of contemporary urban planning, Mumford's basic political philosophy seems inconsistent with ideology of the New Deal, which presumed a centralized, federal authority. Mumford rejected the "false stability of the national state." His organic conception of community entailed a flexible system of power sharing and encouraged a social leveling, such that no one state could claim preeminence nor any individual declare superiority.[117] "Authority under the emerging regime of political relativity is a matter of functional competence," he argued. "Neither size, position, nor physical power—nor a monopoly of all these qualities—by itself determines the importance of a city or a community."[118] The structure of *The City* accords with this ideal of political relativity. In the film, the power of authority (whether the metropolitan city or omniscient commentary) is vitiated, and the individual elements form elastic bonds of cooperation and collaboration.

The dilemma of the progressive position, as Casey Nelson Blake notes, is its tendency toward fascism insofar as the enlightened individual and government planning are construed as solutions to social problems. *The City* never descends into fascistic propaganda despite its persuasive visual and spoken rhetoric, because the structure of the images, presentation of narrative, and character of Copland's music imbue the eutopic city with flexibility, motion, and change.[119] His flowing themes defy the strictures of the barline and avoid predictable, set melodic patterns. Conformity and predictability are heard as part of dystopia—the most regular and regulated music accompanies the futile escape to the country in part 2c—whereas the greenbelt town is melodically fluid and endlessly inventive. The generative theme in part 3 seems to grow from its first melodic turns, slowly expanding its range and rhythms, and thus to suggest the organic and evolving nature of the eutopia. Ultimately, this logical and formal argument distinguishes the film from the New Deal as a comprehensive program of federal reform. Instead *The City* is allied with the less stable but more ambitious program of the Popular Front.

The Second Hurricane and *The City* occupy an indeterminate position along a continuum of left-wing thought, lying somewhere between a committed, consistent radicalism and New Deal liberalism, and this uncertain terrain is precisely what belongs to the Popular Front itself. If the ideal of community presented here does not epitomize the radicalism of the Front, which emphasized the alignments of race and class, neither work can be summarily dismissed as sentimental platitude nor considered a celebration of collective control.[120] Rather, both draw on the radical republicanism of a progressive social critique to present examples of personal and collective expression. In their parables of cooperation, they attempt to counteract the alienation of self and society considered endemic to modern industrial culture. Both are products of artistic collaboration and statements of communitarian values. As such *The Second Hurricane* and *The City* level a meaningful critique of individualism while constructing compelling examples of holistic community.

4 "The Dancing of an Attitude"

"CRITICAL AND IMAGINATIVE WORKS," Kenneth Burke explains in his theory of literary form, "are answers to questions posed by the situation in which they arose." More than that, "they are *strategic* answers, *stylized* answers."[1] Arguing that artistic creations reveal a personal and cultural perspective on social situations, Burke characterizes symbolic acts as "the *dancing of an attitude*."[2] The metaphor captures the ways in which aesthetic expression manifests the individual subjectivity of an artist, the influence of his material conditions, and a public as well as private response to social circumstances. "The dancing of an attitude" is but a figure of speech that relates the personal and political to the aesthetic, but the phrase might well be interpreted more literally in the case of Copland's music for the ballets *Billy the Kid* (1938) and *Rodeo* (1942).

These works not only form the basis of Copland's reputation as a composer of Americana but have also come to define an uncomplicated form of musical nationalism. As concert suites, they are staples on programs with a patriotic theme or commemorative function and favorites for children's concerts. Each of the ballets—or more accurately, snippets from the suites—also has been appropriated by mass culture: the music of television and film has rendered Copland's distinctive rhythms and borrowed melodies part of the commercial realm. Perhaps most familiar are the thirty seconds of "Hoe-Down" from *Rodeo* used in advertisements for beef. Music from *Billy the Kid* greets guests at the Western-themed Wilderness Lodge in Walt Disney World, and as Neil Lerner has demonstrated, *Appalachian Spring* (Copland's third Western-tinged ballet) has established the Hollywood musical code for the American pastoral.[3] Coplandesque gestures resound through such films as *Hoosiers* (1986), which follows the 1950s Cinderella story of a rural Indiana basketball team's improbable victory in the high-school state championship; *Field of Dreams* (1989), a sentimental yarn about an equally improbable baseball field in an Iowa cornfield that grants the wishes of masculine selfhood; and *Apollo 13* (1995), which Lerner aptly describes as "a starkly patriotic and politically reactionary docu-drama" about the ill-fated space mission in April 1970.[4]

It might seem only fitting that Copland's music should accompany such symbols of Americanism as red meat, sports, fathers and sons, or the "new frontier" of space, because *Billy the Kid, Rodeo*, and *Appalachian Spring* themselves engage an equally powerful figure of America: the West. Like the Midwestern prairie or outer space, the West has been construed in popular culture and the national imagination as a setting for romantic reverie, a place for indulging dreams of individual heroism and gratifying chauvinistic cultural desires. It is an enchanted landscape counterpoised to Megalopolis, and Copland's ballets have been interpreted as a "nostalgic escape" from the crises of contemporary America.[5]

Yet *Billy the Kid* and *Rodeo* reference the West not merely to exploit its cultural resonance but also to explore conflicting ideological imperatives within the social thought of the thirties and forties. Surely the West may serve as a repository for conservative cultural values and traditional definitions of Americanism, but evoking the rural past is not the same as embracing it. *Billy the Kid* and *Rodeo* engage the West as an ideology—in Burke's definition, "an aggregate of beliefs sufficiently at odds with one another to justify opposite kinds of conduct."[6] Here the West is not a safe house from modernity but the stage for a contemporary drama of community as told from the perspective of the individual. Whereas such works as *The Second Hurricane* and *The City* focus on the creation and maintenance of social solidarity, *Billy the Kid* and *Rodeo* attend to the individual by questioning whether community demands conformity. *Billy* draws a sympathetic portrait of the outlaw living on the margins of society and considers the irony of progress—its power to destroy as well as create; *Rodeo* confronts the gendered conceptions of self as formed in the unsettled social landscape of frontier life. Interpreted in light of Burke's aesthetic program and the politics of the Popular Front, these ballets and Copland's music for them present ambivalent tales that complicate the standard mythopoetic narratives of the West. In both works, the West—so often regarded as the crucible of American values—serves as the perfect forum for inquiry, because the tensions between liberty and equality, individual freedom and collective security, inhere in the myth and the ballets as in the very ideals of the nation.

Constructing and Countering the Myth of the West

The West is a particularly useful framework for exploring social conflicts and cultural contradictions, given that the myth of the West has its own origins in conflict. As Claude Lévi-Strauss has observed, a crucial function of myth is to mediate contradictory cultural imperatives.[7] Following this insight, David Hamilton Murdoch has argued that the idea of the West was formulated by the Eastern establishment in the late nineteenth century to negotiate the cultural crisis of industrialization.[8] American values had long prized self-sufficiency and unfettered progress, but the evident corruption of laissez-faire industrialism in the years following the Civil War appeared to demand greater regulation by the federal government. Thus a tradition of individualism (conflated with liberal capitalism) and zeal for progress ran up against a demonstrated need for collective security. "In essence," Murdoch explains, "America appeared to be faced with the choice of rejecting a future which her own commitment to progress had wrought, or abandoning her value system. . . . This dilemma cried out for a myth to resolve it."[9] That myth was the West, imagined to be the renewable resource of democracy and fountain of America's youth.

The West had long provided a means to release the mounting pressures of urbanization as experienced in the East, but, as Murdoch notes, "the old fail-safe factor had proved to have built-in obsolescence."[10] The more people availed themselves of open land, the less of it remained. In 1891, the Census Bureau unequivocally declared that the frontier had disappeared. "Up to and including 1880," a census bulletin proclaimed, "the country had a frontier of settlement, but at present the unsettled area has been so broken into by isolated bodies of settlement that there can hardly be said to be a frontier line."[11] Thus the myth of the West was born of the frontier's death. Even after the frontier had passed into history, the imagined West could still be used to justify a continuing reliance on individual rather than collective solutions to the problems of modernity. The West, the prairie, the pioneer, and the cowboy—all were cemented as icons of American progress, and together they came to represent a spirit of endless expansion, whether of national borders, liberal democracy, or industrial capitalism.

The meaning of the West and its closing was forcefully articulated by historian Frederick Jackson Turner, whose 1893 speech "The Significance of the Frontier in American History" linked the development of American society, politics, and culture to the frontier experience.[12] Turner identified the essence of Americanism with westward expansion, arguing that "this perennial rebirth, this fluidity of American life, this expansion westward with its new opportunities, its continuous touch with the simplicity of primitive society, furnish the forces dominating American character," democracy chief among them.[13] "The most important effect of the frontier," Turner claimed, "has been in the promotion of democracy."[14] Drawing implicitly on the philosophy of Thomas Jefferson, who idealized the yeoman farmer as the self-governing individual, Turner equated free land with freedom: "frontier individualism has from the beginning promoted democracy," he explained.[15] But writing within the grip of a severe economic depression marked by agrarian radicalism and labor unrest, Turner acknowledged that "the democracy born of free land" was regrettably "strong in selfishness and individualism, intolerant of administrative experience and education," and given to "pressing individual liberty beyond its proper bounds."[16] Frontier individualism "allowed a laxity in regard to governmental affairs which has rendered possible the spoils system and all the manifest evils that follow from the lack of a highly developed civic spirit."[17] Yet the "proper bounds" of individualism were unclear, and although he acknowledged that in the absence of free land, the government became the guarantor of democracy, Turner remained suspicious of federal authority.[18]

In the 1930s, when democracy itself seemed imperiled by the crisis of the Great Depression, liberal reformers and radical critics argued that the problems of unregulated capitalism could no longer be displaced to the real or imagined frontier. The West and its symbols (partiuclarly the pioneer) were appropriated by the leftist political discourse as tropes linking the social and economic crisis to the pernicious influence of pioneer individualism.[19] In a landmark speech delivered before the Commonwealth Club of California in 1932, for example, Franklin Roosevelt offered the closing of the frontier as a reason why government needed to take an active role in the regulation of the economy. The West had been a haven of opportunity, a place where individual labor ensured self-sufficiency. So long as there was land, the question of the capitalist exploitation of resources (whether human or natural) could be continually deferred. "On the Western frontier," Roosevelt explained, "land was substantially free." As a consequence, "no one, who did not shirk the task of earning a living, was entirely without opportunity to do so."[20] The ability of the prairie to provide had offset the effects of past economic downturns. In response to any depression, Roosevelt continued, "a new section of land was opened in the West; and even our temporary misfortune served our manifest destiny."[21] And yet without limitless space, the West could no longer be called on to solve the problems of industrialization and laissez-faire capitalism. "There is no safety valve in the form of a Western prairie to which those thrown out of work by the Eastern economic machines can go for a new start," Roosevelt noted, urging "a re-appraisal of values" that would privilege the civic good over individual advancement.[22] The postfrontier world demanded a new industrial order, and in *A New Deal* (1932), economist Stuart Chase made the case for economic planning and the revolutionary reform of capitalism, arguing that "laissez-faire rides well on covered wagons; not so well on conveyor belts and cement roads."[23]

Roosevelt's secretary of agriculture (1932–40) and eventual vice president (1940–44) Henry A. Wallace wrote of the frontier and its place in the culture of the Depression from a resolutely left-wing perspective. In *New Frontiers* (1934), Wallace explained that the title of his study referred not to new land "but a new state of heart and mind" to be achieved by the building of "a new social machinery" that would guarantee economic security and social justice.[24] Seeming to accept Turner's thesis that the West had shaped American culture and mores, Wallace nonetheless criticized competitive individualism as encouraged by the frontier experience. "By the raw pioneer rules of first stakes we have encamped as migrants and have taken greedily and unevenly of its wealth," he wrote. "A few of us, in consequence, have much more than we can comfortably or decently spend or handle; yet most of us have too little for comfort, decency and hope of a general progress." Echoing Roosevelt, Wallace maintained that because the "land frontier" was gone, the "Depression can no longer be solved by shipping the unemployed West." Instead, he argued, "we must learn to live with each other. We have no longer enormous, unexploited natural resources awaiting only the touch of young and vigorous hands to be transformed into fabulous, individual wealth."[25]

The "keynote of the new frontier," he declared, "is cooperation."[26] This new charge demanded a rejection of certain values beholden to the frontier. The pioneers had "suffered and forged ahead in the world" by exploiting "not only natural resources but the generations which came after," and Wallace decried their selfish pursuit of individual gain over the collective good. "We glorify these men, grabbers and exploiters that they were, and marvel at their conquests. But they did not know how to live with each other and they did not know how to teach the American nation to live with other nations." He concluded that "frontier free-booter democracy of the purely individualistic type is definitely gone."[27] Similarly, the historian Walter Prescott Webb explained in *Divided We Stand: The Crisis of a Frontierless Democracy* (1937) that "democracy could function under [frontier] conditions, even an extreme democracy, not because it solved problems, but because it seldom had to meet them." Yet "the closing of the frontier brought democratic America to the first test of its ability to govern, to solve problems rather than to enjoy an escape from them."[28]

For those to the left of Roosevelt and New Deal liberalism, the West seemed but a foundation myth for American capitalism, an outmoded ideal that obscured the inequalities of progress. One of the key documents of the Popular Front, the 1932 pamphlet *Culture and the Crisis*, linked a critique of capitalism and support for the Communist ticket in the presidential election to the realities of postfrontier American society. Its authors maintained that the open space of the frontier had enabled capitalist expansion; with the closing of the West, capitalism had lost its ability to recover from inevitable depressions. "In the past," it is noted,

> depressions were followed by prosperity on a larger scale, because of undeveloped forces within capitalism—the expansion of home and foreign markets and the growth of new industries. In the United States the undeveloped lands out West were an additional stimulus to expansion. But these lands are no more, there are no new industries in sight, home markets are saturated, and the competition for foreign markets is enormously aggravated. The decline of capitalism, which has tormented Europe since the World War, is now also an American phenomenon.[29]

Without the West, it seemed that American capitalism simply could not survive.

Culture and the Crisis was written primarily by Lewis Corey, a founding member of the American Communist Party (under the name Louis Fraina) and a leading theorist of the Popular Front.[30] In *The Decline of American Capitalism* (1934), Corey argues that the "major significance of the frontier lay in its influence on the growth of capitalism, in its contribution to the long-time factors of economic expansion."[31] Aided by increasing agricultural production and the building of railroads, the frontier had provided a growing market for capital goods. "The expansion of the frontier was a perpetual re-birth of capitalism," Corey continues, "energizing its upward movement, strengthening capitalism economically and ideologically."[32] After the Civil War, the frontier increasingly functioned as an agent of capitalist expansion rather than a locus of democratic energy; instead of furthering the ideals of the American Dream—"liberty, democracy, equality, mass well-being, opportunity, education, no class stratification, limited government, peace, and progress"—the frontier supported monopoly capitalism.[33] According to Corey, the spirit of American individualism had been perverted by laissez-faire capitalism, and the ruling class had donned the guise of the pioneers' "rugged individualism" as but "a screen for predatory practices and disregard for the masses' need."[34] While the frontier still existed, the inevitable decline of capitalism could be forestalled, as Roosevelt had noted, but the ideology of expansion—of endless growth and production, of pioneering—had survived long after the demise of the frontier, to ill effect.[35]

In his 1931 tract *Counter-Statement*, Kenneth Burke examines such survivals, detailing a political and aesthetic program that explains how the culture of pioneering and the myth of the West continue to inform the attitudes of industrial modernism and retard the development of new, more productive modes of thought. A leading figure on the cultural front, Burke (like Copland) belonged to the generation of American artists and intellectuals born around the turn of the century. In the 1920s he was a frequent contributor to *The Dial* (serving as music editor from 1927 to 1929), *Hound and Horn*, and the *New Republic*; some of his articles were collected into his first book, *Counter-Statement*.[36] There he argued that art was a form of communication with social significance and maintained that the artist and his art were bound to their culture and society, that literature (or music) could participate in a campaign for civic reform. Still, he respected the creative independence of the artist; aesthetics might subsume politics, but the co-option of aesthetics by politics was objectionable. *Counter-Statement* validates the practical possibilities of artistic expression as a symbolic act and considers the ways artistic creation might challenge hegemonic rhetoric and ideology. Because it melds the political with the aesthetic and relates the culture of the past to the conditions at present, Burke's theory of the aesthetic is particularly useful in considering how *Billy the Kid* and *Rodeo* simultaneously enact and interrogate the myth of the West to expose the cultural assumptions of both rural and industrial America.

His program explores "which emotions and attitudes should be stressed, and which slighted, in the aesthetic adjustment to the particular conditions of today."[37] Asserting that life is "an aggregate of survivals and possibilities," Burke suggests that "the artist wholly awake to the contemporary will embody a mixture of retentions and innovations."[38] Earlier modes of thought are often retained even as conditions change, and it is the job of the artist to challenge these retentions, test their continuing value, and synthesize old with new. Whereas society had traditionally been agrarian, Burke explains, the emergent condition of modern life was industrialization. But even the patently new forces of industrialization also tended to resist new ways of thinking, to oppose the innovations of the artist, because the industrialists' "own values are primarily a survival."[39] Such survivals undermined the formation of attitudes more appropriate to contemporary circumstance. By way of example, Burke offers the pioneer. Although self-sufficient individualism "was an adequate adjustment to the conditions of pioneering," he notes, in the industrial context the values of the pioneer were retained in the destructive doctrine of laissez-faire capitalism.[40] Thus the seemingly modern crisis of capitalist overproduction had resulted from the historical attitudes of pioneering.

Uncritically or unconsciously drawing on the obsolete values of the frontier, industrialists had failed to develop more appropriate responses to the destructive cycles of capitalist production.

> Some industrialist leaders, recognizing that improved methods of production may lead to enforced idleness, admit that their industry may eventually be placed upon a seasonal basis, with even several months a year in which the factories are closed. But they do not consider the necessary cultural concomitant of such a change. They would meet the rise of technological unemployment by decreasing the hours of labor. Yet they still hold to the blessedness of toil and are in many cases themselves unceasing workers. They retain in this respect the mental equipment of the pioneer—who had to "glorify" toil if he was to survive.[41]

The artist may counter such retentions by exploring (and even exploding) the dialectic between the practical and the aesthetic. According to Burke, the practical is concerned with "efficiency, prosperity, material acquisitions, increased consumption, 'new needs,' expansion, higher standards of living, progressive rather than regressive evolution, in short, ubiquitous optimism." The aesthetic embraces "inefficiency, indolence, dissipation, vacillation, mockery, distrust, 'hypochondria,' non-conformity, bad sportsmanship, in short, negativism."[42] The aims of the practical seem laudable, Burke accedes, but the practical tends toward fascism, as it rails against the inefficiency of democracy and longs for centralized authority. In a what might be read as a veiled critique of New Deal liberalism, Burke criticizes the desire for a "more 'efficient' form of government, with problems of production and distribution handled as they are by the co-ordinating head of a large factory." This is essentially "the ideal Fascism—guidance in accordance with economic principles—central authority."[43] And although the aesthetic might seem to have few positive qualities, it serves to keep "the practical from becoming too hopelessly itself." The aesthetic "could never triumph" as an organizing principle of society, yet it remains essential as a subversive force that reasserts pluralism in the face of resurgent homogeneity. Opposing the fascist ideal of "perfecting the means of control" over industry and government, the aesthetic endangers "the basic props of industry" and advances a democratic "doctrine of interference."[44]

The aesthetic subverts the power of the industrialists by being politically aligned with the agrarians.[45] In a modern, industrialized world, the agrarians are the radicals, Burke claims, because they have retained "pre-industrialist modes of living and thinking" that preserve alternatives to the accepted industrial ethos. They stand opposed to industrial hegemony and thus may be considered "politically and economically as liberal, or Progressives." In aligning himself with an agrarian sensibility, the artist harnesses the power of the aesthetic to challenge the culture of industrial capitalism. He then works "to formulate the cultural counterpart to industrialism" (presumably the counter-statement of Burke's title) that "will involve the destruction of values" held in common by agrarian and industrial interests, "such as the cluster of emphases stimulating commercial ambition."[46]

This powerful dialectic of industrial and agrarian, city and country, East and West, demonstrates that a rural sensibility need not always be attached to conservative values. In light of Burke's program, Copland's ballets can be seen to embrace elements of the agrarian and to accord with the ideal of the aesthetic as an unruly, subversive force that aims "to discourage the most stimulating values of the practical," a strategy that "would seek—by wit, by fancy, by anathema, by versatility—to throw into confusion the code which underlies commercial enterprise, industrial competition, the 'heroism' of economic warfare."[47] *Billy the Kid* and *Rodeo* throw the code into confusion by questioning the legacy of the pioneer—so often conflated with the West itself—and the cult of individualism, as well as the cultural construction of selfhood. The view of the West in leftist social thought and Burke's definition of the aesthetic provide an interpretive framework for *Billy the Kid* and *Rodeo* that reveals a more ambiguous view of the American past (and present) than is generally found in their current reception. Copland's Western turn can thus be interpreted as a political and aesthetic strategy that tests the values of industrial modernism by incorporating an agrarian awareness without espousing a romantic nostalgia or conservative social agenda.

For and Against the Outlaw in Billy the Kid

In 1938 the poet, writer, and dance impresario Lincoln Kirstein approached Eugene Loring, a young choreographer, with a commission for a new ballet. Some two years earlier, Kirstein had formed the Ballet Caravan, a small company that aimed to invent a new American tradition of contemporary ballet.[48] The Ballet Caravan had already produced a string of successful dances on American subjects when Kirstein turned to Loring with an idea in mind and a book in hand: "Here!" he said, offering Loring a copy of Walter Noble Burns's *The Saga of Billy the Kid* (1926), "See if you can make a ballet of it."[49] To write the scenario, which presents episodes in the life of William H. Bonney culminating in his death, Loring not only read Burns's well-known and largely sympathetic portrait of Billy the Kid but also turned to other sources, including *Pilgrims of the Santa Fe* (1931) by Agnes C. Laut; *Cowboy Songs and Other Frontier Ballads* (1910) by John Lomax; *The Doomsday Men: An Adventure* (1938) by J. B. Priestley; *The Virginian: A Horseman of the Plains* (1902) by Owen Wister; and *Ranch Life and the Hunting Trail* (1888) by rough-rider and former president Theodore Roosevelt.[50] Loring's notebooks are filled with quotations from these sources, copious notes that he must have used in preparing the remarkably detailed scenario.[51]

Most notable among these are the books by Burns, Roosevelt, and Wister. Only the biography by Burns concerns Billy the Kid, but all three volumes speak to the ways in which contemporary cultural attitudes and anxieties were projected onto the West and one of its most notorious outlaws. Roosevelt and Wister's books react to the progress of industrialization and the cultural upheaval of the 1880s, whereas Burns's biography is very much a product of the 1920s. And Loring's scenario does not simply reflect the various worlds described by these authors but also captures the values and conflicts of his own era. In the late 1930s, as hopes of economic recovery were dashed by a new recession and the threat of war loomed over Europe, Loring and Copland collaborated to create a ballet that, in dance and music, considers the ambiguous legacy of Western expansion in the American experience.

Writing within a decade of Billy's death (in 1881), Theodore Roosevelt and Owen Wister were friends who had met at Harvard University. Both traveled during the 1880s, and their books helped to define the immediate cultural context for the emerging legend of Billy the Kid. Roosevelt journeyed west on a hunting trip in 1883; the following year, after having lost his mother to typhoid and wife in childbirth, he returned to his ranch in the Dakota Territory. Despondent over their deaths and frustrated by the defeat of his political faction, he spent two years working as cattle rancher. Wister, too, spent time in the West, and though *The Virginian* is a work of fiction, its account of a young man's experiences in Wyoming recalls the author's own travels in that territory.

Roosevelt and Wister viewed their Western experiences from an Eastern perspective, looking West partly to understand the transformation of the

East.[52] The two men had come of age in an era marked by enormous change and conflict. During the 1880s, a president was assassinated (James Garfield in 1881); Thomas Edison's electric wiring illuminated a square mile of New York City; long-distance phone calls became possible; George Eastman developed the box camera; the internal combustion engine was invented; and the police opened fire on the crowd at the Haymarket labor riots in Chicago, leaving eight people dead and scores injured. The swiftly moving tide of industrialization seemed to be eroding traditional social and economic structures at the same time increased immigration was reshaping cultural norms. A variety of competing political movements sought to address these changes but also fragmented the American civic sphere. In response to such tumult, Roosevelt and Wister invoked the frontier as a past that might redeem the present.[53] Their West was a bulwark intended to protect a rural, Anglo-American, egalitarian sensibility from the advancing industrial, multiethnic social order. Both of these young men also located their ideals of masculinity and adulthood in the figures of the frontier. For Roosevelt, the West nurtured such qualities of American masculinity as fortitude, independence, and determination. Wister imbued his romantic hero with these same characteristics, portraying the cowboy as an unstudied amalgam of gentlemanly decorum and rugged individualism.

Likewise the story of Billy the Kid was presented as a lesson in masculine selfhood, though Billy did not emerge as a man to be uncritically emulated. During the late nineteenth and early twentieth centuries, the legend of the Kid was constructed along the lines of a typical romance—a literary archetype that generally presents a hero's struggle and triumph over villainous evil to establish a dialectical relationship between the characters and the values they embody.[54] But the hero of the Kid's romance was not Billy himself; that role was reserved for Pat Garrett, the sheriff who protected law and order in frontier society. In sources dating from just after the Kid's death through the mid-1920s, Billy is generally presented as an effeminate, selfish, cruel, and savage boy, whereas Garrett is a virile, responsible, sensitive, civilized man.[55] In this early generation of tales about the Kid, Garrett's defeat of Billy resolved a larger cultural conflict, just as the myth of the West itself was called upon to reconcile the American ideal of progress with the inescapable reality of capitalist exploitation. Garrett's triumph could be claimed as a triumph of order over chaos at a time when the American social structure seemed especially unstable.[56]

As times changed, so did the construction of the West and symbolic significance of Billy the Kid. The legend faded from public imagination for a time during and immediately after World War I but resurfaced in Walter Noble Burns's best-selling biography, *The Saga of Billy the Kid*. If in prior decades the Kid had been cast as the villain in a romance meant to reaffirm the traditional aristocracy of wealth and talent, in the 1920s and 1930s he became a way to question modes of thought that seemed obsolete in the modern world.[57] Burns's stance on Billy and the West is ultimately ambivalent; he emphasizes Billy's redeeming qualities, and the boy bandit emerges as an unstable combination of conflicting impulses. Billy is portrayed as a troubled youth, a brave man, and a noble outlaw. Devoted to his friends, he was nonetheless quick to violence against perceived enemies, his generosity matched by a callous disregard for human life.[58]

Writing with an eye toward the present, Burns remarks that these traits are found in the businessman as in the bandit. Billy the Kid had a "desperado complex . . . defined as frozen egoism plus recklessness minus mercy," and men of the same character were found in "business, the pulpit, the drawing room."[59] Desperados of any ilk were unsuited to the circumstances of contemporary society, because the social and cultural conditions of urban industrialism and market capitalism demanded a beneficent morality and a commitment to ethical behavior. Thus Burns acknowledged that "the good 'bad man' had a definite place in the development of the West" but also noted that Billy's passing had "paved the way for peace, stability, law, and order."[60] Billy's death symbolically purged society of a self-destructive individualism. As Stephen Tatum observes, "the tragic pattern of the Kid's life revealed a constructive purpose"—not simply of building a nation but of building a true republic.[61]

Burns reserves the role of tragic hero for Pat Garrett and indeed for civilization itself; whereas Billy is a sympathetic character, he is still a hurdle to be leaped by the advance of civilization. Billy's "life closed the past; his death opened the present," Burns explains. Yet the Kid's death was not to be celebrated without remorse, because Billy exemplifies a certain compelling bravado and appealing individualism that Burns finds lacking in the modern world.[62] This hint of sentimentality or nostalgia does not, however, suggest a purely escapist longing for the past but speaks to the concerns of the present. The pathos of Billy's story as presented by Burns results from a recognition of the seemingly irreconcilable conflict and inevitable compromises between self-expression and social responsibility.

Burns's biography is copiously quoted in Loring's notes for *Billy the Kid*, and the figure of the sympathetic outlaw had a decisive influence on the ballet. Loring seems to focus on Billy's conflicted nature, choosing to cite

TABLE 4.1 Characteristics of Billy the Kid, as Listed by Loring

Against	For
Forgetfullness of crime	Alertness
Egoism	divine inspiration about outlawry that made him the *finished master*
recklessness	Cheerful
without mercy	Hopeful
remorseless deadliness	talkative
murder—process of pressing trigger	laughter
killing	No swagger
—no rules of etiquette	No Braggadico [*sic*]
—no punctilios of honor	quiet
No scruples about assassination	unassuming
	courteous
	courageous

Spelling, capitalization, and punctuation in this table are Loring's

passages that reveal admirable qualities as well as moral failings. In his notebook is a table that encapsulates Billy's dichotomous character as described by Burns. Two columns are labeled "AGAINST" and "FOR" (table 4.1).

Surely the good outweighed the bad in quantity if not in kind; hence Billy elicits sympathy and even pity. Like Burns, Loring leaves these contradictions unresolved. In both the biography and the ballet, Billy is a tragic figure, a child overwhelmed by forces beyond his control or comprehension, while Garrett plays a willing, active, and adult role in building a new civilization.

Loring's take on the Kid is further developed in the narration for a 1953 television production of the ballet. The story is described as "an episode in the progress of America," Billy as "a man who had to be destroyed to establish law and order which he never understood or trusted." Billy lacks the self-determination necessary for pioneering. "This is a country that was built by men like Garrett," Loring explains. "Men and women who are not afraid to push forward—hack their way through forests, plunge through barriers, even with simple means, whip fear, look back only to see how far they had gone and look forward to see how far they had to go."[63]

Kirstein also saw the story of Billy as encapsulating the narrative of civilization and its progress. In his 1937 tract "Blast at Ballet," Kirstein describes the Ballet Caravan version of the legend, placing Billy within the historical experience of Western expansion and contemporary search for civil society. Billy's life is presented "as only a fragmentary, if symbolic, incident in the expansion of our vast frontier," Kirstein writes. "Billy's career was doomed, not by implacable fate," he asserts, "but by the collective necessity of establishing law and order so that people could live in a new place in peace. Billy was used as the symbol of an order of reckless individuals which, however charming or picturesque, was doomed by the historical process of the developing Frontier." Reinforcing Billy's historical contingency and arguing for the necessity of his death, Kirstein concludes that "Billy was not a tragic poet but a little bad-man, like others we know and even like, and are forced to shoot to keep them from shooting us first."[64]

From the opening chords, Copland's music exudes a sense of timelessness and tragedy, of struggle and uncertainty. *Billy* begins with a remarkable sonority: falling parallel fifths are heard in the very high B-flat clarinets, with an unusually low oboe subtly doubling the second clarient.[65] Similar open fifths harmonize the repetition of the opening idea in the flute, now including a triadic fanfare (ex. 4.1). The gapped melody and open intervals create a sense of stasis that suggests both the eternal realm of myth and vast expanse of the prairie. Although the open fifths of the introduction have since become sonic hallmarks of the West, the distinctive opening and its iconic intervals evolved only over a long period of time and in relation to pieces without Western connotations. Copland first wrote out a version of the pentatonic melody in late 1934, when he was working on *Statements*. A sketch from March 2, 1935, presents the melody in fifths with the exact pitches of the final clarinet part. More materials from the opening were developed in August 1935 as a violin piece. In this sketch, as in the music for *Billy the Kid*, Copland set the fanfare-like, triadic gesture above a syncopated ostinato accompaniment. In 1937, when the composer was at work on *Music for Radio*, he wrote out the theme again. Sketch pages dated April and May 1937 show the melody harmonized with thirds and fifths. Thus both the evocative melodic fragment and ostinato were developed in various works before finding a suitable home in *Billy the Kid*, where the sonic spaciousness of Copland's music perfectly matches the title of the introduction, "The Open Prairie."[66]

Copland's music accompanies a procession that references the familiar image of westerning but is here distorted by a grim ambivalence. The dancers and the music struggle to move forward; their migration is labored. Loring describes the opening as a "theme [and] variations with interruptions," a "fugue in action using interruptions for concerted group action."[67] The "theme" is a series of motions highly abstracted from descriptions of pioneering that he found in his sources. Among the gestures are a whip-cracking arm throw and a chopping bend. There is also a stately walk with an ambiguous and contradictory arm motion: a straight thrust forward, palms out in the "stop" position, followed by a pull back with closed fists, elbows drawn in tight to the body. In a similarly conflicted gesture from this kinetic theme, the dancers turn around and walk back, from whence they came. The overall impression is of controlled chaos as dancers move both forward and back, reach up and fall down.

The theme of movements is unpredictable, and the gestures find no simple, direct correlation to each other, nor to Copland's music. Loring varies the order of elements to create a dense visual field that mirrors the fragmented musical materials and the gradual thickening of the orchestral texture. Just as the music begins with very few instruments, so too a single dancer appears first, silhouetted against the backdrop. Small groups of dancers follow across the stage as more instruments enter and fill the sonic space. The polyphonic visual texture and swelling orchestral accompaniment eventually create a sense of claustrophobia. The stage is soon replete with bodies in motion as the musical texture thickens, the melodic fragments accrue, and the dynamic level rises. This is not the open West, the safety valve of American progress. On stage, as in history, the limits of the frontier are quickly reached.

This contrapuntal progression is accompanied by the syncopations of a triple-meter march. Loring was initially taken aback by Copland's musical choice: "I'd always thought of a march in four or six," he remarked.[68] Copland's music, like Loring's choreography, purposefully undermines a sense of forward motion, and the triple meter, along with the lurching rhythms in the brass, strings, and percussion, precludes an easy correspondence of the musical rhythms to a natural, walking cadence. The syncopations accompany the halting, erratic migration of the dancers; the repetitive fragments, uneven rhythms, and static minor-mode harmonies mitigate a sense of progress. A solo flute recalls and extends the triadic melodic motive at measure 9, and in measure 20, the first clarinet, in a piercingly shrill register, transforms the triadic ascent of the melody into a quick, dotted fanfare (ex. 4.1). The musical deformation of the march casts a pall on the procession, and at times it is not entirely clear whether the dancers (as pioneers) are moving determinedly or reluctantly across the stage from right to left, East to West.

The grim migration visually and musically depicted in the Introduction to *Billy the Kid* recalls not only the migration of nineteenth-century pioneers but also the uprooting of Midwestern families during the agricultural depression of the Dust Bowl.[69] In the 1930s, the sentimental vision of the courageous and enterprising family moving westward in search of property and prosperity was displaced by images of migrants forced to leave their lives and land. Although these Depression-era pioneers may have escaped the Dust Bowl, they found

EXAMPLE 4.1. Opening of *Billy the Kid* (brass and winds only), mm. 9–16

new hardships in the West. Their difficult journeys were documented by a group of talented photographers working for the federal government under the direction of Roy Stryker and the Farm Security Administration (FSA). Photographers Dorothea Lange and Walker Evans traveled to migrant camps, visited with transient families, explored abandoned towns, and captured the Western migration on film. Their photographs were shown to middle-class, urban audiences, who were shocked and appalled to see the desperate circumstances of the yeoman farmer—an American archetype long associated with the prairie.

Thousands of New Yorkers attended a gripping and disturbing exhibit of FSA photographs at the First International Exposition of Photography in April 1938, some six months before the premiere of *Billy the Kid*. In his study of FSA photography, historian James Curtis notes that the exhibit revealed rural America to be "on the move, its traditions uprooted by economic chaos, its people driven to the highways in search of food, shelter, and employment."[70] These images undermined the urban viewer's fantasy of westward expansion, reinforcing instead the profound and devastating consequences of the frontier's closing. As Curtis explains, "the open road had long been the setting for real and allegorical journeys in search of wealth, property, redemption, and renewal. Indeed, restlessness and mobility had become synonymous with the American spirit of individualism."[71] The migrants captured by the FSA photographers had not chosen to pursue the American dream, however, but had been compelled by circumstance to flee an environmental and economic nightmare.

The connection between the migrants of the 1930s and the pioneers of a century before was made explicit in a 1935 article for *Survey Graphic* with photographs by Dorothea Lange and text by the radical Berkeley economist Paul Taylor. Titled "Again the Covered Wagon," the article observes that "the present migration . . . follows channels cut historically" by the nineteenth- and early-twentieth-century movements across the plains and into California, "but it moves with the tremendous added impulses of drought and depression behind it."[72] Like their predecessors, these Dust Bowl pioneers found that the people of the West (now Californians rather than Native Americans, long since dispossessed) were not entirely hospitable to new arrivals. Established residents feared that indigent migrants would tax state resources and contribute to the growing labor unrest among agricultural workers. Taylor depicts the West as a site of disillusionment, observing that "the refugees seeking individual protection in the traditional spirit of the American frontier by westward migration are unknowingly arrivals at another frontier, one of social conflict."[73] California's fertile fields produced radical political action, and the Communist Party was deeply involved in organizing farm workers. John Steinbeck's 1936 proletarian novel *In Dubious Battle* captures the violent conflict of the 1933 agricultural strikes, but the most famous portrayal of the Depression in California appears in another Steinbeck novel. *The Grapes of Wrath* (1939) follows the Joad family's move from Oklahoma to California, emphasizing the plight of white, Protestant Americans and thus tapping into a racialized populist spirit not wholly representative of the cultural front.[74]

By contrast, *Billy the Kid* offers a musical display of ethnicity more in keeping with leftist cultural pluralism. The second sequence, "Street in a Frontier Town," captures the racial and ethnic mix of the West in a medley of folk songs and an original tune.[75] Four cowboy tunes can be identified in this section (there are six in the entire ballet): "Great Grandad," "Whoopee Ti Yi Yo, Git Along Little Dogies," "The Old Chisholm Trail," and "Old Paint."[76] Copland found his borrowed tunes in a variety of folk-song collections, three of which had been given to him by Kirstein.[77] Initially uninterested, the composer soon became "hopelessly involved" with the songs while writing the ballet in Paris, drawing primarily on *The Lonesome Cowboy: Songs of the Plains and Hills*, compiled by John White and George Shackley.[78] Copland generally alters his borrowed material, fragmenting, expanding, rearranging, and recasting the melodies and rhythms of the tunes. The basic melodic profiles are preserved; variety comes through rhythmic manipulation and quick cross-cutting between various songs. Among these preexisting melodies lies a newly composed *jarabe*, a jaunty Mexican dance in 5/8 presented by a solo trumpet (ex. 4.2). In "Street in a Frontier Town," the rhythmic reworking and forceful juxtaposition of melodies create an aural

EXAMPLE 4.2. *Jarabe* in "Street in a Frontier Town" from *Billy the Kid* (winds and brass only)

portrait of a bustling thoroughfare where people and their music collide. The *jarabe* arrives at the climax of the sequence and is danced by Mexican women, inflecting the West of *Billy the Kid* with ethnic variety. This is a key difference between Steinbeck's novel and Loring's ballet—and a telling one, given that the Depression-era West was plagued by ethnic conflict. In the 1930s, tens of thousands of Mexican farmworkers were deported as a result of labor unrest and displaced by competition from more recent arrivals, chiefly Anglo migrants from the Southwest.[79]

Violence erupts at the end of the sequence as a group of cowboys saunters onto the scene. Garrett is among them, and the men proceed to "exhibit their talents for lassoing, spitting, shooting crap, or exchanging tales." The *jarabe* is interrupted as a fight breaks out between two armed and drunken cowboys. In the confusion, Billy's mother is shot, and Billy, in a blind fury, exacts revenge by stabbing his mother's killer. This crucial episode recalls a passage from Roosevelt's *Ranch Life and Hunting Trail* that Loring excerpted in his notes for the production. Writing with a clear affection for the cowboys of the open range, Roosevelt nonetheless recognized their disruptive presence in the frontier town. Here is part of the passage that Loring quotes:

> Singly, or in twos or threes, they gallop their wiry little horses down the street, their lithe, supple figures erect or swaying slightly as they sit loosely in the saddle. . . . When drunk on the villainous whiskey of the frontier towns, they cut mad antics, riding their horses into the saloons, firing their pistols right and left,

from boisterous light-heartedness rather than from any viciousness, and indulging too often in deadly shooting affrays, brought on either by the accidental contact of the moment or on account of some long-standing grudge or perhaps because of bad blood between two ranches or localities.[80]

In a surprising display of compassion, Garrett reaches out to console the young boy. The next scene follows quickly as the stage is cleared, and a now-mature Billy stands alone for his "Soliloquy," as Loring termed this solo dance. At once vibrant and volatile, Billy is athletic, graceful, and virtuosic but very much alone and seemingly tormented. He moves off center stage when a posse appears. They have come to arrest him, but Billy kills the sheriff and slips off into the night.

In contrast to the medley of fragmented tunes in "Street in a Frontier Town," the song "The Dying Cowboy" is presented nearly intact in the scene that follows, "Card Game at Night." Perhaps more familiar from its opening line ("Oh, bury me not on the lone prairie") the tune was, according to John White and George Shackley, "the best known of the cowboy airs."[81] The lament appears first in the violins, floating above and within the contrary motion of the descending flute line and ascending cello scales. Although masked to some extent by the dense texture and metric uncertainty, the tune remains little changed, and Copland even preserves the same key (A-flat) as in the White and Shackley compilation. The soft dynamic and languorous melody coupled with the accompanying flute and cello lines reflect the contemplative, lonely side of Billy's life and of the West. The words of the dying cowboy, "Oh bury me not on the lone prairie," echo through the melody to evoke Billy's fate— the death that surrounds him and eventually will claim him.

Yet the card game offers a chance at life. Billy seems to have the opportunity to make a connection with Garrett (as he had once before, briefly, after his mother's death) and perhaps even to be redeemed through human companionship. Loring notes in the scenario that there is "no tension . . . only friendly amusement" between Garrett and Billy.[82] In the narration for the 1953 Omnibus telecast, Loring explains that Garrett had hoped to help Billy, but the dreamy and even dreary setting of "The Dying Cowboy" as well as the echo of its lyrics imply that such a companionable life is not Billy's fate. He exists beyond the bounds of society, and this distance between Billy and the others is a musical relationship as well. The ostinato bass heard throughout the episode rises to meet the descending line, but a vast expanse exists between their opposing contours. The sonic emptiness of the musical texture opens a gulf between the individual and community, the potential and the real.

The reverie is broken as Garrett, having discovered that Billy is cheating at cards, leaves in disgust. It is a crucial and symbolic moment: Billy has broken a basic social compact by ignoring the rules that govern behavior and ensure fair play. Instead he signals his immaturity and rebellion against the strictures of sociality by baldly pursuing his own self-advancement. As a result, he is abandoned by the one person who had ever shown him sympathy. Garrett storms off, and Billy becomes the leader of the cowboy gang. But still "he feels he is really alone," the scenario explains.[83] Billy is truly an individual, isolated from his companions and alienated from the prairie that must have been so foreign to so many of the Dust Bowl migrants. For those unhappy transplants as for the cowboy in the song, the open prairie was a most undesirable final resting place.

Soon Garrett returns in the company of the sheriff, their badges marking their maturity and signaling an allegiance to the laws of society—laws Billy has violated through violence and avarice. They capture Billy, and people gather to celebrate, dancing a "macabre polka" among the bodies of slain outlaws and deputies.[84] Copland's music is appropriately grotesque. The dotted rhythms and shrill scoring perfectly match the scenario, which describes "something frantic, hysterical, yet incomplete about the dancing."[85] The bitonal clash between melody and accompaniment distorts the entire scene; Copland even labels his melody "crudely" (at R 45), reinforcing the ghoulish and vulgar nature of the dance. The townspeople jerk like puppets on strings; arms in the air, elbows bent, they move woodenly, as if animated from above, and dance rigidly in time to the steady pulse of the music. As Howard Pollack notes, the ostinato from the introductory processional returns here as a satiric "oompah bass" that underscores the disturbingly shrill dotted tune.[86] Copland's music suggests that Billy's capture is not something to be so quickly celebrated. In mocking his captors, the music elicits sympathy for Billy, such that the community seems not wholly right to glorify the fall of the errant individual.

Billy manages to escape from prison, and while on the lam dances a heartfelt but tragic *pas de deux* with an imagined sweetheart. Described as "the girl with whom he was thought to be in love," the sweetheart offers "a strange, cool, detached and unemotional" comfort.[87] The same dancer takes both the roles of Billy's mother and sweetheart, suggesting that the comfort Billy desires is that of maternal love. Their dance is both familial and sexual; before she appears, Billy removes his guns and his boots, stripping away the symbols of his masculinity and leaving himself naked and vulnerable before her. Yet there is an unbridgeable gulf between Billy and his mother/lover, a distance again measured in both dance and music. Billy does not even look at his partner as they move together, and she alone in the ballet dances *en pointe*. Copland's music for their duet features another borrowed tune, "Trouble for the Range Cook," a humorous folk song. As Pollack notes, the music has "an ironic edge," sharpened by use of the "comical ditty" as the theme and solos for bassoon and trombone—surprising instruments to feature in a sentimental waltz—accompanied by an oom-pah-pah bass. But the irony is contained: in contrast to the comical tune and its artless setting for winds and brass is another passage of lush, romantic music, complete with soaring *tutti* strings, harps, and affective chromatic turns. This interlude, along with the sweetheart's delicate pointework, suggests a level of refinement and culture that Billy must surely possess (he is, after all, her son and partner) but has yet to reveal outside this dream state. Perhaps he could yet be redeemed.

But it is simply too late, and not long after the wistful duet with his sweetheart, Billy is shot by Garrett. The ballet then ends as it began, with the corps continuing its march across the stage and into the imagined distance. Loring varies the choreography slightly in the closing procession to emphasize the backward-facing turns sweeping through the group. And as the curtain falls, many of the dancers, the pioneers, are looking back.[88] The plodding parade and haunting music capture "the muted nature of civilization's advance," Stephen Tatum comments, leaving "us to wonder whether this progress will liberate and regenerate the self and society or will—as in the Kid's example—destroy or hinder an individual's vital energy and self-expression."[89] The ballet does not resolve the matter, however, inspiring pity for the individual who exists outside society while also demonstrating the need to quell the violent nature of the immature and isolated self. "Murder," program notes for a 1941 performance explain, is "the ultimate expression of a lonely individualism."[90]

In *Billy the Kid*, the outlaw is not vilified; the pioneers are not lionized. Instead, Billy's fractured identity and tenuous relation to society are carefully constructed. The duality emphasized by Burns, Loring, and Kirstein, then captured in music by Copland, reflects a conflicted attitude toward American individualism in the context of progressive politics during the Depression era. The ballet revels in the moral contradictions of the heroic outlaw, who—much like the pioneer—is at once a destructive force to be contained and an essential democratic energy to be released. Ultimately the ballet tries to assess what is lost and gained in the name of progress. In the context of the left-wing rhetoric about the West and it pioneers, *Billy the Kid* questions the ideology of expansion and thus of American capitalism. The romantic narrative of civilization collapses into a more ambivalent tale, one without clear villains or heroes, and in the end the emptiness of the musical texture—the sonic spaciousness so prized as a hallmark of Copland's Western sound—captures the hollow core at the heart of the myth.

Rodeo *and the Errant Individual*

By 1942, when Copland was approached by Agnes de Mille about *Rodeo*, *Billy the Kid* was "already something of a classic," and he was apparently reluctant to write a second Western-themed ballet. When de Mille called with an offer to collaborate, Copland responded "Oh no! I've already composed one of those. I don't want to do *another* cowboy ballet!"[91] Eventually he was convinced that de Mille's approach would be sufficiently different from Loring's and so agreed to compose a ballet score for her, to be performed by the Ballet Russe de Monte Carlo. The story of *Rodeo* features a young tomboy—a cowgirl who wants to ride and rope with the boys. The (male) cowhands have gathered for a rodeo, and the Cowgirl, who has a crush on the Head Wrangler, is an unwelcome participant. Left out of the rodeo events and the romantic couplings, she eventually dons a dress for the celebratory hoedown. Although she has been pining for the Wrangler, she falls for the Champion Roper in the end, and the two come together in a final climactic kiss.[92]

Work on *Rodeo* advanced quickly. De Mille had already choreographed a short piece titled *The Rodeo*, and Copland drew on preexisting music; some of the material used in the ballet began life in 1941 as a piece for band.[93] The manuscript containing Copland's earliest sketches for *Rodeo* is variously titled "Film music from an Imaginary Horse Opera," "Film Sequences," "Band Music," and finally "Rodeo / early sketches." The first page of music is headed "Band Music" and dated November 1, 1941 (when Copland was in Santiago, Chile on his first South American trip). This sketch features the opening of "Buckaroo Holiday" with the same lively octave descent as in the finished ballet but without the syncopated response in the brass. A few pages into the manuscript is another, earlier sketch, dated June 6, 1941, with a slightly different iteration of this opening that lacks the "giddy-up" response but includes the wonderfully dissonant chords scored for brass in the finished version. As Copland was wont to do when using any preexisting music—whether folk song or his own sketches—he retained many of these original ideas in his finished composition.

The pencil short score of *Rodeo* is dated June 20, 1942, on its opening page (ex. 4.3); at the end is a note that the piano version was written in Stockbridge, Massachusetts between June 1 and July 20, 1942.[94] Appended to this score is a most unusual manuscript: a single leaf with three cowboy melodies

EXAMPLE 4.3. Sketch for *Rodeo* (ARCO 47.1)

written out by Agnes de Mille herself. Copland used one of these, a version of "Old Paint," as the central tune in "Corral Nocturne," the second of the ballet's five sections. He found the rest of the tunes used in *Rodeo* (including "Sis Joe," "If He'd Be a Buckaroo," "Bonyparte," "McLeod's Reel," "Gilderoy," and "Tip Toe, Pretty Betty Martin") in two published collections: *Traditional Music of America*, edited by Ira Ford; and *Our Singing Country*, compiled by John and Alan Lomax and edited by Ruth Crawford Seeger.[95]

As Howard Pollack notes, *Rodeo* is unusual in the degree to which Copland preserves his borrowed melodies. Unlike *El Salón México* and *Billy the Kid*, *Rodeo* generally presents folk tunes in their entirety without pervasive metric distortions or melodic fragmentation.[96] Compare, for example, the relatively complete, straightforward presentation of "The Dying Cowboy" in *Billy the Kid* to the "Saturday Night Waltz" in *Rodeo* (exx. 4.4a and b). Although both

EXAMPLE 4.4a. "The Dying Cowboy" from *Billy the Kid*

EXAMPLE 4.4b. "Old Paint" from *Rodeo*

sections focus on a single tune, in *Billy the Kid* the melody is enveloped in a metrically ambiguous fog created by the descending flute lines and rising cello ostinato. Both the source version of "The Dying Cowboy" and its new setting are in 12/8 time, but Copland shifts the melodic points of arrival to obscure the downbeats. Furthermore, the tonal scheme is altered; the ostinato suspends the harmonic motion and conceals the melodic cadences. In "Saturday Night Waltz," by contrast, the tune of "Old Paint" dominates the texture, which is cleanly divided into melody and accompaniment. The syncopated accompaniment provides an gentle lilt, and the simple harmonic design of the tune remains clear. As with the "Hoe-Down" to come, the waltz is basically a transcription and orchestration of the borrowed tune.

Perhaps because borrowed folk songs saturate the ballet and appear nearly intact, *Rodeo* seems unlike other works in the composer's catalogue. This has been explained as resulting from de Mille's influence; the choreographer has been described as a "pervasive and often controlling presence" in the collaboration.[97] Pollack observes that *Rodeo's* "completed score reflected much of de Mille herself—her personality, her movements, her dramatic and musical ideas—thus helping to explain, in the context of Copland's oeuvre, its unique character."[98] Although de Mille certainly had a definite vision of the ballet and invested much of herself in the character of the Cowgirl, the emphasis on her dominant role seems a distorted reflection of the scenario itself, which de Mille described as "the Taming of a Shrew—cowboy style."[99] The relation between the two key authors has been framed as a power struggle for the expression of identity in much the same way that the Cowgirl's individuality seems at stake in *Rodeo*. And like the Cowgirl, the composer is described as adopting a wholly subservient role, directed by a domineering choreographer to write his music to her strictures.

This bit of historiographical slippage between the scenario of the dance and story of its creation speaks to the central issues of gender and agency in the ballet. Although *Rodeo* can certainly be seen to inscribe conventional notions of the gendered self, there are important ways in which the story and music subvert expectations to offer a more ambiguous and challenging view of the Cowgirl and the composer.[100] The ballet appears to showcase the traditional values of womanhood—including a femininity based on physical appearance and a submissive posture toward masculine authority, but the Cowgirl is more in control of herself and her destiny than it might seem. Copland, too, has power over the music he appropriates. The shape of his compositional authority and musical identity remains visible even under the dress of his borrowed tunes. Thus gender and agency are not quite as fixed as it might first appear; instead, *Rodeo* is remarkably protean. Its deceptively simple story may be read and reread with an eye toward its subversive potential, and moments of resistance can be related to the dialectic of Burke's aesthetic as well as to a more contemporary understanding of gendered subjectivity.

To address matters of gender and sexuality in *Rodeo* is not to abandon historical context but rather to enrich it, keeping in mind the biography of the collaborators and the cultural shifts of wartime America. Neither de Mille nor Copland belongs within the heteronormative paradigm assumed to be operating in their ballet. De Mille, whose own experiences are often called on in interpreting the Cowgirl, struggled with her sexuality and with the norms of femininity. Copland was apparently comfortable with his homosexuality, and it seems unreasonable to presuppose that this essential part of his identity found no expression in his music.[101] Moreover, the entire culture of gender relations was in flux during the thirties and forties when the masculine identity as breadwinner was threatened by the Depression, and women entered the workforce during the war. Indeed the growing phenomenon of the working woman (especially the married working woman) was important to de Mille, who linked her very identity to her work.[102]

On the surface, *Rodeo* presents a *Bildungsroman* of conventional femininity: the tomboy matures into a woman and finds heterosexual romance. Yet the very nature and structure of the ballet destabilizes this stereotype and invites readings attuned to a queer sensibility. As a tomboy, the Cowgirl easily fits a typical category of gender (and presumptively sexual) identity that can be recognized as "lesbian." In her study of gender in the mid-century American musical, Stacy Wolf explains that the tomboy "is a character defined by her performance of gender in relation to sex: masculine behavior in a female body."[103] The term itself connotes female homosexuality, and the tomboy character "often conveys signs of lesbian sexuality" through her apparent indifference to or rejection of femininity.[104] In *Rodeo*, the Cowgirl quite literally turns her back on typical displays of heterosexual romance and stereotypical, heteronormative feminine behavior. When the group of women first enters during the rodeo, for example, the cowboys take notice and begin to flirt with the comely girls. The Cowgirl, however, turns away from the preening, and Copland's music gives voice to her disgust by mocking the ladies. The prettily dressed, appropriately demure women flounce across the stage to the resolutely comic tune "If He'd Be a Buckaroo" in the trombone (R 21).

Like the Cowgirl, de Mille was an unconventional woman, at once obviously sensual and sexually inhibited, supremely athletic as a dancer but ungainly offstage. She was herself a tomboy of sorts, ill at ease with the feminine costume of her gender. Her biographer Carol Easton notes that well into her twenties de Mille "still wore the ill-fitting, unbecoming clothes her mother chose for her; her stockings were wrinkled, a hem hung down, a strap escaped its mooring, and her hair was an unruly red frizz that she rarely bothered to comb."[105] Only onstage while dancing did she feel beautiful. Dancing also was bound up with her conflicted attitude toward sexuality. On the one hand, it could be a source of sexual release, but, on the other, dancing meant "freedom from sex," total independence, a physicality apart from sensuality. It was for de Mille nearly a "form of celibacy."[106] She suffered sexual anxieties and experienced troubled romances, including fraught attractions to homosexual men, evenly though she was openly critical of homosexuality.[107] "For a woman as insecure about her sexuality as Agnes to put herself into competition not only with other women but also with men was masochistic," Easton concludes, "and could only feed her fear that she was not 'sexy,' meaning desirable."[108] Uncomfortable with the gender role and sexual identity of stereotypical femininity, de Mille stands with her Cowgirl outside the heterosexual paradigm.[109]

Much as queer identities challenge or subvert straight gender standards, so too the Cowgirl is a strong female presence who defies the strictures of a conventional plot that would contain her. Wolf argues that the charismatic woman in mid-century musicals may be freed from the "heterosexualizing narrative that severely limits her" by virtue of the lopsided dramatic structure.[110] The first act of a Broadway musical, featuring the lead woman and showcasing her individuality (often as a problem to be solved), simply outweighs the second, such that the romantic conclusion is never as compelling.[111] And although the structure of *Rodeo* seems, if anything, to be endweighted, romance is still slighted. More convincing than the final kiss is the Cowgirl's individual bravura display at the rodeo and the final hoedown. The Cowgirl owns the stage, thanks to the singular power of her performance, and does not lose herself entirely in the requisite romantic attachment. She is not controlled by the men around her, is not reduced to spectacle nor constructed from desire, but has agency. As Wolf writes about the heroines of musical theater (including another famous unruly woman, Julie Andrews as Eliza Doolittle in *My Fair Lady*), the female principal is not "a passive, to-be-looked-at object" but claims "the position of self-spectacle."[112]

This sense of self-spectacle, what Wolf characterizes as "an autoerotic quality" of the heroine's performance, emerges most clearly in the Cowgirl's solo episodes. The Cowgirl—not the ranch hands, ropers, or cowboys—sets the tone for the entire ballet at the opening of "Buckaroo Holiday." She is first shown among the men, who stand on stage motionless before sauntering off. The Cowgirl tries to follow but is shooed away. Alone, she begins an aggressive solo in which she pantomimes the rigorous physical motions of riding and roping. The men return and dance in tight formation, but the Cowgirl cannot be brought into line. As de Mille explained in her initial scenario,

> She can't [scored-through, with "fails to" written above] keep her own horse in order. She gets involved in their figurations and causes their horses to shy. She goes threw [sic] them like a bat out of hell. She rides brilliantly but is always trying something a little beyond her, and whether she succeeds or fails she is as cocky as hell.[113]

Even as the cowboys dance in tight formation, the young woman remains an individual. The charismatic female soloist in a corps of men, the Cowgirl disrupts and even dominates the rodeo with her presence. The men are forced to react to her, to contend with her, but they eventually give up and move on.

Left standing alone as various couples pair off and disappear into the twilight, the Cowgirl dances by herself in the following section, "Corral Nocturne." She does not despair, however, and her languid solo exudes a sense of self-reliance and self-fulfillment. In the scenario, de Mille noted that the girl "is lonely," true,

> but she is in love with the land around and the great glowing night sky, and the smells and the sounds. She leaves the fence and moves across the moonlit space. Someone hurries by with an oil lantern. She run[s] through the empty corrals intoxicated with space, her feet thudding in the stillness. She stops spell-bound.

In this autoerotic moment of self-discovery, she performs "a dance of courting," in de Mille's words, "a dance between people and darkness" rather "than between people and people."[114] Eventually the Head Wrangler notices the Cowgirl and approaches, seeming to wait for *her* to advance. But she doesn't reach to him as had the Rancher's Daughter. Instead, she gives him a playful shove and turns away. He shrugs in confusion and exits with the Rancher's Daughter, whom de Mille derisively describes as "the epitome of everything fluffy [and] feminine."[115] Although these moments alone might be seen as but a temporary reprieve from the demands of conventional gender norms, the subversive potential of her solos remains in force throughout the ballet, opening an interpretive space for a queer, rather than hegemonic, reading of the ballet.

The Cowgirl soon enters into a romantic triangle in which one partner— the Champion Roper—seems every bit as unconventional (as queer) as she.

The three sides are drawn at the very outset of the ballet. As the curtain opens, the Cowgirl is seen standing between the Wrangler and the Roper. During the rodeo, she loses control of her horse and careens across the stage into the arms of both men (R 36). Soon enough, it becomes clear that the Cowgirl will have to choose between the two, and this choice confirms her remarkable, nonnormative gender identity and the power of her individuality. In the third section of the ballet (cut from the suite), the Cowgirl again finds herself standing between the two men. She is sitting by herself, watching couples dance together, when the Champion Roper approaches her. He pulls her to her feet, smoothes her hair and, as she bends over and away from him, brushes off her backside. She quickly straightens up—only to encounter the Wrangler suddenly before her. She hesitates, and in the meantime the Rancher's Daughter has appeared. The men stride over to this cliché of femininity, but the Wrangler pushes the Roper aside and claims her as his own.

The "Saturday Night Waltz" then begins, and the Cowgirl lines up with the other girls on one side of the stage, arms outstretched for a partner. Of course no one wants her, and she is left to wander around the circle as the others dance an abstracted, folksy waltz. Once more the Cowgirl is on the outside looking in at the conventional couplings, at least until another outsider—the Champion Roper—comes back over to her. The two stand side by side, and he places an elbow on her shoulder, leaning into her in a gesture of empathy and companionship. As the other couples move offstage, the Cowgirl and Roper begin to dance. Their spirited stepping contrasts markedly with the more classical *pas de deux* that the Wrangler and Rancher's Daughter perform in the background. As the dance historian Sally Banes observes, the graceful balletic style of the Wrangler and his partner mark them as "elitist and snobbish—whereas the Roper and Cowgirl always dance together in an American folk idiom."[116] The pairing of the Roper and Cowgirl, wherein both dance the same steps, also evokes the ideal of companionate marriage—an equal partnership that by extension suggests a democratic social vision.[117]

At one point, the Cowgirl runs off stage then returns in a new costume: she now wears a dress and has a bow in her hair. But even so, she is not "coy, skittery, and evasive" like the other women, and her clothes are comparatively plain. Just as bold and brash as ever, she joins in the hoedown—an energetic, physical dance that is the stylized equivalent of the rodeo in its competitive display of individual effort. De Mille described the hoedown as "a dance competition where the chorus movement is interrupted for brilliant solo improvisations, each dancer tryi[ng] to top the rest with humor or swiftness or rhythm or ingenuity of invention, men against men, men against the woman." This is an egalitarian contest, and the Cowgirl proves herself equal to any man. "The girl more than holds her own," de Mille explains; in fact "she outdances the lot." Her exuberance is untamed and her individuality celebrated. "She is unconquerable," de Mille writes.[118]

Both the Head Wrangler and Roper notice the Cowgirl and seek to prove themselves worthy of her attention. In a version of the scenario found among de Mille's papers that does not exactly describe events in the ballet as performed, the romantic entanglements—including a homosocial attraction mediated by the girl—are explained in more detail. At the hoedown,

> The wrangler becomes slightly interested and he decides to flirt with her. The roper acts as her aide and second, cueing her for all her moves. Finally when the wrangler is about to kiss her the roper steps in and decides that since he has done all the work in keeping up her courage and encouraging her and companioning her he might as well keep her and he takes her, to her great astonishment and ultimate delight.[119]

The three dance together for a bit, with the Cowgirl in the middle, but the Roper moves away for his solo. He dances an elaborate set of steps—rustic, energetic taps rather than delicate ballet or careful footwork, and entrances the Cowgirl. Arguing against an interpretation of *Rodeo* as a narrative of conformity, Banes sees the Roper's dance as the constructive expression of individuality and freedom. "The Roper charms the Cowgirl with that powerful symbol of uniqueness"—his creativity—"and he draws her into his dance, showing her the way to live in society but on her own terms."[120] His skill and invention matches her own and proves that theirs would be a partnership of equals.

The Cowgirl's own creativity is underscored by Copland's music, the composer acting as her aide and second, particularly in the raucous "Hoe-Down." Largely a transcription of "Bonaparte's Retreat" (also known as "Bonyparte"), the music for this final section is still recognizable as Copland's own.[121] Indeed the music of the hoedown could never be mistaken for a traditional dance, thanks to the clever orchestration, quick cross-cuts between phrases, and tonal shifts that are hallmarks of Copland's style. Like the Cowgirl, Copland preserves his own personality while wearing borrowed clothes, assimilating the tunes so thoroughly that the preexisting melodies come to sound like his own invention. As a result, the composer remains a unique individual.

The "Hoe-Down" begins with a brusque triplet motive taken from the opening of the fiddle melody as performed by "Fiddler Bill" Stepp and transcribed by Ruth Crawford Seeger in *Our Singing Country*. Copland expands this introductory gesture, which in the original score leads directly into a plunging sixteenth-note descent, across four measures. A brass fanfare ensues, and the strings "tune," their open fifths recalling the beginning of "Saturday Night Waltz" as well as the opening of "Bonaparte's Retreat" as found in Ford's *Traditional Music of America*. Copland did not use this particular version of the tune as his main source for the "Hoe-Down" but nonetheless seems to have been inspired by its recurring fifths.[122] The triplets return for four measures but are then interrupted (at R 3) by an accompaniment pattern that Copland freely adapted from Ford's collection. At the opening of that volume is a "simple system of accompaniment" featuring "chords and patterns . . . played since pioneer days, and handed down with the old American fiddle tunes."[123] Naturally Copland chose the accompaniment in D major, key of "Bonyparte" in *Our Singing Country* and of the "Hoe-Down." Only at R 5 does "Bonyparte" truly begin.

Copland transcribes the tune—but not exactly. As performed by "Fiddler Bill" Stepp and transcribed by Ruth Crawford Seeger, "Bonyparte" falls into two phrases: A, the rushing triplet followed by an octave compass, and B, a narrow, rhythmic drone outlining the tonic triad (see ex. 4.5).[124] Phrase B shifts register in its second, expanded appearance, and the rising tessitura lends the tune a sense of mounting excitement. In Copland's transcription, however, B first appears in a high register, delicately scored for violins, oboes, and clarinets (R 6). The phrase returns a second time (R 8) in a lower tessitura for eight measures, evenly divided between the violins and winds. The full orchestra then enters (R 9) for a bold statement—the strings *fortississimo*—of B with the syncopated drone in the brass. This orchestration gives the drone potent rhythmic energy and a visceral presence. Phrase A returns for two and a half more statements (R 10–11) that grow ever more virtuosic. The music pulls back from the expected climax, however, as the introductory triplet motive returns. The anticipated cadence at R 12 is averted, and "McLeod's Reel" begins.[125]

Between two appearances of "McLeod's Reel" (at R 12 and R 14), the minor-tinged "Gilderoy" is quoted in the solo oboe then solo clarinet. The closing theme (R 16–17) of this interlude features vigorous scalar runs that seem to paraphrase the phrase-endings of "Arkansas Traveler" (Ford, p. 46) with only the slightest adjustments: in addition to transposing the tune (from D to A major), Copland changes the final gesture from $\hat{3}$–$\hat{1}$–$\hat{2}$–$\hat{3}$–$\hat{1}$, as in the original, to a pair of falling thirds, $\hat{3}$–$\hat{1}$–$\hat{2}$–$\hat{7}$–$\hat{1}$, another common figure in these

EXAMPLE 4.5. "Bonyparte" from *Our Singing Country*

fiddle tunes (see, for example, "Uncle Joe," across the opening from "Arkansas Traveler" on p. 47).

After a decisive, "whooping" conclusion at R 17, the D-major accompaniment pattern returns, seeming to prepare for or introduce the culmination of the romantic drama. The Wrangler makes his move, sidling toward the Cowgirl for a kiss, yet both the Cowgirl and Copland's music reject his sexual overture. The vamp that attends his approach (ex. 4.6) is comic, mocking the exaggerated masculine swagger of his advance. The loping, chromatic descent in the trombone (which recalls a similar trombone solo in *El Salón México*) is not confident and assured, as the Head Wrangler might have once appeared to the besotted girl, but awkward and unseemly. The tempo slows and dynamic softens as he draws near, and the staccato rhythms seem ever more hesitant and flaccid. The Wrangler leans in to kiss her to an improbable E-flat major triad, which, as Howard Pollack points out, recalls the key of the romantic waltz.[126] The otherworldly quality of the moment is reinforced by the scoring for celesta. But the Roper

EXAMPLE 4.6. "Hoe-Down" from *Rodeo* (concert suite), R 18–19

quickly intervenes, returning her to reality. He shakes his head, then kisses the Cowgirl himself—quite passionately.

Her "happy ending is not that she finds love," Banes concludes, "but that she bucks conformity by choosing a partner on her own terms." The Cowgirl couples with the Roper "because he, too, inhabits a world of singularity, excitement, and noisy disorder."[127] His noise—the exuberance of the aesthetic—is expertly captured in Copland's setting of the high-spirited, virtuosic fiddle tune. As the Cowgirl and the Roper dance a final flurry of steps, the orchestra flirts with musical danger in the form of extreme virtuosity. The music rushes ahead, nearly out of control. Long passages in unison demand enormous skill of the players as well as the conductor; articulations are precisely marked, as is the use of open strings—idiomatic to the fiddle, but not the violin. The tempo is fast, the rhythms tricky. Such virtuosity is dangerous, thrilling, and visceral. In stark contrast to the Rancher's Daughter and the Head Wrangler, who had performed a quiet, reflective waltz, the musical pairing of the Cowgirl and the Roper is unabashed, intense, and resolutely physical.

Neither lives entirely outside society, however, and the stereotypical heterosexual narrative is present, even as an alternative is posed. The neat lines and group dancing that might be interpreted as oppressive do not define the Cowgirl or curtail her individuality but form a vision of the practical, stable community committed to order.[128] The Cowgirl is the aesthetic force who, like Billy the Kid, disrupts this stability by pursuing her own desire and passion. She does not threaten to undermine the social construct—the aesthetic cannot triumph, as Burke explains—merely to change it, to reconfigure her community so as to allow her singularity. Thus *Rodeo* envisions frontier democracy as a negotiation of individual and civic welfare, of personal expression and public good. The Champion Roper cooperates with the Cowgirl to achieve a shared end; the social dancing reveals a constructive spirit; the Cowgirl does not compromise herself to the romantic union but retains her identity even as she is integrated into the community. In *Rodeo*, the unruly aesthetic energy can continue to exist, because the Cowgirl and her society have alternatives to violence: the organized rodeo and social dance provide opportunities for competition that are creative, not destructive, and there are others who share her same passions. Unlike the frontier ideology so roundly criticized by Henry Wallace and other progressives, this egalitarian, democratic West was entirely fit to serve as a usable past for present reform.

Both *Billy the Kid* and *Rodeo* present enormously charismatic and sympathetic individuals who express themselves outside the limits established by their communities. One fails, having transgressed too far, but another succeeds. Such are the possibilities of the aesthetic as a subversive force, here given room to roam through the unsettled social landscape of the West, a place of potential, where presumptive American values—whether unrestrained individualism, capitalist progress, or conventional gender identity—could be constructed and critiqued. The ballets revel in the disruption of the aesthetic, privileging the disorderly and unruly within the play of traditional and innovative values as well as the conflicts between the individual and his or her community. Ultimately, the aesthetic is akin to the disorder of the Popular Front, which rejects statist authority and embraces the complexities of leftist politics, standing outside the conventional political boundaries to challenge the presumed structures of American society.

5 In Wartime

BY 1939, THE economic crisis of the Great Depression had begun to improve and the political situation in Europe to worsen. If progressives hadn't yet taken note of events across the ocean, they had to appraise the global situation in August 1939, when the Soviet Union signed a nonaggression pact with Nazi Germany. Many within the American Communist Party were disillusioned by the treaty, which the leadership labored to explain, and the community of anti-Stalinist liberals grew in size and influence.[1] For the twenty-two months that the pact was in effect, the CPUSA struggled to navigate the hairpin turns of Comintern policy and to toe the newly militant, antiwar line dictated by Moscow. But some progressives were reluctant to condemn Stalin, either for the show trials or the pact, and while there is no specific evidence of Copland's reaction to either the treaty with Hitler or shifts in Communist Party policy, it is clear that he did not divorce himself from Communist causes and organizations in the 1940s.[2] "All of us think that Stalin knows what he's doing," Harold Clurman wrote to Copland only days after the agreement was signed, "and all of us think we know what Stalin is doing and approve."[3] Of course history has proved this utter folly, but in 1941 the issue became largely moot after Germany invaded Russia, and Roosevelt joined hands with Stalin in the Grand Alliance.[4]

In wartime, the desire to make music accessible was concretely political, as Copland explained in an article for the progressive journal *Twice A Year.*

> The new musical audience will have to have music which it can comprehend. That is axiomatic. It must therefore be simple and direct. . . . The need to communicate one's music to the widest possible audience is no mere opportunism. It comes from the healthy desire in every artist to find his deepest feelings reflected in his fellow-man. It is not without its political implications also, for it takes its source

partly from that same need to reaffirm the democratic ideal that already fills our literature and our stage. It is not a time for poignantly subjective lieder, but a time for large mass choral singing. It is the composer who must embody new communal ideals in a new communal music.[5]

The mention of "large mass choral singing" recalls the priorities of the Composers Collective nearly a decade earlier (as well as the Soviet predilection for choral music) and suggests how the radical aesthetic agenda advanced by that relatively short-lived group of politically aligned composers continued to operate long after the Collective itself had disbanded. Copland noted that the "main tendency in music today" involved "a simplification of style for the sake of once more making contact with the large mass of listeners,"[6] and his own works epitomized this tendency. During the war years his music found its largest audience to date: pieces such as *Lincoln Portrait*, the *Fanfare for the Common Man*, and *Appalachian Spring* no doubt appealed to many Americans by dint of their grandeur and patriotic sentiment. But the evident cultural nationalism of Copland's wartime compositions and their popular renown has perhaps eclipsed the political implications of the accessible style as an affirmation of a "democratic ideal." For Copland, that ideal continued to be founded on the principles of the Popular Front as a progressive social movement.

The wartime Front married support for Roosevelt and the American military effort to the familiar causes of antifascism, labor solidarity, and social democracy.[7] Even after the demise of the Party apparatus (the Comintern was disbanded in May 1943; the American Communist Party a year later) the Popular Front enjoyed renewed energy, especially in late 1943, when the labor movement mounted an impressive electoral campaign for Roosevelt.[8] Yet rather than simply cheer the Allied cause or avow America's presumed moral authority in the world, many on the Left looked to complete the unfinished project of American democracy. And throughout the Great Depression and World War II, as progressives tried to imagine the possibilities of social change, they often looked to another, earlier war—the Civil War. The Civil War became an important trope during these years, with particular significance within the Popular Front, serving as a source of reflection and site of meditation on what Michael Denning has termed "the decline and fall of the Lincoln Republic."

Progressives often used the Civil War "to tell a tale of the 'big money,'" Denning explains, "of lost opportunities, of a republic that became an empire."[9] The American republic had been saved, true, but the promise of the Lincoln Republic—the emancipated state founded on the principles of social justice, which negotiated a balance between individual freedom and civic responsibility—had been betrayed in the nineteenth century by the rise of industrial modernism and laissez-faire capitalism. The crises of the Depression and war seemed an opportunity to pursue certain causes easily associated with Lincoln, including civil rights, racial equality, and economic equity. The New Deal was to be a second emancipation, the war against fascism to usher in a second reconstruction of American democracy and inaugurate the century of the common man. Thus the story of the decline and fall of the Lincoln Republic expresses both a sense of loss and of hope.

The notion of the Civil War as a crucial episode in the ongoing struggle for emancipation and the image of Abraham Lincoln as a revolutionary leader inform four of Copland's most popular wartime compositions. *Lincoln Portrait, Appalachian Spring, Fanfare for the Common Man,* and the Third Symphony all speak to the concerns of a nation at war while imagining the possibilities of peace. *Lincoln Portrait* uses Lincoln's own words to renew the call for social and economic justice, affirming with Carl Sandburg "the people, yes." Originally set in the context of the Civil War, *Appalachian Spring* honors the individual sacrifice for the common good; the *Fanfare for the Common Man* and the Third Symphony follow Copland's own precept by envisioning "new communal ideals in a new communal music." Although these works might not seem at first blush to be as politically motivated as Copland's music from the 1930s or as easily attached to a left-wing perspective, in fact his wartime compositions bespeak an enduring alignment with the progressive politics of the cultural front.

Lincoln Portrait *and the Legacy of the Lincoln Republic*

Some ten days after news of the attack on Pearl Harbor had circulated throughout the country, the conductor André Kostelanetz wrote to Jerome Kern, Virgil Thomson, and Aaron Copland with a commission. He hoped for three works that would have "a correlated idea in that they are to represent a musical portrait gallery of great Americans."[10] Kostelanetz suggested George Washington, Paul Revere, Walt Whitman, Robert Fulton, Henry Ford, and Babe Ruth as suitable subjects to memorialize in music.[11] Thomson chose Fiorello LaGuardia, the mayor of New York City from 1934 to 1945, along with the journalist Dorothy Thompson, his colleague at the *Herald Tribune*. Copland proposed Walt Whitman. But Kern had already selected Mark Twain, and because Kostelanetz did not want two writers in the group of three portraits, Copland turned to Lincoln.

Whitman and Lincoln were hardly random choices: they dominated the historical imagination of the Left—Communists, Democrats, and the Popular Front alike. Both men were embraced as representatives from the American past of contemporary social democratic values. And both were associated with the Civil War, opposed to slavery, and committed to preserving the Union. Whitman was beloved by the literary Left and frequently cited as a model for the politically engaged artist as well as an early advocate for sexual and social democracy. Lincoln was awarded pride of place in the American revolutionary tradition.[12] Karl Marx himself championed Lincoln as an agent of change. Believing that the emancipation of the American proletariat would come only with the abolition of slavery, Marx wrote to Lincoln in 1865, on behalf of the First International, to congratulate the president on his reelection.

> The workingmen of Europe feel sure that, as the American War of Independence initiated a new era of ascendancy for the middle class, so the American anti-slavery war will do for the working classes. They consider it an earnest of the epoch to come that it fell to the lot of Abraham Lincoln, the single-minded son of the working class, to lead the country through the matchless struggle for the rescue of an enchained race and the reconstruction of a social world.[13]

Marx's letter set the terms for the discussion of Lincoln within the American Communist Party. In 1936 Earl Browder, then Party secretary and chief architect of the Communist Popular Front, praised Lincoln for having overcome a natural pacifism "to lead to victory a long and bloody civil war whose chief historical significance was the wiping out of chattel slavery, the destruction of private property rights in persons, amending the Constitution in the only way it has ever been fundamentally amended." Lincoln embodied "the revolutionary traditions of Americanism" now claimed by Communists. "*We are the Americans,*" Browder announced, "*and Communism is the Americanism of the twentieth century.*" Surveying the American radical tradition in the opening chapter of his book *What Is Communism?* Browder concluded with the "prophetic lines of Walt Whitman: 'We have adhered too long to petty limits. . . the time has come to enfold the world.'"[14]

A portrait of Lincoln hung behind the podium at the 1936 Communist national convention, and the Party platform of that year invoked his legacy. Arguing that Roosevelt was unwilling or unable to counter such conservative foes as the Republican Party, the Liberty League, and the Ku Klux Klan, the platform called for an alliance of the workers, farmers, and middle classes "to fight for and establish a People's government—a government of, for, and by the people." The struggle for social democracy in the 1930s was presented as a third American revolution, the first having been led by Washington, the second by Lincoln. "The Communist Party continues the traditions of 1776, of the birth of our country," the 1936 platform explains, "of the revolutionary Lincoln, who led the historic struggle that preserved our nation. In the greater crisis of today only the Communist Party shows a way to a better life now, and the future of peace, freedom, and security for all."[15] Thus revolutionary socialists saw Lincoln as a radical leader committed to protecting the people. The Great Emancipator who had freed the slaves was seen as capable of liberating all Americans from economic insecurity and social stratification.

In 1938 this image of Lincoln was drafted into the Spanish Civil War on the side of the Republic and its elected government. The Abraham Lincoln Battalion was an interracial volunteer force of some 2,800 Americans—over half of whom were members of the Communist Party—who ventured to Spain and who were, for a time, led by an African American, Oliver Law. Along with the George Washington Battalion and the John Brown Battery, the Lincoln Battalion formed part of the Fifteenth International Brigade, organized by the Comintern.[16]

The sixteenth president was also coupled in the public mind with Roosevelt, who turned to Lincoln early and often during his twelve years in office (March 4, 1933, to April 12, 1945).[17] In a 1934 "Fireside Chat" on the role of government in the regulation of capitalism, for example, Roosevelt quoted Lincoln to urge management and labor to support the recovery programs of the New Deal. "I believe with Abraham Lincoln," he asserted, "that 'the legitimate object of government is to do for a community of people whatever they need to have done but cannot do at all or cannot do so well for themselves in their separate and individual capacities.'" Indicating his willingness to challenge powerful economic interests, Roosevelt argued against

a return to that definition of liberty under which for many years a free people were being gradually regimented into the service of the privileged few. I prefer and I am sure you prefer that broader definition of liberty under which we are moving forward to greater freedom, to greater security for the average man than he has ever known before in the history of America.[18]

At Lincoln's birthplace in June 1936, Roosevelt declared: "Here we can renew our pledge of fidelity to the faith which Lincoln held in the common man," concluding his brief remarks with a quote from Lincoln on the nature of democracy—the same quote Copland would later use in *Lincoln Portrait*. "As I would not be a slave," Lincoln wrote, "so I would not be a master. This expresses my idea of democracy. Whatever differs from this, to the extent of the difference, is no democracy."[19] During his second term in office, Roosevelt—and the Democratic Party—began to challenge the Republican hold on Lincoln's legacy, suggesting that the former president's ideals were more in line with Democratic policies, and Roosevelt continued to refer to Lincoln.[20] In 1938 the president described Lincoln as having "fought for the morals of democracy" and "faced opposition far behind his battle lines from those who thought first and last of their own selfish aims." Dedicating the Peace Memorial at Gettysburg in the summer of that year, naturally Roosevelt mentioned Lincoln in his address, relating the task before the American people in 1863 to that at present.[21] Playwright Robert Sherwood, author of the successful play *Abe Lincoln in Illinois*, was hired as a presidential speechwriter in 1940.[22] And once the United States had entered the war, Lincoln became a touchstone of authority for the administration as it worked to clarify the aims of the war effort, justify the mobilization, prepare the public for a protracted struggle, and console a nation in mourning.[23] After the bombing of Pearl Harbor in December 1941, the Office of War Information produced posters with a quote from Lincoln's Gettysburg Address obviously intended to motivate Americans to war as much as to commemorate the dead (see fig. 5.1).

Both the New Deal and World War II were repeatedly imagined to be extensions of the Civil War insofar as the incomplete project of economic reform and social justice that had begun with Lincoln was finally to be finished.[24] The poet Carl Sandburg, best known during the 1930s for his highly regarded and enormously popular biographies of Lincoln, went so far as to describe the New Deal as the second emancipation. Roosevelt's ambitious government programs were just as outrageous, Sandburg maintained, and just as essentially right, as abolishing slavery. He compared wage labor to slavery by drawing historical parallels between the Emancipation Proclamation and the remarkable proposals in the National Industrial Recovery Act (NIRA). Presented by Roosevelt to Congress in May 1933, the NIRA was passed a month later, the culmination of Roosevelt's remarkable Hundred Days of legislative activity. This central piece of New Deal legislation created the National Recovery Administration, which adopted some of the provisions dear to the Left and particularly to organized labor; it established maximum hours and minimum wages in industry, for example, and guaranteed the right of collective bargaining.

"When Lincoln freed the slaves," Sandburg explained, "he was making the first decisive gesture of authority looking toward an American society with an institution abolished in which humans were exchanged as money as between

FIGURE 5.1. Color poster no. 44-PA-191 (artist Allen Saalberg); "We here highly resolve . . ."; records of the Office of Government Reports, record group 44, National Archives at College Park, College Park, MD

buyers and sellers." Likewise, New Deal legislation sought to establish "certain guarantees" regulating the "two classes, the sellers of wage-labor and the buyers thereof." In justifying Roosevelt's bold economic proposals, Sandburg referenced Lincoln's proclamation to suggest that some truths might lie beyond reason.

> What Lincoln did when he issued his Emancipation Proclamation was curious, contradictory, preposterous. The persons of cold logic and flashlight minds who tried to penetrate the document, and with fine discrimination lay bare its anatomy, had hard going. Likewise, there are proposals and announcements in connection with the N[ational] R[ecovery] A[dministration] which are curious, contradictory, preposterous, if they are to be subjected to merely cold logic.

It was not logical analysis that would validate the New Deal programs, Sandburg argued; rather, the "history, people, constructive events and incalculable explosions of violence" would "determine the values of the NRA proclamations as they did that of Lincoln on January 1, 1863." Lincoln's "mere act of proclamation projected an idea that gained momentum from the instant it was spoken," and this momentum had seemingly led in the following century to President Roosevelt's own bold legislation. "Those who live by selling their labor for wages, paid by those who buy labor," Sandburg concluded, "are having their status changed."[25]

The pairing of Roosevelt and Lincoln in rhetoric about the Depression and war owes much to the work of Sandburg and his monumental biographies of Lincoln. *Abraham Lincoln: The Prairie Years* (1926) was followed in 1939 by *Abraham Lincoln: The War Years*, which received the Pulitzer Prize. These were the most celebrated volumes among a spate of works on Lincoln from this era, including Stephen Vincent Benét's *John Brown's Body* (1928), an epic poem about the Civil War; E. P. Conkle's *Prologue to Glory*, a successful play produced by the Federal Theater Project in 1938, and his radio series *Honest Abe*, produced by the Columbia Broadcasting System in 1940–41; as well as Robert E. Sherwood's play *Abe Lincoln in Illinois*, which ran for well over four hundred performances, won a Pulitzer Prize in 1939, and became a successful motion picture in 1940. Lincoln also was venerated in music. Copland's teacher, Rubin Goldmark, had composed a Lincoln work during World War I *(Requiem Suggested by Lincoln's Gettysburg Address*, 1916). Other works to set Lincoln in music include Robert Russell Bennett's *Lincoln: A Likeness in Symphony Form* (1929); Daniel Gregory Mason's Symphony No. 3, "A Lincoln Symphony" (1936); Elie Siegmeister's *Abraham Lincoln Walks at Midnight* (1937), titled after the poem by Vachel Lindsay; Earl Robinson's "Abe Lincoln" (1936), a song with text by Alfred Hayes (author of "Into the Streets May First"); and Robinson's Lincoln cantata *The Lonesome Train* (1942).[26]

Thus as a potent symbol in wide circulation, and one attached to left-wing reform politics, Lincoln was a fitting subject for Copland's musical portrait, which he began to write in late February 1942. That same month marked Lincoln's 133rd birthday (on February 12), and as essayist Robert L. Duffus observed in a piece for the *New York Times*, "it is natural that Lincoln's birthday in 1942 should make an American draw parallels between Lincoln's great war and our own great war."[27] Official celebrations included a pilgrimage to Lincoln's tomb in Springfield, Illinois, by the British ambassador Lord Halifax and Lynn V. Stambaugh, national commander of the American Legion, a conservative organization that in the years following World War II attacked Copland for his leftist politics. In his address, Stambaugh noted that "the details of the picture are changed" in the current war, but "the motivating principle is the same." He explained that "we are fighting, as a nation of free men, to preserve the Union and all that it means to a war-torn, maddened world." While Americans longed "for the ultimate victory," he continued, "soon, along with the desire for victory, we shall begin asking what shall be the character of the peace that is to follow the war. As night follows days, so will the problems of the peace come to us."[28] In Washington, D.C., President Roosevelt laid a wreath at the Lincoln Memorial, and the Gettysburg Address was recited in Congress, where representatives also compared the Civil War and Second World War in their remarks. As House Majority Leader Representative John W. McCormack (D-Mass.) declared, "Lincoln preserved the Union from internal danger, and it is our duty to preserve the Union from external danger."[29]

Unlike Thomson and Kern, who composed purely instrumental portraits, Copland wrote for speaker and orchestra—inspired, perhaps, by the example of Soviet oratorios with spoken text and the quotations in Robinson's song. ("I'm stealing some of your thunder," Copland told his one-time pupil.")[30] He recalled having found his texts in an immensely popular biography of Lincoln by Lord Godfrey Rathbone Benson Charnwood.[31] "I happened upon a paperback biography of Lincoln by an Englishman named Lord Charnwood," Copland explained in a radio interview from 1968.

> In his book I found letters and speeches of Lincoln that supplied me with my text. I deliberately avoided quoting well-known sayings of Lincoln, except for the peroration. And I carefully chose those words of Lincoln's which seemed to me to be true not only for his own time, but for ours as well.[32]

This retrospective account is not wholly accurate, however. Copland seems to have taken his texts not from Charnwood's book but from a collection of Lincoln's writings edited by Philip van Doren Stern.[33] Among the manuscripts for *Lincoln Portrait* are notes that link the narration to pages in Stern's compilation, and from these, it is clear that Copland first found quotations in the introductory biographical essay by Stern, then located the full speech or address elsewhere in the volume.[34] His choices draw from a variety of Lincoln's writings, including the 1862 message to Congress and final debate with Stephen A. Douglas in the United States Senate race of 1858. The only quote not yet located in either the Charnwood biography or Stern collection is the short passage on democracy ("As I would not be a slave, so I would not be a master") likely written in 1858, around the time of the debates with Douglas (see table 5.1). Although Copland's source is not certain, the aphorism

TABLE 5.1 *Lincoln Portrait*, Sources for the Narration

Narration for *Lincoln Portrait*	Sources
"Fellow citizens, we cannot escape history." That is what he said, That is what Abraham Lincoln said:	Annual Message to Congress, December 1, 1862. Charnwood, 327. *Life and Writings of Lincoln*, 148–49, 745.
"Fellow citizens, we cannot escape history. We of this Congress and this administration will be remembered in spite of ourselves. No personal significance or insignificance can spare one or another of us. The fiery trial through which we pass will light us down, in honor or dishonor, to the latest generation. [. . .] We—even we here—hold the power and bear the responsibility." He was born in Kentucky, raised in Indiana, and lived in Illinois. And this is what he said: This is what Abe Lincoln said: He said:	Ibid. Charnwood lacks "The fiery trial. . ."
"The dogmas of the quiet past are inadequate to the stormy present. The occasion is piled high with difficulty, and we must rise with the occasion. As our case is new, so we must think anew and act anew. We must disenthrall ourselves, and then we shall save the country."	Annual Message to Congress, December 1, 1862. Charnwood, 327. *Life and Writings of Lincoln*, 745.
When standing erect he was six feet four inches tall. And this is what he said: He said:	Description by William Herndon, quoted in *Life and Writings of Lincoln*, 73 ("tall" substituted for "high" in original).
"It is the eternal struggle between [these] two principles—right and wrong—throughout the world . . . It is the same spirit that says, 'You toil and work and earn bread—and I'll eat it.' No matter in what shape it comes, whether from the mouth of a king who seeks to bestride the people of his own nation and live by the fruit of their labor, or from one race of men as an apology for enslaving another race, it is the same tyrannical principle!" Lincoln was a quiet man. Abe Lincoln was a quiet and a melancholy man. But when he spoke of democracy, This is what he said: He said:	Lincoln's reply to Stephen A. Douglas, Seventh Joint Debate, October, 15, 1858. Not quoted in Charnwood. *Life and Writings of Lincoln*, 70, 530. Exclamation point added by Copland.
"As I would not be a slave, so I would not be a master. This expresses my idea of democracy.	On slavery in a democracy, c. August 1858.

Whatever differs from this, to the extent of the difference, is not democracy."	Not located in either source; quoted in Carl Sandburg, *The People, Yes* along with previous quotation, 136–37.
Abraham Lincoln, sixteenth President of these United States, is everlasting in the memory of his countrymen, for on the battleground at Gettysburg, this is what he said: He said: ". . . that from these honored dead we take increased devotion to that cause for which they [here] gave the last full measure of devotion: that we here highly resolve that these dead shall not have died in vain; that this nation, under God, shall have a new birth of freedom; and that government of the people, by the people, and for the people, shall not perish from the earth."	Gettysburg Address, November 19, 1863. Charnwood, 363. *Life and Writings of Lincoln*, 158, 788 (wording on p. 158: "that the nation shall, under God, have . . .).

Lord Godfrey Rathbone Benson Charnwood, *Abraham Lincoln* (1916; 17th repr., New York: Henry Holt, 1928).
The Life and Writings of Abraham Lincoln, ed. Philip van Doren Stern (New York: Random House, 1940).

is one of Lincoln's more familiar writings. And this same quote appears in Carl Sandburg's *The People, Yes* (1936) along with the previous passage ("—the same spirit that says . . .") of Copland's narration. Same quotes, same order: perhaps Copland had Sandburg's poem at hand.[35]

Copland's choice of texts may also have been influenced by Stern's essay. For instance, Stern quotes from Lincoln's 1862 message to Congress ("Fellow citizens, we cannot escape history. . .") to argue that "Lincoln was keenly conscious of the tides of opinion throughout the world" and "was in full sympathy with liberal thought." He then describes a split along class lines in British public opinion about the American Civil War; the social elite "was in almost complete sympathy with the South," according to Stern, "but the British working people were in hearty accord with the aims of the North."[36] In citing Lincoln's words from this section of Stern's essay, Copland was perhaps drawn not only to this particular passage but also to the way in which Stern allies Lincoln with working-class sentiment.

As Copland explained, he chose passages not for their familiarity—although the Gettysburg Address is used at the end—but for their contemporary relevance. All of his selections evoke the political and moral challenges to American democracy posed by slavery in the Civil War and fascism in World

War II. Naturally, the narration for *Lincoln Portrait* speaks eloquently on the subject of slavery, but it also can be seen to reflect a contemporary concern for economic justice and support the international fight against fascism. The second passage, with its mention of past dogmas and plea for new modes of thinking, echoes a leftist call for the creative social and political reform of American capitalism, and the third references not a racial but a class-based conflict. Yet another quotation that Copland wrote out in his notes—but chose not to set—explicitly raises the issue of civil liberties. In the manuscript drafts for the narration, Copland cobbled together the following from an 1860 letter that Lincoln wrote to his friend Henry Asbury and an address Lincoln delivered that same year at the Cooper Union in New York City. "The fight must go on. The cause of civil liberty must not be surrendered at the end of one or even one hundred defeats. . . . Let us have faith that right makes might, and in that faith let us to the end dare to do our duty as we understand it."[37] As had Browder and Sandburg, Copland quotes Lincoln to cast the Civil War as one battle in a continuing struggle for freedom.

Copland quotes music as well as text in *Lincoln Portrait*, setting two traditional American tunes: the eighteenth-century ballad "Springfield Mountain" (the title recalls Lincoln's hometown though the song is set in Massachusetts) and Stephen Foster's minstrel song "Camptown Races." The first was adapted from S. Foster Damon's *Old American Songs* (1936).[38] Actually, Damon's volume contains only a bawdy parody of "Springfield Mountain," known as "The Pesky Sarpent," though as Howard Pollack notes, Copland may also have known "Springfield Mountain" from another source, the *Treasury of American Song* (1940) by Olin Downs and Elie Siegmeister, or even from a recording that Copland had reviewed in 1939.[39] "Camptown Races" is not found in *Old American Songs*, which does, however, include a number of minstrel tunes. Copland himself revealed these borrowings in the program notes for the premiere performance in May 1942.

First to appear in *Lincoln Portrait* is "Springfield Mountain." After a static, pandiatonic opening featuring Copland's own plaintive double-dotted theme, the ballad enters in the clarinet. The tune and its setting exemplify Copland's pastoral idiom: the arching, disjunct melody is set above a conjunct bass line; the harmony is diatonic; the texture homophonic, even chorale-like; and winds predominate.[40] These musical codes evoke nostalgia, a longing for home *(nostos)* tinged with a sense of loss *(algia,* mournfulness). Thus in one short musical phrase, Copland establishes a sense of time and place, of Lincoln's time and place, long ago in rural America.

After the introduction of "Springfield Mountain" and a suggested return to the minor mode, the key suddenly brightens to E major, the tempo quickens, and a new theme appears. Fragments of "Camptown Races" are altered and abstracted, but the melodic and rhythmic profile of the tune remains recognizable. There's a surface similarity to Prokofieff's "Troika" from *Lieutenant Kijé*: both feature repetitive string accompaniments, *pizzicato*, sleigh bells, and frequent quick cuts between folk-like melodies that vary in character. But the dotted rhythms, wind timbres, and familiar melody root us in an American context. Perhaps as in *Kijé*, Copland's music also suggests a journey, either from adolescence to adulthood or from Illinois to Washington. High spirited and rough-hewn, like the young Lincoln of popular memory, "Camptown Races" appears only in this first, purely instrumental section. It does not return in the section with the narrator, who assumes the voice of President Lincoln, and if the exuberance of the tune is associated with youth, its disappearance might signal maturity. "Camptown Races" was also used in nineteenth-century political races, as Howard Pollack points out.[41]

Moreover, as a blackface minstrel song written in dialect, it recalls the subjects of race and slavery—key issues in Lincoln's presidency. With its gapped melody and rhythmic syncopations, "Camptown Races" perhaps even preserves some traits associated with African-American music in the antebellum South. These have already passed through Stephen Foster's white, commercial filter and are now subject to a process of modernist abstraction. While Copland quotes the unobjectionable "Springfield Mountain" almost exactly, he fragments the minstrel tune. As a result, the borrowing calls up its original cultural context—the antebellum South and blackface minstrelsy—but not its problematic lyrics. It is easy enough to recognize the quotation or at least sense its familiarity, but the melody is so changed that it is difficult, if not impossible, to hear the actual song or its derogatory dialect. Thus is Copland able to exploit the song's connotations without becoming complicit in its offensive racial politics.

In his choice and setting of these tunes, Copland captures the two sides of Lincoln as portrayed in Sandburg's biography: the solemn wartime president and the humble "rail splitter" from the backwoods. After each melody is presented separately, the two are brought together in counterpoint, offering a complete musical portrait of Lincoln as man and president. Just as the music then seems to approach a final cadence in C major, the harmony shifts to A-flat. This unexpected move propels the music forward and prepares for the entrance of the speaker, who intones "Fellow citizens, we cannot escape history."

The first passage of narration is introduced by the open, ascending intervals of a fanfare based on "Springfield Mountain." At the end of the spoken excerpt, the dotted idea first heard at the very opening of *Lincoln Portrait* returns as a *marcato* interjection in the winds, brass, and strings (ex. 5.1). The expressive tone of triumph is soon vacated, however, as the music moves into the darker tonal realm of F minor. To introduce the next quotation (the passage that begins, "the dogmas of the quiet past . . ."), an anticipated cadence in C major is avoided by another move to A-flat—now as a true key area, A-flat major. The dotted motive is extracted and repeated: the first violins and cellos reiterate a single pitch in a double-dotted rhythm, while the second violins, violas, bass, and other horn parts descend and ascend in the same rhythm through the interval of a fourth. The oblique motion captures the spirit of determined resolve and bold assurance in the text. At the end of this passage, the dotted motive is transformed as a fanfare in C major—a stunningly bright key that illustrates Lincoln's plea for a break with the past and new course of action.

Throughout this section with narrator, Copland's original text seems to recapitulate the contrast and combination first presented by the purely instrumental themes. The simple, even folksy, descriptions of what Lincoln looked like, of where he was born and raised, are paired with a more stately and formal declaration that repeatedly introduces Lincoln's words and so serves as aural quotation marks: "This is what he said, he said. . . ." The redundant phrase recalls a similar formulation—"And God said, saying. . . ."—that appears frequently in the Hebrew Bible.[42] Surrounded by Copland's original text, Lincoln's own words sound both human and divine, pragmatic and idealistic.

Just before the final passage presents the famous closing lines of Lincoln's Gettysburg Address, the sense of time shifts. Until this point the narrator had seemed to exist in the present, but now memory is invoked: "Abraham Lincoln, sixteenth President of these United States, is everlasting in the memory of his countrymen." This shift emphasizes the role of *Lincoln Portrait* as a memorial to the past president and to the honored dead. "Springfield Mountain" returns as a stately lament, its opening intervallic profile now a clear evocation of "Taps," the bugle call used by the Union Army during the Civil War to signal lights out and later adopted for military funerals. Set for solo trumpet, the tune—along with the text—paints a picture of the commander-in-chief grieving for his fractured nation.

The somber mood is eventually broken as Lincoln's final exhortation is answered by a restatement of the rising fanfare melody in the entire orchestra,

EXAMPLE 5.1. Dotted "fanfare" motive in *Lincoln Portrait*

again in C major. "The challenge was to compose something simple, yet interesting enough to fit Lincoln," Copland recalled of his compositional process. "I kept finding myself back at the C-major triad!"[43] The final chord is a quick, accented eighth-note followed by rests: cut short, the sound nevertheless lingers in the air, as does Lincoln's call for "a new birth of freedom."

Many different people have narrated *Lincoln Portrait* since the premiere in 1942. The first was William Adams, a radio actor well known for portraying FDR on the radio series *March of Time*, which (like the movie newsreels) dramatized current events. Adams had also vocally portrayed Abraham Lincoln on the series *Cavalcade of America* (1935–38).[44] In 1943 under Serge Koussevitzky's baton, Will Geer read Lincoln's words, apparently with great enthusiasm.[45] Geer was a noted character actor active in left-wing politics: he had played Mr. Mister in the premiere of Blitzstein's *The Cradle Will Rock;* openly supported the 1939 cotton strike in the San Joaquin Valley; led Folksay, a troupe of performers that included Woody Guthrie; and (like Copland) had worked with Orson Welles at the Mercury Theatre.[46] Geer was blacklisted for such activities, later appearing on television in the 1970s as Grandpa on the series *The Waltons.*

By all reports, Geer was less than satisfactory as the narrator in *Lincoln Portrait*. "Your Lincoln piece is my dish," composer and friend William Schuman wrote to Copland after a performance with Koussevitzky and the Boston Symphony Orchestra in March 1943. But, Schuman explained,

> Will Geer is not very good and exactly what you didn't want. He meant well but unfortunately acted out Lincoln in speech and gesture. During the talk he stood very, very tall with one hand on the lapel of his coat and used the free arm for gesticulation in the manner of ham oratory. Most people (including Agnes de Mille and Victor Wolfson) thought Geer quite poor.[47]

Copland wrote to André Kostelanetz: "my friends have been writing me about the performances in Boston and New York and from what I can gather Will Gear [*sic*] must have been rather on the hammy side."[48] Consequently the composer added a warning in the published score to deter such mimicry. "The Speaker is cautioned against undue emphasis in the delivery of Lincoln's words," reads a note to the narrator. In an enduring condemnation of Geer's performance, Copland explained that "it is the composer's wish that the Speaker depend for his effect, not on his 'acting' ability, but on his complete sincerity of manner. How Lincoln spoke these words we can never really know,—but certainly we can all sense how *not* to read them."

Who reads the text, and how it is read, necessarily influences how the piece is perceived. The presence of General "Stormin'" Norman Schwarzkopf inevitably enhances the image of Lincoln as wartime leader, even though his delivery is rather flat and expressionless. James Earl Jones emphasizes the threefold repetition of "people" in the final line—"of the *people*, by the *people*, and for the *people*"—rather than the shifting prepositions, and in stentorian tones exhorts the listener to action with the righteous anger of an abolitionist. Nebraskan Henry Fonda, on the other hand, carefully measures his intonation to capture Lincoln's humanity, rendering the text plainly but movingly.[49]

Another notable narrator was Coretta Scott King, who read the text in May 1968 on a memorial concert for her slain husband. Dr. Martin Luther King might have read the text himself, as explained in a program note for subsequent performances with Mrs. King in February 1969 (during what was then Black History Week, coinciding with the birthdates of Abraham Lincoln and Frederick Douglass). According to the program for the Washington National Symphony, "for Memorial Day, 1965, we had invited the Reverend Dr. King to narrate the Copland piece in the first symphony concert ever presented on Washington's Mall. Though accepting in principle, Dr. King could not keep the date due to the press of his activities. He agreed to perform with the National Symphony at some future time and the 1965 performance was narrated by Adlai Stevenson."[50] In the 1950s, Copland witnessed "a fiery young Venezuelan actress" narrate a performance in her home country. After the final lines "the audience of 6,000 rose to its feet as one and began shouting so loudly that I couldn't hear the end of the piece." The military dictator Marcos Pérez Jiménez was deposed shortly thereafter, and Copland was "later told by an American foreign service officer that the *Lincoln Portrait* was credited with having inspired the first public demonstration against him—that, in effect, it had started a revolution."[51]

The context in which the work is performed also matters. During the spring of 1942 as Copland was composing *Lincoln Portrait*, Kostelanetz recalled that "our nation was in one of the darkest days in its history."

> Our Pacific Fleet had been all but destroyed. MacArthur, driven from Manila, was making a last-ditch stand on Corregidor. In Europe, our allies were beaten or facing defeat. France had fallen, Britain was reeling under a hail of fire bombs, and Russia was fighting at the gates of Moscow. Copland finished the rough sketch around Lincoln's birthday, reworked and polished it that disastrous spring.[52]

This history, which Kostelanetz recounted from the distance of more than a decade, holds true. Rough pencil sketches dated February 24, 26, and 27 show that Copland had already composed the double-dotted opening theme and decided to use "Springfield Mountain." He refined these ideas over the next three weeks, at some point adding "Camptown Races." The rough pencil sketch was completed on March 17, 1942.[53] (Copland also arranged the "Internationale" for Koussevitzky during the first week of March.)[54] Orchestration began on April 13, and Kostelanetz had the finished score in hand by April 19. During this time the Battle of the Java Sea (February 27–March 1, 1942) was a crushing defeat for the Allies, and the Japanese seized the Dutch East Indies. On March 11, General Douglas MacArthur evacuated Corregidor, famously announcing "I shall return." The situation in Europe was equally grim. During late April, Britain suffered through the devastating Baedecker air raids—so named, because Hitler had sworn to destroy historic British cities listed in the famous guide, page by page. Yet, Kostelanetz continued, "by the time [Copland] finished it in April the tide was starting to turn in the Pacific. Doolittle's daring men bombed Tokyo; U.S. forces were grouping to push westward. Americans were breathing a bit easier." Just before the premiere on May 14, 1942, the United States scored a victory in the battle of the Coral Sea (May 4–8), and *Lincoln Portrait* was met with loud applause. "Lincoln's warning fell on victory-deadened ears," according to the conductor.

But the fortunes of war were to turn again. When Kostelanetz led another performance on July 15, 1942, on a concert dedicated to Army-Navy relief in Washington, D.C., it was clear to all Americans that the war would be long, hard, and costly. The narrator was Carl Sandburg; the First Lady and members of the Roosevelt administration were in attendance. Though the tide had seemingly turned in the Pacific, thanks to a crucial victory at the Battle of Midway, Kostelanetz noted that

> it had sunk in that in Europe we were in a war that saw no end. Hitler stood astride a continent and was reaching over Africa, perhaps the world. His U-boats were taking a frightful toll of Allied shipping. America was grimly determined—but the road ahead was bloody and dark.

"Even as I raised my baton," Kostelanetz remembered, "President Roosevelt was in conference with Admiral King and General Marshall to chart our course." On this occasion, Copland's music and Lincoln's words "sounded with a terrible new clarity," the conductor remarked. At the end of the performance was silence.[55]

Such silence might seem the result of shock and awe, a silencing the self by force of a singular rhetoric. And thus the music of *Lincoln Portrait* might present a curious (or even disturbing) contradiction to the Popular Front position that would inspire collective action, not submission. Admittedly, Copland's music is grand and even, perhaps, overwhelming, but it is only in the postwar context that this sounds like bombast. Only in the wake of victory does *Lincoln Portrait* seem to trumpet that victory. In the midst of World War II, at a time when the Allied position was especially weak, the ecstatic C-major outburst represents something more like hope on the verge of breakthrough. Having accompanied the sorrow of loss and memorialized the dead (whether at Gettysburg or Pearl Harbor), Copland's music now confirms Lincoln's claim that government by, for, and of the people would not only endure but triumph; and this was to be the triumph of the people, of a democratic—and even social democratic—form of government. Representing hope, Copland's music stands at odds with the historical moment of its enunciation, promising deliverance from its present circumstance and resounding defiantly from the depths of despair. This difference between hope and celebration, between solidarity and authoritarianism, is measured by the different responses of audiences during the war. In the wake of Allied success, *Lincoln Portrait* was met with applause; it tipped toward an authoritarian grandeur that hallows victory in order to forget the hallowed dead. And its use since, particularly to commemorate success (as in the recording with Schwarzkopf after the first Gulf War) rather than struggle and loss, has seemingly shifted its cultural signification in this direction.[56] But at a time of defeat and uncertainly, *Lincoln Portrait* means something else entirely. After the Allied setbacks in 1942, it was met with charged silence, the final sforzando, C-major triad a wordless voice of providence and hope issued from an outdoor stage in Washington D.C., some 500 yards away from the Lincoln Memorial.

On Loss and Mourning in Appalachian Spring

"Spring is the loveliest and the saddest time of year," Martha Graham said, describing *Appalachian Spring* some thirty years after its premiere.[57] The ballet concerns a young couple just starting out—the new life of spring—but also suggests the sadness of death before rebirth. And like *Lincoln Portrait*, *Appalachian Spring* is also about war. This may seem surprising given the gentle, tuneful cast of the music, but even more so than either *Billy the Kid* or *Rodeo*, *Appalachian Spring* exists as two distinct works that differ greatly in character and tone. In fashioning the suite Copland cut most of the dark, nervous, brooding, and violent music from the ballet; thus, for most listeners, *Appalachian Spring* is less a dramatic elegy than bucolic essay. Yet Graham and Copland, two artists aligned with the cultural front, both had the Civil War in mind as the context for the ballet, and their collaborative effort meditates on the decline and fall of the Lincoln Republic. Ultimately, however, *Appalachian Spring* is not a tragedy, and the ballet holds out hope for a better peace after a bitter war.

As had Copland in music, Martha Graham embraced modernism in dance as an appropriate idiom for art and political expression. Her politics were squarely aligned with the Popular Front, embracing a multiethnic vision of America, antifascist agenda, and commitment to social democracy.[58] These values emanate from such works as *Panorama* (1935), which explores the Puritan ethos and the subjugation of African Americans, and *Imperial Gesture* (1937), a ballet performed to benefit the democratic cause in the Spanish Civil War.[59] Like many of the other radical moderns, Graham had little personal connection to the revolutionary struggles of the working class: she could trace her ancestry back to the Mayflower and grew up in a world of privilege. Yet she could be critical of her own heritage, and her unsentimental view of the past can be seen as a rejection of a parochial Americanism.

Graham's work, like Copland's, reflects a form of progressive Americanism rooted in the national imagination. In *American Document* (1938), for example, Graham turns to the texts of American history: passages from the Declaration of Independence, Abraham Lincoln's Emancipation Proclamation, and a lament by Red Jacket of the Senecas are read by an Interlocutor, acting as master of ceremonies.[60] The Interlocutor speaks from the stage to introduce the various sections, which include "Declaration 1776," "Occupation," "The Puritan," and "Emancipation," and the spoken text ensures that the audience knows exactly what each represents. The values of the Front inform the dance. "Declaration 1776" celebrates the multiethnic character of America, whereas "Occupation" and "Emancipation" relate to the cause of social justice and ethnic tolerance in referencing the conquest of Native Americans and exploitation of African Americans. These sequences focus on the dark side of the American experience, but the ballet ends with an affirmation. As the left-wing dance critic Edna Ocko proclaimed, *American Document* epitomized a new approach to political dance—a turn away from biting cultural critique and toward more positive social expression affirming the rights of the individual and harmony of the community.[61]

This critical yet affirmative approach to American history characterizes the leftist perspective of *Appalachian Spring*. Although the ballet has often been regarded as primarily sentimental and nostalgic, in fact it bears some relation to contemporary cultural politics.[62] Howard Pollack has found in the abstract narrative of domesticity echoes of an earlier scenario explicitly related to the crisis of the Civil War, and reading the finished ballet with its original story in mind opens the door for an interpretation that restores a sense of social engagement to the realm of Americana. Certainly *Appalachian Spring* evokes the rural American past, but not as a "hermetic" space, "removed and safe" from the contemporary context, as has been suggested.[63] Instead, it captures the anxiety of individuals and their community involved in a war with the potential to (re)define the character of American democracy. It is a ballet about what might have been and what might yet be: the Lincoln Republic—the equitable, just, and radically democratic society—had not materialized after the Civil War, but World War II afforded another opportunity to reclaim this lost legacy, to renovate and refashion the American collective.

The Civil War was a presence in the very first script Copland saw after having been commissioned by Elizabeth Sprague Coolidge to write a ballet for Martha Graham.[64] Titled "House of Victory," this original scenario was subsequently revised with Copland's participation. Graham developed two more scripts, based on the same general ideas, which she sent to the composer during the summer of 1943. Both of these revisions, simply titled "NAME," differ slightly from "House of Victory" and from each other, but the Civil War underlies the drama in all three.[65] As in the final ballet, the scenario focuses on a young couple—initially the Daughter and the Citizen rather than the Bride and Husband—who establish a household in rural America. The cast of characters varies, however, between the draft scripts and the finished ballet, and in general *Appalachian Spring* is more abstract than its original concept. Nonetheless, it is worth examining the scenario in some detail, because, as Pollack has shown, the spirit of the original story still animates the final dance. *Appalachian Spring* follows the pattern of the "House of Victory/NAME" scripts to knit together past, present, and future in a melancholy but hopeful portrait of personal sacrifice for the greater good. (See table 5.2 for a comparison of the narrative schema of the draft scenario and final version.)

In the script titled "NAME?" the Daughter is described as a child "of this country," an American who remains "in our blood." Her companion the Citizen is "the abolitionist, a man descended from the clan of John Brown or perhaps the ancestor of Brown." Evoking the abolitionist cause as well as the contemporary circumstance of the draft in World War II, Graham writes of the Citizen:

TABLE 5.2 Comparison of NAME? script, *Appalachian Spring* (ballet), and *Appalachian Spring* (suite)

Section	NAME?	*Appalachian Spring*	Suite Reh. nos.
1	Prologue		1–6
	Mother and Indian Girl	Entrances	
2	Eden Valley	Pioneer Woman and	6–16
	Daughter's solo, "joyous psalm"	Followers	16–19
	Citizen's entrance	Husband's solo	19–23
	Duet for Daughter and Citizen	Duet for Husband and Bride	
3	Wedding Day		23–35
	Part I		
	Sister and children	Revivalist and Followers	
	Citizen solo		
	Citizen and daughter enter	Pioneer Woman and	35–55
	house	Followers	
	Part II		
	Love duet inside house		
	"Charivari" outside	Bride's solo	
	Fade to black with Mother		
	alone		
		Wedding and procession	
4	Interlude		
	"telescoped day"	Bride's and husband's solos	55–67
			[reordered, one
			variation cut]
5	Fear in the Night		cut
	Fugitive's solo	Revivalist's solo	[ARCO 55.3,
			73–78]
6	Day of Wrath		cut
	Mother rises in anger	Pioneer Woman rises	[ARCO 55.3,
	Citizen's solo, "an exhortation"	Husband's solo	78–88]
	Children play at war	Revivalist and Followers	
	All exit	Husband's solo	
7	Moment of Crisis		cut
	Women, "feeling of hysteria"	Bride's solo	[ARCO 55.3,
	Daughter "breaks the spell"		88–96]
8	The Lord's Day		67–end
	Company assembles	Husband returns	
	Church service	Company, except Bride	
		Bride's solo	
	Love Duet outside	Duet for Husband and Bride	
	Citizen and bride enter house	Husband and bride enter house	

NAME? script c. June/July 1943; *Appalachian Spring Suite* (Boosey & Hawkes, 1945). Table adapted in part from William Brooks, "*Simple Gifts* and Complex Accretions," in *Copland Connotations: Studies and Interviews*, ed. Peter Dickinson (Rochester, N.Y.: Boydell Press, 2002), 109. Used by permission. See also Marta Robertson, "'A Gift to Be Simple': The Collaboration of Aaron Copland and Martha Graham in the Genesis of *Appalachian Spring*" (Ph.D. diss., University of Michigan, 1992), 221.

He is the man who fights when he does not like to fight, simply because he knows he must do so to bring about the things in which he believes. As such he may be wrong and he may be cruel and violent and to be feared. But he is a power to be reckoned with, a man who brings reform. He is tragic in his dedication as well as heroic.

In addition to the couple, there is the Mother, whose own youth was the youth of the country; the Indian Girl, who represents the primitive "as part of the romance of our youth as a land"; two children, a younger sister, townspeople, and the Fugitive, "the man who is hunted, persecuted." He "is represented in the Civil War period by the slave" but "exists at all times."

As in *American Document*, Graham included spoken text in her scripts for what would become *Appalachian Spring*. The Mother was to speak first and introduce the setting with a biblical quotation: "And the Lord God planted a garden eastward in Eden." Departing from the biblical story of creation, however, it is the Daughter—the woman—who is the first inhabitant of Eden. She walks out of the house with "an eagerness for destiny that is the unconscious partner of youth." Next the Citizen appears, and the Mother charges him with the stewardship of the community, intoning, "and the Lord God took the man and put him into the garden of Eden to dress and keep it." The wedding between the Daughter and Citizen follows. Graham envisioned dividing the scene in two: a love duet inside the house portraying private intimacy; and a community celebration outside—a simple party that then develops "into something wilder and infinitely older" with an element of "violence, a wild kind of beauty" and an "animal vitality." The Indian girl brings the two scenes—inside and outside, private and communal, domestic and feral—into dialogue as she dances with each of the men in the company. "She is the dream of the men," Graham explains, and "the dream of the eternal woman, gentle, generous, utterly loving and innocent." As both scenes increase in intensity the lights fade to black, and only the face of the Mother remains illuminated.

An Interlude was to follow for the company. Graham imagined that this section would have "the simplicities of a telescoped day in which people behave as though working and playing together in a common bond of time and place." It is purely lyrical, and Graham suggested to Copland that the scene have a "song-like quality" that might be matched to "a rondo form in theme and variations." Copland seemed inspired by this suggestion. The Interlude, which in the finished ballet features solos by the Bride and her new Husband, is accompanied by the variations on the Shaker tune "Simple Gifts."

The reverie is short-lived, however, and a major structural break occurs here, dividing the ballet in half: before and after. "Up to this time there has really been no violence as such," Graham writes. But "now all is changed." The Fugitive bursts onto the stage, "as though catapulted by fear." He dances a grotesque and tortured solo that is not without "a certain dignity." The Citizen watches before rushing over to catch the Fugitive as he falls to the ground, but the Indian girl gets there first, and she holds the Fugitive "in a way reminiscent of the Pieta." Here is the original sin of the American republic—the sin of slavery, of bondage and persecution figured in the bodies of the Fugitive and the Indian Girl. Although the scene might be understood to depict a loss of innocence, the omniscient figures of the Mother and Indian Girl suggest that the idea of innocence was always an illusion: it was not innocence but ignorance that had protected Eden and her young couple.

At this point, the Mother rises from her chair for the first time in the ballet, turning to the Citizen and exhorting him to "take the wine cup of this fury at my hand." The Citizen then rises himself, moved "into terrible action." Graham describes his dance as having "the qualities of the Harper's Ferry incident without being literally John Brown." The abolitionist motivates the men to war, and in the following sequence, "Moment of Crisis," only the women gather on stage. They are restless and anxious, but the tension is broken by the Daughter as she begins to dance "in some simple way" that is "like a song, any kind of song." In his copy of the scenario, Copland wrote "Shaker" in the margin next to Graham's description of this dance, indicating perhaps that he planned to use the Shaker melody "Simple Gifts."[66] The entire company then returns for what appears to be a religious service, and Copland again noted "Shaker song" in the script. In this final scene, titled "The Lord's Day," the Daughter and Citizen are reunited, but it is not obvious that he has truly returned; she may only remember him, and the church service is perhaps a memorial rather than a thanksgiving.

The most familiar scenario for *Appalachian Spring*—the one widely known and often referenced—comes not from the ballet but from the suite. At the premiere of the ballet, the program contained only the following note:

Part and parcel of our lives is that movement of Pennsylvania spring when there was "a garden eastward of Eden."

Spring was celebrated by a man and woman building a house with joy and love and prayer; by a revivalist and his followers in their shouts of exultation; by a pioneering woman with her dreams of a promised land.[67]

After the premiere, as Marta Robertson has discovered, the first paragraph was omitted.[68] She also notes that the much longer and more detailed description of the ballet frequently cited in annotations or general discussions of *Appalachian Spring* was devised by Edwin Denby and published in connection with the premiere of the suite in October 1945. His text provides a more elaborate story that facilitated the work's transition from a ballet (with visual narrative content) to concert suite (as disembodied orchestral music).

> The action of the ballet concerns "a pioneer celebration in spring around a newly-built farmhouse in the Pennsylvania hills in the early part of the last century. The bride-to-be and the young farmer-husband enact the emotions, joyful and apprehensive, their new domestic partnership invites. An older neighbor suggests now and then the rocky confidence of experience. A revivalist and his followers remind the new householders of the strange and terrible aspects of human fate. At the end the couple are left quiet and strong in their new house."[69]

While the original ballet was written during a time of war, Denby's narrative and Copland's suite seem to reflect the postwar cultural context: the threat of violence is now but a memory, both in the dance and in the music itself, since Copland cut the more troubled passages from the score in composing the suite.

In the finished ballet, the figure of the Mother is replaced by the Pioneer Woman—a clear evocation of the American frontier that invests the *Appalachian Spring* with a sense of historical as well as generational time. The Citizen has become two characters: the Husbandman, who represents an intimate, domestic relation with the Bride; and the Preacher, who preserves the activism and passion of the abolitionist. Graham eliminated the spoken text, allowing the action to remain more abstract than in *American Document* or the original scripts for *Appalachian Spring*, but Copland's music, especially for the sections "Fear in the Night," "The Day of Wrath," and "Moment of Crisis," retains a sense of conflict, uncertainty, and even violence, explicitly related in the scenario to the Civil War.[70] Although the score is justly celebrated for its lucid scoring, enchanting rhythms, and folksy melodies—all of which suggest an American Eden—it is worth recalling that the ballet is actually set east of Eden, the land of Cain's banishment. And so where there is light, there is also darkness.

Even the very opening of the ballet, justly celebrated as a sonic depiction of the pastoral landscape, points to a snake in the garden by foreshadowing discord. The simple A-major triad outlined in the clarinet is taken up in first inversion by the flute in measure four; while the strings sustain the tonic A, the flute moves on in measure six to the dominant E-major triad, arpeggiated in second inversion. Within the pandiatonic stasis, the pitches of the tonic and dominant triads begin to pile up one on top of the other, creating a delicate yet substantial dissonance that imbues the opening with a luminous tension. This is a prologue with a past: in the scripts from which Copland worked, a light shone only on the face of the Mother, who sat "terrifyingly still," thinking of her youth and of the land. These finely honed dissonances capture the unsentimental nostalgia Graham described, suggesting the memory of a hardship that the Mother—or, in the final ballet, the Pioneer Woman—must have endured. Her presence at the very outset in this dreamy but tense sonic realm implies that the entire ballet is a memory; perhaps the Pioneer Woman is, or was, the Bride who lost her young husband in the war, whose hopes were dashed but who remains resolute, who stands as the emblem of American innocence and experience.

The dissonant potential of the opening is realized three measures before R 19, when the Bride and Husband back out of the house together. This is their first interaction. Both fall to their knees, as if in prayer, to a wrenching, chromatic line in the strings that recalls the theme from the *Piano Variations* in its intense angularity and linear dissonance (ex. 5.2). The passionate yet troubled music then accompanies their duet (R 19 to R 23). After the couple has received the blessings of the Pioneer Woman and Revivalist, the Bride then dances her solo. At one point she moves over to the Pioneer Woman, who rises from her chair and pantomimes handing the young woman a baby. The Bride sits in the rocker and cradles the imagined child, ending her solo as a supplicant at the feet of the Pioneer Woman.[71]

Soon the couple is married, and the newlyweds dance to variations on "Simple Gifts."[72] Here is the lyrical interlude that Graham had proposed in the "House of Victory/NAME" scripts. The Husband and Bride dance a sequence of solos with smiles on their faces while the Revivalist watches over them, and during the climactic, fourth variation, the couple dances together in a high-spirited duet that represents their happy union. At the end of the variations, they move inside the house, but the domestic tranquility does not last long. Soon the Revivalist removes his hat and approaches the Bride and Husband, who bow their heads before him. But the Revivalist is not there as a preacher. Instead in this section, "Fear in the Night," he adopts the character of the Fugitive, thrashing across the stage to nervous, repetitive broken triads that swirl throughout the ensemble.

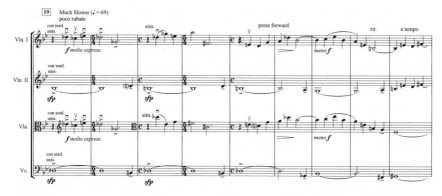

EXAMPLE 5.2. *Appalachian Spring*, first duet between Bride and Husband, R 19

The music of "Fear in the Night" (R 73–78) marks a clean break in the dramatic and musical narrative, just as Graham had planned in her scenario, and Copland's music also departs entirely from the pastoral mode and from anything heard in the preceding sections. In the first half of the ballet, melody was generally the most important element: the rising theme at the opening, the love theme, the tune of "Simple Gifts"—all have melodic integrity and interest that lend a sense of narrative progress to the score. Story and music seem to offer promise and hope. Despite its dissonance, for example, the opening triadic theme captures a sense of potential; it grows slowly and naturally, measuring out the limits of the sonic space. Similarly, the theme and variations have a narrative arch. The melody is carefully introduced; the orchestration swells; rhythms expand and contract. In the ballet (the variations were reordered for the suite), "Simple Gifts" is first presented by the viola and first violin in counterpoint. But this variation has come too soon, anticipating the theme itself, and before the tune is heard in full, the solo clarinet interrupts for a complete, unaltered statement of the theme. The first full variation is then enriched by the presence of the bassoon and flute; in the second variation the viola and bassoon add a dotted rhythm. The strings take over the theme in the vigorous third variation. Music and choreography build to a climax in variation 4, as the couple dances a joyous duet and the texture thickens with stretto entrances of the borrowed tune, now *sonore*, in the strings. After the climax, the clarinet returns with a more subdued statement of the melody. Thus, there is in this sequence a natural cycle of development: the tune expands and flourishes, then contracts. "Fear in the Night," which follows on the heels of "Simple Gifts," lacks just this sense of organic development as repeated rhythmic fragments and static harmonies suspend musical and narrative time.[73] Dance and music are fractured. Recalling nothing so much as Copland's music from part 2b of *The City*—the Megalopolis—the quick cuts between short musical snippets, jagged contours, and insistent rhythms suggest a present danger.

At the end of his solo, the Revivalist takes the role of the abolitionist, pointing to the Husband and calling on him to address to the situation, to react to the injustice he has been shown. Rising chords from the opening are now transformed into a fanfare (R 78) that begins the sequence "Day of Wrath." The Pioneer Woman rushes off the bench where she had been sitting and falls to her knees, while the Husband, too, dances onto the stage; he and the Pioneer Woman kneel in prayer. Throughout the sequence this rising fanfare line repeats, but what it might announce seems never to arrive. At R 79, the Pioneer Woman reenters the house, the Bride taking her place on the bench, hand to her head in confusion or despair. Pointing dramatically off stage, the Pioneer Woman seems to order the Husband away. He follows her command but stops two measures later at the same time the rising line is also abruptly arrested. There is to be no reprieve, however, and the low strings begin another ascent. The rest of the strings join in unison as the piano and winds sweep up an enormous span of scales, ushering him off to war.

Harsh, dissonant chords at R 83 accompany a twirling, leaping solo for the Husband. A fractured version of the love theme echoes in the strings, and the Husband falls to the ground. He rises, waves goodbye to the Bride and the Pioneer Woman, then moves outside the fence—the only character to traverse the boundaries of the community, in what seems to be a metaphor for death. At R 84 the playful melody from the "Wedding Day" sequence (R 24) returns, but the five-measure phrase is truncated, the tune left hanging in mid-air (ex. 5.3). In the manuscript score, Copland marks the passage "Little Girls," recalling Graham's description of the original wedding scene in her "House of Victory/NAME" scripts. There she indicated that the younger sister should run across the stage "in an excited an adolescent way." But now innocence is lost, and the searing music of the Husband's departure, of his death, returns in the string choir. Although the girls' theme makes a more extended appearance between R 85 and R 86, it again trails off into nothingness. The melody is but a reminiscence—fragmented and diffuse—a representation, perhaps, of what was and might have been.

In the next section, titled "Moment of Crisis," the Bride is anxious, even frantic, as she rushes around the stage seeming to search for something, accompanied by buzzing sixteenth-note figures in the clarinet and bassoon. As in "Fear in the Night" there is no melody, no sense of harmonic motion, no depiction of musical progress. Short phrases and quick jumps between the agitated

EXAMPLE 5.3. "Wedding Day" theme at R 84 (labeled in ARCO 55.3 "Little Girls")

sixteenth-note patterns paint a disturbing picture of musical and emotional unrest. Eventually music and dance are quieted (R 95), and the love theme sneaks in below the frantic sixteenth notes. But unlike the initial scenario in which the Daughter restored calm and order, here the Husband provides solace, at least momentarily. He returns, and the couple briefly dances together again. Both the music—another variation on "Simple Gifts"—and gestures recall their nuptials, but again this seems a memory rather than a reunion, and soon they drift apart. The final, resolute variation finds the Pioneer Woman dancing with the Followers; the community is the context, the cause and the effect of the individual drama. As did so many American women during World War II, the young Bride forfeits her private happiness to fulfill a public obligation, and she watches her husband wave goodbye forever.

The Husband leaves the Bride at the fence, looking out. As the company forms a congregation, kneeling in prayer at the back of the stage, the Bride dances her final solo at R 67 ("The Lord's Day"). At its end she brings her hands to her lips, then reaches out to the sky. The Husband comes up behind her and holds her briefly, but the Revivalist breaks the reverie by touching the Husband's shoulder. The couple retires to the house, and the Bride takes her place in the rocker once occupied by the Pioneer Woman. With the Husband behind her, gone but not forgotten, she looks out on the empty stage and reaches out as the final triad is outlined in the clarinet. The music fades to silence. *Appalachian Spring* thus ends as it began; the music of the prologue returns as an epilogue, with the love theme delicately scored for solo flute and the rising A-major triad in the clarinet. But the Bride is no longer a memory of the Pioneer Woman's own youth; instead, she has her own memory now. She sits where the Pioneer Woman had been, and she, too, sits alone, without the child that had seemed promised to her. With the changing generations, the context seems to shift, such that the Bride looks upon another war, seeing into her future as our present. Just as the Second World War was so often linked to the Civil War, so too the Bride functions as the tie that binds the experiences of communities, of the home front in the mid-nineteenth and mid-twentieth centuries. She embodies the link between two decisive wars, and in recalling the generative opening triads at the very end of the ballet, Copland's music collapses history.

Fanfare for the Common Man, *the Third Symphony, and the Second Reconstruction*

Along with *Appalachian Spring*, the *Fanfare for the Common Man* is undoubtedly one of Copland's most familiar pieces. It frequently opens programs of American music and is performed at Fourth of July celebrations; it even kicked off the 2000 Republican convention as an unambiguous celebration of partisan patriotism. Such accrued associations threaten to obscure the relationship between the *Fanfare* and progressive politics, a relationship that emerges with particular significance in the finale of the Third Symphony (1946). On the surface, a fanfare for the common man seems the musical epitome of wartime populist nationalism, but there is a distinction to be made between populist rhetoric and populist politics.[74] The symbol of the people was adopted by various ideological positions, and their shared language does not necessarily communicate a shared politics. As distinct from mainstream or conservative populisms, the left-wing politics of the Popular Front persisted through the war years to advance the values of democratic laborism, multiethnic tolerance, and antifascist solidarity.

These values can be heard to resonate in Copland's *Fanfare for the Common Man* and the Third Symphony. Like *El Salón México*, the *Fanfare* and symphony were influenced by the idealization of a foreign culture—in this instance, the Soviet Union. The goodwill progressives had long felt toward

Russia was intensified by the wartime alliance between the United States and Soviet Union. From the tangled circumstance of the romance with all things Soviet sanctioned by the cultural front and Second World War, a few specific elements may be extracted as especially influential to the development and eventual fulfillment of progressive aesthetic ideology in the Third Symphony. These elements include the descriptions of proletarian music in *Modern Music* in the 1930s, the example of the Russian symphonists, Copland's relationship to Serge Koussevitzky throughout the war years, and the progressive vision of the postwar world.

During the early 1930s, Soviet Russia was the subject of a remarkable number of books and articles praising the country's communitarian principles and its presumed attempt to integrate art with the life of the people. As he had done in constructing an ideal of Mexico, Waldo Frank advanced the image of the Soviet Union as a holistic society that vitalized both the community and the individual. "There are no separate things in Russia," Frank wrote in his 1932 travel journal *Dawn in Russia*, "no separate persons. Every object, however small, is linked, by the consciousness of him who made it or who uses it, with life itself. . . . And every person is in full flowing action with the folk about him. Therefore he is vital."[75] Edmund Wilson recognized that "Americans and Europeans are both becoming more and more conscious of Russia, a country where a central social-political idealism has been able to use and inspire the artist as well as the engineer."[76] And John Dewey, who traveled throughout the Soviet Union in 1928, came away with the thought that "perhaps the most significant thing in Russia, after all" was "not the effort at economic transformation, but the will to use an economic change as the means of developing a popular cultivation, especially an esthetic one, such as the world has never known."[77] The Communist system was thus credited with aesthetic as well as political import, and Soviet music was portrayed as having real social significance—a state of affairs that American artists and intellectuals on the cultural front had achieved only in theory. The "great significance of the revolution" for the Russian musicologist Yevgeny Maksimovich Braudo (identified for the readers of *Modern Music* as Eugene, an "art critic") was the "vast new social perspectives" it had opened for artists. Music in the Soviet Union, he explained, aspired "to achieve maximum accessibility to the new mass audience."[78] The critic Ashley Pettis reinforced the presumption that art was a powerful force in Soviet society, claiming that "in this much discussed country, the enormous vitality, determination and hope of the people find outlets not only in work but in many forms of expression, the most vital of which seems to be music."[79]

Copland's attitude toward a new degree of accessibility in concert music was undoubtedly influenced by the descriptions of Soviet music in the pages of *Modern Music* as well as his involvement in the Communist movement. He also had personal connections to Russian culture through his friend Nicolas Slonimsky and the conductor Serge Koussevitzky, both Russian émigrés. Koussevitzky, a leading figure on the cultural front, was one of the "major and continuing influences" on Copland's life.[80] Composer and conductor shared a philosophy of music that emphasized the close ties between art and culture, the need to communicate with the audience, and the leading role of the artist in society. Each sought music of the highest artistic quality, accessible to a large public, simultaneously reflective of a uniquely American culture and a vital progressive community. Their musical ambitions gained new political significance as the politics of progressive reform merged with wartime cultural patriotism, and during the war years, the two articulated a Popular Front blend of American cultural nationalism and pro-Soviet sentiment.

Copland and Koussevitzky worked together on the National Council of American-Soviet Friendship, an organization formed in 1943 under the direction of the author Corliss Lamont.[81] Lamont had previously chaired the first Congress of American-Soviet Friendship, held November 7 and 8, 1942—dates that marked the twenty-fifth anniversary of the Bolshevik Revolution. Vice President Henry Wallace was the featured speaker on the second day, which had been proclaimed "Stalingrad Day" by Mayor LaGuardia.[82] The National Council was devoted to strengthening the "friendly relations between the United States and the Union of Soviet Socialist Republics through the promotion of better understanding between them." And this understanding was considered "as essential to winning the war as U.S. Treasury War Bonds" and "indispensable to the achievement of a lasting peace."[83] Koussevitzky chaired the Council's music committee, and, as Howard Pollack notes, "at least as early as 1944, Copland served as vice chairman of the council's music committee."[84] At the same time, Copland and Koussevitzky also were members of the Sub-Committee on Musical Interchange with the Union of Soviet Socialist Republics, a group formed in June 1943 within the State Department Music Advisory Committee as a natural outgrowth of efforts to enhance musical and cultural relations with Latin America.[85]

Copland and Koussevitzky believed in the democratization of music and its significance in the war effort. As Koussevitzky optimistically wrote in a 1939 article for the *New York Times*, "The concert world, formerly the guarded sanctum of the elite, has now become a familiar world to millions of men and women," a fact that would have "profound significance" for the "immediate and more distant future."[86] Copland also applauded the idea that "democracy has entered the realm of music" as "a thrilling fact, which eventually will change every phase of our musical life."[87] And both men agreed that concert music, especially in the context of war, needed to be culturally germane. "As we know," Koussevitzky explained during a speech at Town Hall in 1943, "this is a war of the people as much as of the armies and of the artists as much as of the soldiers, every atom of artistic effort must be mobilized and thrown into action." Music was capable of "preserving the burning spirit and the lasting aspirations and ideals," and Russia provided a "matchless example" as a country "where art is a mighty weapon in the war."[88]

Their shared political and aesthetic positions influenced Copland's major work for Koussevitzky, the Third Symphony, which was composed on a commission from the Koussevitzky Music Foundation at the height of the war. Copland "knew the kind of thing Koussevitzky liked to conduct and what he wanted from me" for the commission, namely a work "in the grand manner" with broad appeal.[89] Copland was affected not only by Koussevitzky's words but also his actions, including the Boston Symphony Orchestra's programming of symphonic music by Serge Prokofieff and Dmitri Shostakovich. These Soviet symphonists seemed to some Americans to be writing music consistent with the sociopolitical and aesthetic goals of the cultural front. To those already in accord with a progressive social critique, the political implications of Soviet symphonic music were clear, and wartime concerts also adopted frankly ideological frameworks. The Berkshire Music Center student orchestra, for example, gave the American concert premiere of Shostakovich's Seventh Symphony on a 1942 Tanglewood program dedicated to Russian war relief.[90] The first performance of his Eighth Symphony by Artur Rodzinski and the New York Philharmonic was prefaced by a paean to America's Soviet ally, delivered by a member of the Foreign Economic Administration. The Boston Symphony Orchestra (BSO) gave an all-Russian program at Carnegie Hall on November 22, 1943, that featured Copland's arrangement of the "Internationale," and in the spring of 1944 the Soviet ambassador traveled to Boston amid public fanfare to hear Koussevitzky and the BSO perform Shostakovich's Eighth Symphony.[91]

Shostakovich had, in Copland's estimation, met the challenge of the mass audience, though with varying degrees of musical success.[92] Compelled "by the very circumstances under which he lived to address his works to a large mass audience—an audience that could of necessity only understand music which was simple and direct," Shostakovich presented a stylistic example to be followed.[93] In Copland's opinion, the First Symphony "teaches us a lesson.

It shows how the composer can bridge the gap between himself and the great mass of people, by speaking a musical language which they can understand." That the music was not without its flaws only proved that simplicity was a sophisticated strategy serving a lofty and elusive aim. "To be both simple and direct in the musical idiom of your own day, and at the same time create great music, is one of the most difficult things in the world to achieve. . . . It seems to me a goal worth trying for."[94] Copland praised the Seventh Symphony for its "consciously adopted musical style which is accessible to listeners everywhere," and although he found "obvious weaknesses" in Shostakovich's music, he credited the Soviet composer with addressing the problem of accessibility. "It is the *tendency* he represents," Copland concluded, "rather than the music he writes, that makes Shostakovich a key figure of the present time."[95] If he sometimes criticized Shostakovich's compositional technique, however, Copland had no reservations about the cultural politics of communitarianism and aesthetic of accessibility that the composer and his symphonies seemed to place before the American public.

Copland applied the principles he lauded in Shostakovich's music to his own Third Symphony by adopting a simplified musical rhetoric and by trying to embed the work in the cultural context of wartime America. Perhaps the clearest evidence of the relationships among the Third Symphony, the politics of the wartime cultural front, and a left-wing aesthetic ideology is found in the quotation of the *Fanfare for the Common Man* at the opening of the symphony's finale. In resetting the *Fanfare*, Copland explained only that he wanted to give the Third an "affirmative tone," because the symphony was "intended to reflect the euphoric spirit of the country at the time."[96] But there is more to this borrowing than its uplifting tone. The *Fanfare* explicitly relates to the war effort and directly invokes a progressive political agenda as advanced by Henry Wallace.

The *Fanfare* was originally composed for the 1942–43 Cincinnati Symphony Orchestra concert season. The conductor Eugene Goossens commissioned a series of fanfares for brass and percussion from a group of American composers, including Virgil Thomson, Roy Harris, Walter Piston, and Aaron Copland.[97] Goossens proposed the commission to Copland in a letter of August 30, 1942, asking for a piece to be played in the following season. "It was my idea to make these fanfares stirring and significant contributions to the war effort," he wrote, "so I suggest that you give your fanfare a title as, for instance: 'A Fanfare for Soldiers,' or 'A Fanfare for Airmen,' or 'A Fanfare for Sailors,' or some such heading. . . . I am asking you this favor in a spirit of friendly comradeship, and I ask you to do it for the cause we all have at heart."[98] Copland listed his own potential titles for the fanfare at the bottom of another letter from Goossens, proposing multiple conclusions to the phrase "Fanfare for the . . ." including "Day of Victory," "Future Heroes," "Post-War World," and "Four Freedoms." Struggling to express his ideas about the war, Copland drafted some unwieldy titles: "Fanfare for a solemn ceremony in which man's spirit is rededicated to the proposition of a better world" and "for a rededication of man's spirit to the creation of a better world." Other abandoned titles appear on the manuscript sketches: "Fanfare to the Spirit of Democracy" and "Fanfare for the Rebirth of Lidice."[99]

These ideas speak to Copland's political values and his interest in the war. Goossens's suggestions were fairly prosaic (his own composition was called *Fanfare for the Merchant Marine*), but most of Copland's titles encapsulated grander hopes of a postwar world in keeping with a progressive vision of social justice and international solidarity. His titles also recall the rhetoric of President Roosevelt and Vice President Wallace. The "Four Freedoms" were defined in Roosevelt's 1941 State of the Union address calling for increased American involvement in the international war effort.[100] These freedoms, which were to be the foundation of a new "moral order," comprised freedom of speech and of religion, and freedom from fear and from economic want.

Wallace further developed these four freedoms in a speech on May 8, 1942, broadcast nationally on CBS radio. This address, "The Price of Free World Victory: The Century of the Common Man," gave Copland his final title, *Fanfare for the Common Man*. Copland explained to Goossens that his unusual dedication was inspired by "Vice President Wallace's speech in which he talked about the next century being the century of the common man."[101] Wallace used the phrase "common man" repeatedly, as in the following passage: "Some have spoken of the 'American Century.' I say that the century on which we are entering—the century which will come out of this war—can and must be the century of the common man. Perhaps it will be America's opportunity to suggest the freedoms and duties by which the common man must live."[102] Articulating the communitarian agenda behind progressive political action, Wallace noted that one of these duties was "the supreme duty of sacrificing the lesser interest for the greater interest of the general welfare. . . . There can be no privileged peoples." He compared the American and Russian revolutions as struggles "for the common man in terms of blood," two examples of a "long-drawn-out people's revolution" that also included the latest conflagration.[103]

Wallace's mention of the "American Century" references a well-publicized article by Henry R. Luce of the same title.[104] Looking beyond the war even before the United States had officially entered it, Luce had urged Americans to "accept wholeheartedly our duty and our opportunity as the most powerful and vital nation in the world and in consequence to exert upon the world the full impact of our influence, for such purposes as we see fit and by such means as we see fit."[105] He depicted American democratic culture as a product for export and portrayed American internationalism not as an exchange but a bequest, "a sharing with all peoples of our Bill of Rights, our Declaration of Independence, our Constitution, our magnificent industrial products, our technical skills." Appropriating Lincoln's words to advance his own conservative, jingoistic position, Luce presented his vision as an "internationalism of the people, by the people and for the people."[106] In contrast, Wallace held that "no nation will have the God-given right to exploit other nations. . . . We in the United States are no more a master race than the Nazis." He envisioned a "century of the common man" and believed that a people's revolution would build an "economic peace that is just, charitable and enduring."[107] Both Luce and Wallace invoked America, the people, and democracy in considering the future world order, but Luce's formulation owes more to a chauvinistic nationalism and the individualist stance of classic liberal capitalism, while Wallace embraces a radical collectivism and progressive ideal of social justice.

Copland himself publicly professed only a vague, patriotic motivation behind the striking title of the *Fanfare*. "It was the common man, after all, who was doing all the dirty work in the war and the army," and who, Copland concluded, "deserved a fanfare."[108] In so dedicating his work, he seemed to address both enlisted men and everyday Americans. The armed forces were unquestionably full of very common men; although the draft in World War II was generally considered a fair system, a disproportionate number of draftees came from the underprivileged classes.[109] The draft also transformed patterns of domestic life as industries scrambled to fill positions left open by men departing for war. Women and African Americans—the former excluded from military service and the latter discriminated against by draft boards—took jobs in American manufacturing and were thereby brought into the war effort and the workforce. Wartime models of production benefited organized labor, and union membership soared during these years.[110] Such famous slogans as "Loose lips sink ships" captured the total commitment demanded of every individual, whose slightest inattention was portrayed as endangering the lives of American soldiers. A culture of involvement permeated the home front as people were made to feel that their actions directly affected events overseas. Moreover, the common man of the Popular Front imagination was a citizen of a multiethnic America, and such diversity was widely portrayed as a national value that distinguished the United States from the racially defined cultures of Nazi Germany or Imperial Japan—this despite the disturbing contradiction of American internment camps during the war.

Wallace's speech quickly became a cultural phenomenon. It was first delivered to the Free World Association, a Popular Front group founded by European émigré Louis Dolivet and dedicated to the basic tenets of progressive political ideology, including antifascism and anti-racism. The address was also broadcast nationally, excerpted and printed in newspapers around the country, reproduced as a pamphlet, and even published as a small book.[111] The *Publishers' Weekly* ran a short article on the remarkable success of the speech, reporting that nearly two million copies were printed and distributed to farmers, university deans and presidents, church groups, writers, journalists, publishers, and the Office of Civilian Defense.[112] Not only was Copland familiar with Wallace's text, but the Cincinnati audience at the premiere of the *Fanfare* on March 12, 1943, would likely have also recognized the source of the title.

In November of 1942, Copland sent the manuscript of the completed *Fanfare* to Goossens, who responded that

> its title is as original as its music, and I think it is so telling that it deserves a special occasion for its performance. If it is agreeable to you, therefore, I shall reserve it for our pair of concerts on the 12th and 13th of March, for the common man will be paying his income tax two dates later (if he has anything left to pay it with), and this seems to me a fitting occasion to perform your tribute to him.[113]

Goossens wrote again after the premiere to report the work's success, adding that "the witty nature of the piece was much appreciated, particularly when I told them I had deliberately programmed it as near March 15th as possible."[114] Copland was not amused and responded that "the title was not meant to be funny."[115] His gentle rebuke ("it was a swell idea to have played it around March 15th," Copland conceded) prompted an immediate apology from Goossens, who assured the composer that he recognized the pieces to be "a very solid, serious contribution."[116]

The connection between tax season and the *Fanfare for the Common Man* can be understood as more than a happenstance of chronology or an attempt at clever programming. In his speech, Wallace emphasized Roosevelt's construct of "freedom from want," arguing that we who live in the United States may think there is nothing very revolutionary about freedom of religion, freedom of expression, and freedom from the fear of secret police. But when we begin to think about the significance of freedom from want for the average man, then we know that the revolution of the past 150 years has not been completed, either here in the United States or in any other nation in the world. We know that this revolution can not stop until freedom from want has actually been attained.[117]

Such exalted wartime rhetoric had practical and monetary implications for the American people. Guaranteeing the "four freedoms" in the coming "century of the common man" meant higher taxes in 1942.[118]

Although today the *Fanfare* may be one of Copland's best-known works, in 1943 it was simply a minor commission not often heard until its reappearance in the Third Symphony.[119] There, a revised quotation of the *Fanfare* is tonally and structurally integrated with the finale—a well-wrought, modified sonata-allegro form beholden to Copland's traditional standards of musical workmanship. The *Fanfare* serves as a slow introduction, forecasting keys and relationships developed in the course of the finale, and it returns at significant formal junctures to articulate the sonata structure, rendering the plan of the movement more audible and thus accessible to the broad audience Copland had in mind. The rhetorical trajectory of the *Fanfare*, which moves from darkness to light, ambiguity to certainty, is also assimilated into the overall narrative of the finale, and consequently of the symphony as a whole. The *Fanfare* serves as the catalyst that transforms the tentative opening of the finale into a triumphant conclusion for the entire symphony.

In the original *Fanfare*, the famous rising theme is expanded and developed over three iterations delimited by percussive interjections. These three sections traverse a fairly broad harmonic expanse in a short span of time, and the overall harmonic motion involves a coloristic ascent from flat tonal areas to brighter, sharp keys. The *Fanfare* begins with a plaintive opening statement in the key of B-flat major, tinged with a persistent subdominant harmony that emerges most audibly in measures 30–34. The tonic is eventually cast aside in the final measures as the harmony slides down a whole step from B-flat to A-flat for a concluding statement of the memorable rising theme. Despite a suggested return to B-flat, the closing progression breaks away, moving abruptly from an A-major chord to an F-major one in two aggressive ascents (ex. 5.4). The piece ends on a glorious D-major chord that sounds piercingly bright given the darker tonal realm from which it has emerged.

EXAMPLE 5.4. *Fanfare for the Common Man*, mm. 40–45

In the introduction to the fourth movement of the symphony, the winds begin with an expansive yet tentative presentation of the rising theme in A-flat. A shorter, seven-measure statement by the brass follows in C major. As in the original *Fanfare*, the longest and most developed presentation is saved for last. The theme appears in B major at R 86 before moving through a chromatic, subdominant-colored progression in B-flat that leads to a quotation of the *Fanfare's* closing measures with the original harmonies intact. Example 5.5 shows the initial ascent and final cadence for each thematic statement of the *Fanfare* as heard at the opening of the symphony's finale.[120]

The *Fanfare* assumes a determinant structural role in the fourth movement, and these subtle yet significant changes in orchestration, order of thematic presentation, and tonal design serve to integrate the *Fanfare* with the finale as a whole. For instance, the finale begins *attacca* after the third movement's quiet, reflective close, and the reorchestration of the *Fanfare* for *pianissimo* winds more effectively links the third and fourth movements before the triumphal presentation of the rising theme enters in the brass. Furthermore, the third movement initiates a pattern of half-step harmonies: its final measures slide from the tonic, A major, to a final chord on A-flat—the key of the *Fanfare's* entrance. Beginning at R 85, tonalities continue to descend by semitone from C major, through B major (R 86) and B-flat major (R 87). On reaching B-flat major, the quotation of the original *Fanfare* is exact, and the ending on D major is preserved as a transition to the finale's first theme in that same key. The extended tonal distance traveled in the symphonic version of the *Fanfare* focuses greater attention on the entrance of D major, which is

EXAMPLE 5.5. Reduction of the *Fanfare* with the Third Symphony

ever more brilliant as the first stable, sharp tonal area heard since the close of the third movement in A major.

In keeping with the historical function of fanfares, the entire borrowing serves as an introduction to the finale's modified sonata-allegro form (see ex. 5.6). Copland described the form of the fourth movement in his program note for the symphony's premiere.

> The components of the usual form are there: a first theme in animated sixteenth-note motion; a second theme—broader and more song-like in character; a full-blown development and a refashioned return to the earlier material of the movement, leading to a peroration. One curious feature of the movement consists in the fact that the second theme is to be found embedded in the development section instead of being in its customary place. The development, as such, concerns itself with the fanfare and first theme fragments. A shrill *tutti* chord, with flutter-tongued brass and piccolos, brings the development to a close. What follows is not a recapitulation in the ordinary sense. Instead, a delicate interweaving of the first theme in the higher solo wood-winds is combined with a quiet version of the fanfare in the two bassoons. Combined with this, the opening theme of the first movement of the Symphony is quoted, first in the violins, and later in the solo trombone.[121]

Fragments of the *Fanfare* announce the start of each new formal section, marking points of arrival and supplementing the basic, abstract design with an audible narrative of thematic return.

Writ large onto the sonata-form structure, the harmonic design of the *Fanfare* influences tonal relationships between themes and sections. For instance,

EXAMPLE 5.6. Structural outline of the Third Symphony, finale

EXAMPLE 5.7. Finale of Third Symphony, R 125

the "full blown development" begins in B major, a key first presented in the introduction, and the subdominant coloring of the original *Fanfare* maps onto the finale's tonal plan through the use of G major as the key of the second theme. The recapitulation also superimposes the first theme of the first movement, the second theme of the finale—now a stately tune that recalls the chorale finales of Beethoven's Ninth and Brahms's First, or the climax of Shostakovich's Seventh—as well as fragments of the *Fanfare* in B major (ex. 5.7).[122] This key refers back to a tonality first heard in the *Fanfare* at the beginning of the finale and relates as dominant to the key of the first movement (E major), the first theme of which is heard in the second violins.

The thematic superimposition, tonal recapitulation, and cyclical recall bring the finale and the symphony to an apotheosis appreciable both analytically and aurally. The average listener, unfamiliar with the details of sonata-allegro form or harmonic closure, might still sense the culmination of the teleological process set in motion by the quotation of the *Fanfare* at the finale's opening. Thus, the Third Symphony apparently achieves the composer's stated goal of writing accessible yet sophisticated music connected to its cultural context. The symphony's grand (even grandiose) ending presents a musical picture of victory in the wake of America's success in World War II, reflecting "the euphoric spirit of the country at the time," as Copland noted.[123] And the rhetoric of triumph might seem to herald the dawn of the American century.

Yet the relationship between the symphony and the *Fanfare* is not nearly so straightforward, because in many respects the *Fanfare* actually stands apart from the finale as a disruptive, rather than integral, force. It remains a nagging presence, a call to action that urges the movement on toward a triumphant conclusion, which—despite tending toward bombastic grandeur—does not simply celebrate victory. The overblown quality of the ending gives lie to the apparent rhetoric of conquest and suggests a more complicated ideological perspective that might be linked not to Luce's unequivocal embrace of American preeminence but to the magnanimous populism behind Henry Wallace's "century of the common man." The process by which the *Fanfare* is absorbed into the symphonic discourse manifests a clear tension between musical integration and individuation, hegemony and solidarity.

Read against an analysis of structural assimilation, the *Fanfare* plays a rhetorically ambiguous role, and its status is more tenuous than it might first appear. The *Fanfare* emerges tentatively from near silence at the opening of the fourth movement. Thanks to the delicate scoring, soft dynamic, and lack of percussive interjections, its arched profile seems remarkably static—not unlike the opening of *Appalachian Spring*. This indecisive quality is reflected in Copland's contradictory expression marking "molto deliberato (freely, at first)." Only the intrusion of the pounding timpani and *forte* brass at R 85 revivify the *Fanfare*, described now simply as deliberato. The tonal journey of the introduction is at once more perilous and more heroic than in the original, as the borrowed version moves through an expanded range of key areas (from four flats to five sharps) before reaching a predetermined conclusion on D major. Yet the apparent triumph is short lived. The final D-major chord of the *Fanfare* is abruptly cut off and allowed to fade into silence; a fermata extends a quarter-note rest before the first theme enters in D major. Scored again for *pianissimo* winds and strings, thematic fragments of the *Fanfare* are transformed into a plaintive accompaniment to the first theme, which soon acquires a buoyant character. Staggered entrances of the first theme generate the momentum of the sonata form proper, which leaves the *Fanfare* behind in its wake.

The slow introduction establishes a rhetoric of unrealized promise that returns throughout the finale. Throughout the course of the movement, the *Fanfare* repeatedly enters as musical tension and drama builds, only to be cast aside by the appearance of a new idea. At the opening of the development, for example, the *Fanfare* and the first theme are combined with full fervor: brass and winds present the rising strains of the *Fanfare* while the strings press forward with the busy sixteenth-note motion of the first theme. At R 103, however, the expected climax is averted. The harmony, which had been driving toward a cadence, is left hanging in B major as the flute and bassoon take over the *Fanfare*, now *pianissimo*, in F major.

The first theme reappears at R 112 and leads at R 117 to a sustained, *fortississimo* dissonance presented by the entire orchestra and underscored by flutter tonguing as well as a battery of percussion. This aggressive, clangorous chord is a destructive force that threatens to crush the entire movement. But as the brutal sonority finally fades away, the first theme hesitantly returns in the piccolo, the *Fanfare* in the bassoons and subdued brass. These two themes initiate the recapitulation, which acquires an ethereal, transcendent quality (R 118–24) thanks in part to the presence of harps and celesta. The reverie succeeds in resurrecting the musical progress of the movement; the dynamic level suddenly rises, and the tempo quickens. At R 125 the second theme returns, now less jaunty and more earnest, and the glorious closing phrase of the *Fanfare* emerges in the brass at R 126. This marks the point at which the *Fanfare* is rhetorically integrated with both the structure and the narrative of the symphony. Now its rising strains are but another strand in the thematic web of the recapitulation, and its triumphant ending, so long subverted, is allowed to stand unchallenged. The closing chord on D major (at R 127) marks the return to the tonic key, and the second-theme chorale returns at R 127 in the style of a mass song—with a homophonic texture, open fourths and fifths as accompaniment, and a deliberate, even rhythm—to fulfill the promise of the reconstructed *Fanfare*.[124]

But the symphony does not simply dissolve into utopian harmony. Sharply accented intervals in the winds and strings as well as violent blows to an anvil provide a strident accompaniment to the second theme at R 127 that resists being completely assimilated into the musical texture. In addition, distinct themes from various movements return in the wake of the mass song such that no one theme bears the weight of nor claims credit for the symphonic celebration. The ideological implication of the finale's formal process suggests an ethical ideal of collaboration and collectivity more easily realized in music than in life. "Action of an external sort must eventually lead to combat in one form or another," Kenneth Burke explained.

> Such action is no longer harmony; it lacks the symphonic quality whereby the notes of coexistent melodies can at the same time both proclaim their individual identity and function as parts in a whole. Action in the realm of normal experience involves patterns of striving, competition, and conquest which reach their ultimate conclusion in war.[125]

Within the symbolic realm of music, however, action can effectively be stripped of its inherent drive to violent conflict, because the musical metaphor may depict a participatory, rather than purely competitive, mode of interaction.[126]

This concert of ideas is especially apparent in the first version of the symphony, before Copland cut an eight-measure passage preceding the coda (at R 129 in the 1967 published score).[127] In the original version, the first theme of the first movement is heard *fortissimo* in the piano and upper strings while the winds recall the first theme of the fourth movement—its only recapitulation in the tonic key. The basic profile of the *Fanfare* appears in the cellos, bassoons, contrabassoons, and trombones. This thematic layering contrasts with the preceding, homophonic section (R 127 to 129) and leads into the grand motivic assemblage of the coda.

The ideological imperative of the finale as a drama of reconciliation and cooperation reflects the general progressive concern for the relationship of self to society as well as the specific conflict between opposing populist rhetorics in the postwar era. By the time the symphony was premiered in the fall of 1946, the United States had emerged victorious from World War II, and the "American Century" had seemingly begun. But the legacy of victory was less certain to progressives, who distrusted Truman and vested their hopes in Henry Wallace and his short-lived Progressive Party.[128] Copland's Third Symphony manifests the contradictory populisms of Luce and Wallace, negotiating between the assertion of American dominion and the progressive call for worldwide social justice. With its quotation of the *Fanfare for the Common Man*, the finale attempts to construct a musical and ideological vision of triumph without conquest.

Conclusion

IN A 1946 review of Copland's Third Symphony, Virgil Thomson praised the composer's accessible style and defended the piece against those unconvinced of its sincerity.

> Many have found the piece confusing. It is the very simplicity of Copland's musical language, in fact, that has long made his music seem difficult. Laymen and even musicians are so accustomed to composers' exploiting prefabricated stylistic complexities that obscure more thought than they express that they easily mistake transparency for willfulness. I have known him and his work too long to believe him capable of obfuscation. The will that is involved is a determination to communicate, to share with others through music thoughts and feelings that by their common humanity all men can recognize. Copland aspires, I assure you, to no Jove-like pronouncements. Nor is he any double-tongued oracle. He is much more, for all his skill and personal enlightenment, Henry Wallace's "Common Man."[1]

Thomson was the only reviewer to suggest a connection between Copland's musical style and progressive politics by alluding to the source of the *Fanfare's* title in the speeches of Henry Wallace. But if at first he praised the lucidity and sincerity of the Third Symphony, Thomson later derided the music's relation to Wallace's speech and, by extension, to left-wing politics. In a review from 1947, he compared Copland's symphony to

> the speeches of Henry Wallace, striking in phraseology but all too reminiscent of Moscow. And not of Moscow as a source of vigorous political ideas, either, but of Moscow as the very spirit of international pietism. . . . I am disappointed at feelings that show so little variation, save in the manner of their expression, from the patriotic-versus-pastoral formula that the Russians evolved for war-time radio usage.[2]

At this point—just some seven months later—Thomson heard "something false" in the Third, and, referring back to his 1946 review, suggested that his initial reaction had not been unequivocally positive. "The present writer has referred to this troublesome quality as an 'editorial tone,'" Thomson recalled, meaning that "he is not convinced that the feelings expressed in the work are entirely spontaneous and personal."[3] Less than a year earlier, however, he had written that "there is nothing insincere in the work."[4] Thomson's perception of the symphony had obviously changed—as had the American cultural context.

The profound transformations in American society and politics that accompanied the end of World War II affected not only the critical reception of the Third Symphony but also Copland's view of the relationship between the composer and his environment. He articulated his reaction to the ideological circumstance of the Cold War at the 1949 Conference for World Peace, a "last hurrah" of the cultural front at which Copland and Wallace were seated together for the opening banquet.[5] In a speech delivered at a panel on the arts, Copland explained that

> artists, by definition, hate all wars—hot or cold. But lately I've been thinking that the cold war is almost worse for art than the real thing—for it permeates the atmosphere with fear and anxiety. An artist can function at his best only in a vital and healthy environment for the simple reason that the very act of creation is an affirmative gesture. An artist fighting in a war for a cause he holds just has something affirmative he can believe in. That artist, if he can stay alive, can create art. But throw him into a mood of suspicion, ill-will, and dread that typifies the cold war attitude and he'll create nothing.[6]

Soon enough, Copland himself came under suspicion in the anticommunist fervor of the McCarthy era. Coverage of the Peace Conference in *Life* magazine ran Copland's picture under the heading "Dupes and fellow travelers dress up communist fronts,"[7] and his participation was included on the list of Communist activities compiled by the House Un-American Activities Committee.

The stimulating and fruitful alliance of musical creativity and political engagement that characterized the thirties and forties for Copland was shattered by the culture of McCarthyism and postwar redefinition of liberal democratic politics in terms of fierce individualism.[8] In the late 1940s, the anti-Stalinist left merged with a growing anticommunist movement to create a new intellectual establishment explicitly hostile to the politics and aesthetics of the cultural front.[9] Anticommunist liberalism, as codified in *The Vital Center* (1949) by Arthur J. Schlesinger Jr., disavowed the collectivism of the cultural front and reasserted the ultimate integrity of the individual.[10] Schlesinger disparaged "doughface progressivism" as an unsophisticated, sentimental faith in progress and the virtues of human nature.[11] At the center of postwar liberalism was the New York intellectual circle around the *Partisan Review*, including Hannah Arendt, Daniel Bell, Saul Bellow, Clement Greenberg, Philip Rahv, Dwight Macdonald, and Diana and Lionel Trilling.[12] In general, their attitude toward art was defensive: the high culture of art, literature, and music had to be protected from the contaminating force of middlebrow public taste, the aesthetic separated from the social. Already in 1939 Clement Greenberg had articulated the position of this emergent avantgarde as "art for art's sake," avoiding subject matter and content "like the plague"—a far cry from Copland's own call that same year for an accessible style of "imposed simplicity."[13] As this particular mode of modernism took hold in the postwar era, the aesthetic of accessibility often was replaced by a cultivation of the intentionally difficult. Postwar artistic elitism frequently prized academic segregation more than cultural connection.

This fissure between art and life perhaps explains the compositional difficulties Copland experienced in his later years, for it is undeniable that his output slowed. His musical philosophy was repudiated by the cultural politics and aesthetic ideology of 1950s liberalism, and the progressive ideals that had proved so motivating in the era of depression and war were, within the tenets of anticommunist ideology, considered at best naïve and at worst seditious.[14] Despite his music's continued presence in the concert hall, Copland recognized that the younger generation of composers had little use for the grandly accessible style and collectivist aesthetic that had characterized so much artistic activity during the era of the cultural front. As Leonard Bernstein famously remarked, after the war young composers "gradually stopped flocking to Aaron," which was to Copland "heartbreaking." Bernstein explained further: "Aaron's music has always contained the basic values of art, not the least of which is communicativeness. As these virtues became unfashionable, so did Aaron's music."[15]

Copland's awareness of the new musical scene is evident in his 1967 revision to *Our New Music*, published under a revealing new title, *The New Music*. The shift from possessive pronoun to definite article subtly acknowledges his removal from the musical vanguard. Surveying the new music scene of the fifties and sixties, Copland wrote:

Gradually, toward the end of the '40s, it became evident that a new avant-garde position was in the making. In retrospect, it is clear that fresh ideas began to take hold at the war's end: there was to some extent the same atmosphere of renewal and refreshment that I described as present at the end of the First World War: suddenly it became evident that the post-war generation of 1945 was unwilling to accept the revolution of 1920 as its own; it wanted to make its own revolution in music.[16]

The new text also serves as an apologia. Copland describes having been intoxicated in the thirties by the "heady wine of suddenly feeling ourselves—the composers, that is—needed as never before." He emphasizes his involvement with the U.S. government and interest in serialism, thus aligning himself with examples of political involvement and aesthetic expression more acceptable to the postwar ethos.[17]

The disappointment and hope that Copland expressed in his speech at the Peace Conference is captured in his opera *The Tender Land* (1952–54, rev. 1955). Inspired by the landmark documentary book by James Agee and Walker Evans, *Let Us Now Praise Famous Men* (1941), the opera seems to bid farewell to the world of the Popular Front and to the folkloric idiom that had brought Copland so much success.[18] But before taking leave of such sentiment, *The Tender Land* first envisions a generous and nurturing community, as do so many works from the era of depression and war. The libretto, by Copland's paramour Erik Johns (writing under the *nom de plume* Horace Everett), centers around Laurie Moss, a young girl who lives on a farm with her mother, grandfather, and younger sister. Laurie is about to graduate and is excited as well as anxious about her future. Just before her graduation party, two drifters arrive: Martin and Top. They are looking for work and are invited to stay on the farm. Act 1 culminates in "The Promise of Living," a quintet sung by the Moss family along with the new arrivals. To the soaring strains of the nineteenth-century hymn "Zion's Walls" and Copland's own memorable countermelody, mother, daughter, grandfather, and the two young men celebrate their solidarity, as in the finale of Copland's earlier play-opera *The Second Hurricane*. "The promise of growing / with faith and with knowing / is born of our sharing / our love with our neighbor," they sing. "The promise of ending / in right understanding / is peace in our own hearts / a peace with our neighbor."

That peace is disrupted at Laurie's graduation party. As it happens, a local girl had been assaulted earlier in the day, and Ma Moss harbors doubts about the strangers who have suddenly appeared on her farm. She confesses her suspicions to a neighbor. In the meantime, Laurie has quickly become smitten with Martin, but her mother and grandfather accuse him and Top of the attack. Even though the allegations are proven false when it is revealed that the culprits are already in custody, for Grandpa Moss, Martin, and Top are "guilty all the same"—a clear reference to the politics of McCarthyism.

The simple and secure world created in the first act and celebrated in "The Promise of Living" is thus shown to be an unattainable ideal, and the fragile community of the farm is shattered by internal conflict and an oppressive insularity. As Howard Pollack has noted, promises go unrealized. Laurie had believed that her grandfather would stop meddling in her life and that she would find love; her mother wished for Laurie to stay on the farm; Martin dreamt of settling down. But in a climate of fear and suspicion, none of these things comes to pass.[19] Martin departs without saying goodbye to Laurie, and when she nevertheless chooses to leave the farm and strike out on her own, she does so without romantic dreams of either her past or her future. Instead, she is like Voltaire's (and Bernstein's) Candide—no longer innocent, but not perhaps without hope.[20] As Laurie prepares to leave, she asks her distraught mother to "try to see, / how changed this day must seem for me. / How changed I too have come to be." And so too was the culture of the Cold War utterly changed from that of the Popular Front.

Copland was in the midst of writing *The Tender Land* when, in January 1953, *Lincoln Portrait* was abruptly pulled from President-elect Dwight D. Eisenhower's inaugural program because its composer was identified as a "fellow traveler" of the Communist Party. Representative Fred Busbey argued that Copland possessed a "known record" of "activities, affiliations, and sympathies with and for causes that seemed . . . more in the interest of an alien ideology than the things representative of Abraham Lincoln." Busbey offered no musical rationale but based his objections on purely political grounds: Copland's attachment to allegedly Communist causes was considered unpatriotic and, in the argot of postwar politics, un-American. "With all the music of fine, patriotic, and thoroughly American composers available to the concert committee of the Inauguration Committee," Busbey explained, "I not only questioned the advisability of using music by a composer with the long record of questionable affiliations of Mr. Copland . . . but protested the use of his music."[21]

The list of affiliations that Busbey used to justify removing *Lincoln Portrait* was reportedly compiled by the House Un-American Activities Committee. Among other things, Copland had "signed a statement to President Roosevelt defending the Communist Party"; belonged to the American Committee for

Democracy and Intellectual Freedom, "a Communist front which defended Communist teachers"; judged a song contest sponsored by the American League Against War and Fascism; was affiliated with the Artists' Front to Win the War; belonged to the Committee of Professional Groups for Browder and Ford; performed at benefits for the *New Masses* and the American Music Alliance of the Friends of the Abraham Lincoln Brigade; and was a speaker at the Cultural and Scientific Conference for World Peace. Busbey's information also connected Copland with the National Committee for People's Rights, the National Committee for the Defense of Political Prisoners, the Citizens Committee for Harry Bridges, the American Committee for the Protection of Foreign Born, the National Federation for Constitutional Liberties, and Frontier Films.[22]

To resurrect this list of affiliations and take its contents as more than mere allegation is in no way to legitimate McCarthyism or anticommunist politics. Quite the opposite. To consider seriously and sympathetically the evidence that Copland and his music were aligned with leftist politics is to challenge anticommunist historiography, which has sought to disguise the lasting significance of the Popular Front as a creative force in American culture. With the cultural politics and aesthetic ideology of the Front restored as the context for Copland's music during the thirties and forties, we should not be surprised by events in the fifties, nor even by any enduring discomfort with the connection between Copland and left-wing politics.

In the wake of the cancellation, Copland issued a public statement, wrote directly to President Eisenhower, and offered a private explanation to the League of Composers, which had protested the decision on the composer's behalf.[23] "I want the League to know that I have no past or present political activities to hide," Copland wrote in February 1953, a few weeks after the controversy had surfaced.

> I have never at any time been a member of any political party: Republican, Democratic, or Communist. I have never joined any organization which did not have as one of its primary purposes the cultural interests of America, especially as related to music. I have never sponsored any cause except as a loyal American, proud of his right to speak his mind on controversial subjects, even to protest when some action seems unworthy of our democratic traditions. Supreme Court Justice [Hugo] Black put it this way in a recently written decision: "Individuals are guaranteed our undiluted and unequivocal right to express themselves on questions of current public interest. It means that Americans discuss such questions

as of right and not on sufferance of legislatures, courts, or any other governmental agencies. . . ."[24]

I don't think I need comment on the implications of this little episode, for its sinister overtones must be clear to everyone. We, the intellectuals, are becoming the targets of a powerful pressure movement led by small minds. It is surely a sign of the times that a musical organization like our own should have become involved in an affair such as this.[25]

In April, Copland was put on a State Department blacklist that banned his music from the nearly two hundred official American libraries worldwide.[26]

In May 1953, the composer received a telegram from Senator Joseph McCarthy. Copland testified before McCarthy and the Senate Permanent Subcommittee on Investigations in a closed hearing on Tuesday, May 26, 1953.[27] The transcript reveals the composer to have been patient, polite, and shrewd. He often answered Senator McCarthy by puzzling over the questions, choosing his words carefully, and frequently responding "I don't know" or "I don't remember." As Pollack perceptively notes, "Whether or not Copland prevaricated under questioning, he clearly was not altogether forthcoming."[28] When pressed to confirm his affiliations with a long list of "fronts," Copland hedged, first implicitly denying the charge that organizations on the lists could be fairly characterized as "Communist front organizations," then parrying the thrust of the query by trying to distinguish between membership and affiliation.

The hearing concluded with McCarthy reminding Copland that he was still under subpoena and suggesting that he would be called again. The composer was not in fact asked to return, and although he had some trouble securing a passport in the early 1950s, he suffered less severe consequences than many other artists and intellectuals connected to leftist politics and the Popular Front. Soon enough, he reestablished himself as a leading figure in American music.

The various allegations made against Copland always concerned his political activities: Busbey and McCarthy focused on the organizations to which the composer belonged and the causes with which he was associated, not the music that he wrote. But his music can indeed be heard to resonate with his politics and to express a rather liberal ideal of Americanism—liberal here indicating neither a partisan perspective nor political program but a magnanimous view of our national character. Even the stylistic pluralism that characterizes Copland's oeuvre as a whole, and which has vexed many critics, falls in line with this admittedly diffuse image of the United States as a pluralistic society of many voices. Copland's music projects an individual subjectivity and speaks with an identifiably American voice, but the accent is hard to place; as a result, it seems especially easy to invest his works with a whole host of values, then draft compositions into the service of widely varying ideologies. And although his music from the 1930s and 1940s has come to define an "American" sound, just what might characterize "American" has—especially since World War II—been largely dictated by the restrictive ideological tenets of anticommunist politics and ideology. The Cold War seems to have succeeded in divesting progressive sentiment from the symbols of Americanism, whether the people, rural life, or the American past. These myths and symbols of America—stolen back and forth by various ideologies during the Popular Front era—were eventually ceded to the hegemony of the American century.

Perhaps Copland's music from this era endures (when so much else does not) partly because it has been largely emptied of political significance, preserved as an empty sign, free of historical burdens, to be employed by the culture industry and both political parties for their own purposes.[29] The ballets are now suites; the common man is everyone and anyone; rural America is the heartland. Recently, the conservative editorialist and Cold War veteran William Safire has heard in Copland's music the reinscription of American exceptionalism. "Here is the sort of lesson I think needs teaching," Safire declares. "In the 20th century especially, American artists broke free from their formal European masters." Copland is mentioned, presumably because his music exemplifies those traits Safire ascribes to Americanism: "spare; daring; profoundly plain-spoken." One wonders, though, whether this list of qualities says more about a particular political ideology than the general qualities of American expression. "We are getting far enough away from this," Safire concludes, meaning his set of national characteristics, "to see how much it shapes our revolutionary character and affects our self-image today."[30] Given that his comments were made in the midst of another war—one led by a rather plain-spoken president, marked by an atmosphere of fear, and justified as an evangelical extension of our supposed national values to the world—it seems possible to accept these same adjectives of Americanness but hear in Copland's music something rather different from what the columnist might have in mind.

Copland's Americanism—the qualities of his musical expression and their social implications—remains indebted to the progressive politics of the Popular Front, and his music from the 1930s and 1940s evinces an alignment with the politics of progressive reform, including a fundamental sensitivity toward those less fortunate, support of multiethnic pluralism, belief in social democracy, and faith that America's past could be put in service of a better future. The symbols deployed—whether the West, folk song, patriotism, or the people—are invested with these ideals, and as a socially symbolic act, his music wrestles in the imaginative and aesthetic realm with the very real political complexities and cultural contradictions of its era. Ultimately, to appreciate the progressive political implications behind Copland's music from the Depression and war is to oppose the complacent (even complicit) view that music is, in the first instance and last analysis, only music. For indeed the music—the compelling, entrancing, and engaging aesthetic expression—lies to some extent in its relevance, in a cultural connection that may be endlessly transfigured, renewed, and reinterpreted, but never completely severed.

Notes

Abbreviations

CCLC   Aaron Copland Collection. Music Division, Library of Congress, Washington, D.C.

CCLC online   Aaron Copland Collection. American Memory Collection, Library of Congress, online at http://www.memory.loc.gov/ ammem/achtml/achome.html.

C & P I   Aaron Copland and Vivian Perlis, *Copland: 1900 Through 1942* (New York: St. Martin's/Marek, 1984).

C & P II   Aaron Copland and Vivian Perlis, *Copland Since 1943* (New York: St. Martin's Press, 1989).

NYPL   New York Public Library for the Performing Arts, New York, New York.

Pollack, *Copland*   Howard Pollack, *Aaron Copland: The Life and Work of an Uncommon Man* (New York: Henry Holt, 1999).

Materials in the Aaron Copland collection are reprinted by permission of the Aaron Copland Fund for Music, Inc., copyright owner.

Introduction

1. Harold Clurman, *The Fervent Years: The Story of the Group Theatre and the Thirties* (New York: Alfred A. Knopf, 1945), 120.

2. Ibid.: "historically cruel," 120; "something new," 116.

3. F. Scott Fitzgerald, "Echoes of the Jazz Age" (1931), in *The Crack-Up*, ed. Edmund Wilson (New York: New Directions, 1945), 19–20; on the significance of 1927 see Robert A. M. Stern, "Relevance of the Decade 1929–1939," *Journal of the Society of Architectural Historians* 21 (1962): 84–102; also, Stern, Gregory Gilmartin, and Thomas Mellins, *New York, 1930: Architecture and Urbanism Between the Two World Wars* (New York: Rizzoli, 1987), 29; and Warren Susman, *Culture as History: The Transformation of American Society in the Twentieth Century* (New York: Pantheon, 1984), 186–89.

4. Josephine Herbst, "A Year of Disgrace" in *The Starched Blue Sky of Spain and Other Memoirs* (New York: HarperCollins, 1991), 97.

5. Clurman, *The Fervent Years*, 20.

6. Aaron Copland, "Composer from Brooklyn," *Magazine of Art* (1939); repr., *Our New Music: Leading Composers in Europe and America* (1941; rev. and enlarged ed. *The New Music, 1900–1960*, New York: W. W. Norton, 1968), 158, 159.

7. Ibid., 159.

8. Pollack, *Copland*, 115–21.

9. Copland to Nadia Boulanger, October 16, 1927, as quoted in C & P I, 140.

10. On Copland's turn away from the jazz idiom, see Beth E. Levy, "Frontier Figures: American Music and the Mythology of the American West, 1895–1945" (Ph.D. diss., University of California, Berkeley, 2002), 220–52.

11. "Where Do We Go from Here?" *Modern Music* 4, no. 1 (1926): 9–14.

12. Copland, "Music Since 1920," *Modern Music* 5, no. 3 (1928): 19–20.

13. Copland, "The Composer in America, 1923–33," *Modern Music* 10, no. 2 (1933): 91.

14. Copland, "Composer from Brooklyn," 160.

15. Ibid. As a general phenomenon, the move away from an iconoclastic, ironic, and experimental modernism in the 1920s toward a more politically conscious and socially responsive modernism in the 1930s was not confined to the United States. Copland's adoption of a newly accessible idiom was preceded by and related to similar aesthetic stances taken by German, Mexican, Russian, and French composers in response to the politics and ideologies of the interwar period. The situation in these countries is discussed in sources such as Stephen Hinton, *The Idea of Gebrauchsmusik: A Study of Musical Aesthetics in the Weimar Republic (1919 to 1933) with Particular Reference to the Works of Paul Hindemith* (New York: Garland, 1989); also Hinton, "Hanns Eisler and the Ideology of Modern Music," in *New Music, Aesthetics, and Ideology/Neue Musik, Asthetik und Ideologie*, ed. Mark Delaere, Helga De la Motte, and Herman Sabbe (Wilhelmshaven, Germany: Florian Noetzel, 1995), 79–85; Richard Taruskin, "Back to Whom? Neoclassicism as Ideology," *19th-Century Music* 16 (1993): 286–302; Joseph Auner, "Schoenberg and His Public in 1930: The Six Pieces for Male Chorus, op. 35," in *Schoenberg and His World*, ed. Walter Frisch (Princeton, N.J.: Princeton University Press, 1999), 85–125; Leonora Saavedra, "The American Composer in the 1930s: The Social Thought of Seeger and Chávez," in *Understanding Charles Seeger, Pioneer in American Musicology*, ed. Bell Yung and Helen Rees (Urbana: University of Illinois Press, 1999), 29–63; Inna Barsova, "Between 'Social Demands' and the 'Music of Grand Passions': The Years 1934–1937 in the Life of Dmitry Shostakovich," in *Shostakovich in Context*, ed. Rosamund Bartlett (New York: Oxford University Press, 2000), 79–98; Pauline Fairclough, "The 'Perestroyka' of Soviet Symphonism: Shostakovich in 1935," *Music & Letters* 83 (2002): 259–73; Laurel E. Fay, *Shostakovich: A Life* (New York: Oxford University Press, 2000); Leslie A. Sprout, "Music for a 'New Era': Composers and National Identity in France, 1936–46" (Ph.D. diss., University of California, Berkeley, 2000).

16. Arthur Berger described Copland's simplified style as involving "a rehabilitation of the triad" *(Aaron Copland* [New York: Oxford University Press, 1953], 65).

17. Copland, "Composer from Brooklyn," 160–61.

18. Ibid., 161.

19. "Conversation with Aaron Copland," in *Perspectives on American Composers*, ed. Benjamin Boretz and Edward Cone (New York: W. W. Norton, 1971), 140.

20. Copland letter was prompted by Berger's article, "Copland's Piano Sonata," *Partisan Review* 10, no. 2 (1943): 187–90; see also Berger, *Reflections of an American Composer* (Berkeley: University of California Press, 2002), 13–15.

21. Copland to Berger, April 10, 1943, CCLC.

22. Copland, "Composer from Brooklyn," 168.

23. Ibid., 162.

24. Copland, *Music and Imagination* (Cambridge, Mass.: Harvard University Press, 1952), 99.

25. Transcript of the Seventeenth Program, February 24, 1937, Composers' Forum-Laboratory (Second Series), Aaron Copland, Composer, p. 7; the Composers' Forum-Laboratory, 1935–40; Records of the Federal Music Program; Records of the Works Progress Administration, Record Group 69; National Archives at College Park, College Park, MD.

26. Berger, *Aaron Copland*, 28–29.

27. Copland, "The Musical Scene Changes," *Twice a Year* 5–6 (1941): 342, 343.

28. Copland, "Workers Sing!" *New Masses*, June 5, 1934, 28; repr. *Aaron Copland: A Reader*, ed. Richard Kostelanetz (New York: Routledge, 2004), 88.

29. Several recent studies consider the problem of resurrecting the 1930s in the wake of anticommunist ideology and attempt to reinterpret the political dimensions of Depression-era aesthetics with sympathy and subtlety. See in particular Cary Nelson, *Repression and Recovery: Modern American Poetry and the Politics of Cultural Memory, 1910–45* (Madison: University of Wisconsin Press, 1989); Alan Filreis, *Modernism from Right to Left: Wallace Stevens, the Thirties, and Literary Radicalism* (Cambridge: Cambridge University Press, 1994); Robert Shulman, *The Power of Political Art: The 1930s Literary Left Reconsidered* (Chapel Hill: University of North Carolina Press, 2000); and Alan M. Wald, *Exiles from a Future Time: The Forging of the Mid-Twentieth Century Left* (Chapel Hill: University of North Carolina Press, 2002). In the field of art history, see Erika Doss, *Benton, Pollack, and the Politics of Modernism: From Regionalism to Abstract Expressionism* (Chicago: University of Chicago Press, 1991).

30. Jennifer DeLapp discusses the political dimensions of the dichotomy between tonality and serialism in her dissertation, "Copland in the Fifties: Music and Ideology in the McCarthy Era" (Ph.D. diss., University of Michigan, 1997), 100–6; on the Cold War ideological support for abstract art and political misgivings about realism, see Doss, *Benton, Pollack, and the Politics of Modernism*, 363–416. On government involvement in postwar cultural propaganda, see especially Frances Stonor Saunders, *Who Paid the Piper? The CIA and the Cultural Cold War* (London: Granta, 1999).

31. On Copland's testimony, see DeLapp, "Copland in the Fifties," 134–43.

32. C & P I, 218.

33. Michael Denning, *The Cultural Front: The Laboring of American Culture in the Twentieth Century* (London: Verso, 1997), 4.

34. I am not the only—nor even the first—to situate Copland and his music within the framework developed by Denning. In her dissertation, Sally Bick considers Copland's relation to Hollywood, exploring his attitude toward composing for film in the context of the cultural front and examining the score for *Of Mice and Men* (1939). See Sally M. A. Bick, *Composers on the Cultural Front: Aaron Copland and Hanns Eisler in Hollywood* (Ph.D. diss., Yale University, 2001).

35. See in particular Aaron Copland, "The Composers Get Wise," *Modern Music* 18 (1940): 18–21, which considers the matter of performance fees for concert composers.

36. Denning concentrates on migration narratives, various styles of proletarian literature, musical theater, and the blues.

37. Denning, *The Cultural Front*, xix–xx. Denning credits Alan Trachtenberg with the distinction between an extrinsic and intrinsic political expression. Following Fredric Jameson, Denning preserves a dialectic between Trachtenberg's "politics of affiliation and allegiance" and the "politics of aesthetics" (473–74, n. 9). See Trachtenberg, "Introduction," *Paul Strand*, ed. Maren Strange (New York: Aperture, 1990), 4, and Jameson, *The Political Unconscious: Narrative as a Socially Symbolic Act* (Ithaca, N.Y.: Cornell University Press, 1981), 39–44.

38. Or what Jameson, following Louis Althusser, terms "mechanical effectivity" (Jameson, *The Political Unconscious*, 25).

39. See Denning, xx and 473–74, nn. 9–10.

40. Ibid., 79. Jameson's discussion of symbolic action relies in part on Kenneth Burke's *The Philosophy of Literary Form: Studies in Symbolic Action* ([Baton Rouge]: Louisiana State University Press, 1941). For an eminently readable and graciously concise discussion of the relation between Burke's literary philosophy and Jameson's notion of symbolic significance, see William C. Dowling, *Jameson, Althusser, Marx: An Introduction to "The Political Unconscious"* (Ithaca, N.Y.: Cornell University Press, 1984), 122–23.

41. Ibid., 41. Jameson adopts the model of "structural causality" from Althusser. See Jameson, *The Political Unconscious*, 23–49.

42. Ibid., 39.

43. This while always respecting the difference between the political and the musical. As Lydia Goehr has noted, "between the desire to reduce music to politics, on the one hand, and to preserve the purity of music, on the other, lies a delicate middle position. This position asks us to reconcile two seemingly opposed desires: the demand that we be true to the *political* in music while also remaining true to the *musical* in music" ("Political Music and the Politics of Music," *The Journal of Aesthetics and Art Criticism* 52 [1994]: 102).

44. Clurman, *The Fervent Years*, 290. Emphasis mine.

45. Richard Taruskin notes "the irony of the situation—that important features of the American national identity in music originated in circumstances that would later be branded 'Un-American'" (Taruksin, *The Oxford History of Western Music*, vol. 5, *The Early Twentieth Century* [New York: Oxford University Press, 2005], 651). The irony remains whether the left-wing culture of the 1930s and 1940s is seen as wholly the product of Communist Party policy (and thus of the international Soviet) or

as an indigenous American social-democratic movement related but not reducible to Communism. An additional irony of Copland's position as "Dean of American composers," a position of musical influence and institutional authority, is explored by Nadine Hubbs, who opens her study of gay American composers with this compelling contradiction. "Questions have scarcely arisen about Copland's queer identity vis-à-vis his (apparently incongruous) identity as national cultural spokesperson," she notes before examining in admirable detail the roots of "American" music in early-twentieth century gay male culture (Hubbs, *The Queer Composition of America's Sound: Gay Modernists, American Music, and National Identity* [Berkeley: University of California Press, 2004], 3).

1. Communism and the Cultural Front

1. Transcript of interview with Vivian Perlis, September 16, 1979, p. 324, typescript, CCLC.

2. C & P I, 218.

3. Ibid. Perlis situates Copland in the general context of left-wing musical activities in "Interlude III," 217–30.

4. Pollack, *Copland*, 270.

5. Ibid., 270–87.

6. As quoted in Julia Smith, *Aaron Copland: His Work and Contribution to American Music* (New York: E. P. Dutton, 1955), 120. See also Pollack, *Copland*, 271.

7. Following convention, I capitalize Progressivism in connection to the movement at the turn of the century but, like Edmund Wilson, do not when referring to left-wing politics during the Depression. The literature on the Progressive Era is vast. For a brief overview, see Richard L. McCormick, "Public Life in Industrial America," in *The New American History*, ed. Eric Foner (Philadelphia: Temple University Press, 1997), 107–32; also, idem, *The Party Period and Public Policy: American Politics from the Age of Jackson to the Progressive Era* (New York: Oxford University Press, 1987); John Whiteclay Chambers, *The Tyranny of Change: America in the Progressive Era, 1890–1920* (New York: St. Martin's Press, 1992); Richard Hofstadter discusses Progressivism as a buttress for capitalism in *The Age of Reform: From Bryan to F.D.R.* (New York: Knopf, 1955); on Progressivism as a response to modernity, see Robert H. Wiebe, *The Search for Order, 1877–1920* (New York: Hill & Wang, 1996).

8. Herbert Croly, *The Promise of American Life* (New York: Macmillan, 1909).

9. On the connection between the Progressive movement in the years before World War I and Jewish leftism, see Arthur Liebman, *Jews and the Left* (New York: John Wiley & Sons, 1979), 184–87. In *The Triumph of Ethnic Progressivism: Urban Political Culture in Boston, 1900–1925* (Cambridge, Mass.: Harvard University Press, 1998), James J. Connolly complicates the notion of Progressivism as a universalized, white, Protestant perspective by demonstrating that various forms of ethnic progressivism united minority groups in a struggle of "the people" versus "the interests" (3).

10. Richard H. Pells, *Radical Visions and American Dreams: Culture and Social Thought in the Depression Years* (1973; repr., Middletown, Conn.: Wesleyan University Press, 1984), 1–10. The work of the critics known as the Young Americans is

discussed in Casey Nelson Blake, *Beloved Community: The Cultural Criticism of Randolph Bourne, Van Wyck Brooks, Waldo Frank and Lewis Mumford* (Chapel Hill: University of North Carolina Press, 1990).

11. Van Wyck Brooks, "America's Coming of Age" (1915); as quoted in Pells, *Radical Visions*, 7.

12. On Claire Reis, see Carol J. Oja, *Making Music Modern: New York in the 1920s* (New York: Oxford, 2000), 214–21.

13. Stuart D. Hobbes, *The End of the Avant Garde* (New York: New York University Press, 1997); also Walter Kalaidjian, *American Culture Between the Wars: Revisionary Modernism and Postmodern Critique* (New York: Columbia University Press, 1993), 8–9. Hobbes notes that the avant-garde "had significant intellectual connections with American traditions of social criticism" (8).

14. Pells, *Radical Visions*, 1–42. On progressivism and the "lost generation" of American modernists, see also Judy Kutulas, *The Long War: The Intellectual People's Front and Anti-Stalinism, 1930–1940* (Durham, N.C.: Duke University Press, 1995), 18–51.

15. Pells, *Radical Visions*, 13.

16. In a letter to his parents from Paris, Copland writes: "please don't forget to send me my magazine 'The Dial,' if you have not done so already" (June 21, 1922, CCLC).

17. See Pollack, *Copland*, 100–106.

18. Edmund Wilson, "The Literary Consequences of the Crash," in *The Shores of Light: A Literary Chronicle of the Twenties and Thirties* (New York: Farrar, Straus and Young, 1952), 498–99.

19. Copland, "Composer from Brooklyn," *Magazine of Art* (1939); repr., *Our New Music: Leading Composers in Europe and America* (1941; rev. and enlarged ed. *The New Music, 1900–1960*, New York: W. W. Norton, 1968), 161. The comment is found in a new section appended in 1967 to the original 1939 autobiography.

20. Malcolm Cowley, *Exile's Return: A Literary Odyssey of the 1920s* (1934; repr. New York: Penguin Books, 1956), 287–88.

21. Edmund Wilson, "An Appeal to Progressives," *New Republic*, January 14, 1931, 235–38.

22. Throughout his article, Wilson capitalizes Communism but not progressivism, and I follow suit to distinguish this more radical platform of social, cultural, and economic reform from an earlier Progressivism that presumed the continuance of capitalism.

23. Wilson, "An Appeal to Progressives," 235.

24. Ibid., 237.

25. Ibid., 238.

26. George Soule, "Hard-Boiled Radicalism," *New Republic*, January 21, 1931, 265.

27. On the relationship between progressivism, defined as America's "own characteristic radicalism" (390), and the New Deal, see R. G. Tugwell, "The New Deal: The Progressive Tradition," *Western Political Quarterly* 3 (1950): 390–427. President Franklin Delano Roosevelt was careful, according to Tugwell, never to be too closely

associated with the progressive agenda, lest he be tagged as "red." Roosevelt "never dared go so far as to say, for instance, that capitalism no longer worked to secure the objectives of progressives—the efficient production, the equitable apportionment and the enjoyable consumption of goods; nor did he state that some modified arrangement, some quite drastic alternative, might work better. Something of this sort would doubtless have had more appeal to the underprivileged and to the philanthropically inclined, including those who thought of themselves as progressives; but he felt the danger to be very great" (397). In terms of the connection between a progressive agenda and the Jewish community, it is worth noting that the antisemitic conservative right referred to the New Deal itself as the "Jew Deal" and suggested that Roosevelt himself was Jewish. See Beth S. Wenger, *New York Jews and the Great Depression* (New Haven, Conn.: Yale University Press, 1996), 130–31.

28. This brief account of the Popular Front draws most directly on Harvey Klehr, *The Heyday of American Communism: The Depression Decade* (New York: Basic Books, 1984) and Fraser M. Ottanelli, *The Communist Party of the United States* (New Brunswick, N.J.: Rutgers University Press, 1991).

29. Earl Browder, address delivered at the Institute of Public Affairs, University of Virginia, July 17, 1936, in *The People's Front* (New York: International Publishers, 1938), 111. On the People's Front, see ibid., 19–64.

30. "'Free, Prosperous, Happy . . .': The Text of the Communist Election Platform," *New Masses*, July 14, 1936, 19. See also Donald Bruce Johnson, *National Party Platforms*, vol. 1, 1849–1956 (Urbana: University of Illinois Press, 1978), 330–31 and 360; Barbara Zuck, *A History of Musical Americanism* (Ann Arbor: UMI Research Press, 1980), 106; Michael Denning, *The Cultural Front: The Laboring of American Culture in the Twentieth Century* (London: Verso, 1997), 125–34.

31. As Ellen Schrecker notes, "there is an important distinction to be made here between the Communist party and the communist movement. The two were closely linked, but not quite the same. The movement was a political subculture, a loosely structured constellation of left-wing individuals, ideas, and organizations of which the party was the institutional core" (Ellen Schrecker, *Many Are the Crimes: McCarthyism in America* [Princeton, N.J.: Princeton University Press, 1998], 5–6). Denning's model of the Popular Front as a native social movement denies the Communist Party pride of place but shares the notion of a broader left-wing coalition (or culture) outside the control of the Party and its orthodoxies.

32. Charles C. Alexander, *Here the Country Lies: Nationalism and the Arts in Twentieth-Century America* (Bloomington: Indiana University Press, 1980), 193.

33. Histories of the CPUSA that emphasize the authority of the Moscow-dominated Comintern over all aspects of American communism are often called "traditional" histories; among these are Lewis Coser and Irving Howe, *The American Communist Party: A Critical History* (Boston: Beacon Press, 1957); Theodore Draper, *The Roots of American Communism* (New York: Viking, 1957); *American Communism and Soviet Russia: The Formative Period* (New York: Viking Press, 1960); and Klehr, *The Heyday of American Communism*. Klehr maintains that "to understand Communist actions in America, it is not enough to study the CPUSA. Indeed simply by focusing on national events, one cannot comprehend why the Communists acted as they did

during any era. It was abroad, in Moscow, that the decisive formulations were made which the Americans labored to apply to American conditions. Communist policies and language are incomprehensible unless one recognizes that they were largely responses to Comintern directions" (11).

Among the new historians, also referred to as the revisionists, are Maurice Isserman, *Which Side Were You On? The American Communist Party during the Second World War* (Middletown, Conn.: Wesleyan University Press, 1982); Mark Naison, *Communists in Harlem during the Depression* (Urbana: University of Illinois Press, 1983); Ottanelli, *The Communist Party of the United States*; and Kutulas, *The Long War*. Robbie Lieberman adopts a similarly broad view of American communism, defining the movement as "much larger than the CPUSA itself, including all those who shared the ideals of the party or were involved in its activities" (Lieberman, *"My Song Is My Weapon": People's Songs, American Communism, and the Politics of Culture, 1930–50* [Urbana: University of Illinois Press, 1995], 14). Writing specifically about the Popular Front as the policy of the Comintern, Ottanelli emphasizes the indigenous nature of the Front and the ability of the CPUSA to adjust its strategy to suit the American context: "for United States Communists, the Seventh Congress of the Communist International in the Summer of 1935, far from simply reflecting Moscow's order to adopt a new policy, represented an encouragement to pursue and expand the course they had already been following for at least two years" (Ottanelli, *The Communist Party of the United States*, 80).

The differences between these two models of history are summarized in Isserman, *Which Side Were You On?* vii–xii; Michael E. Brown, "The History of the History of U.S. Communism," in *New Studies in the Politics and Culture of U.S. Communism*, ed. Michael E. Brown, Randy Martin, Frank Rosengarten, and George Snedeker (New York: Monthly Review, 1993); Maurice Isserman, "Three Generations: Historians View American Communism," *Labor History* 26, no. 4 (1985): 517–45; and Kutulas, *The Long War*, 4–17. For a particularly vicious account of the revisionist history and its authors that nonetheless makes the distinctions between the two camps quite clear, see John Earl Haynes and Harvey Klehr, *In Denial: Historians, Communism, and Espionage* (San Francisco: Encounter Books, 2003), 11–57.

34. Denning, *The Cultural Front*, 5.

35. Ibid.

36. Ibid., 4–6.

37. Ibid., 102.

38. Ibid., 22–24.

39. Ibid., 24–27.

40. Ibid., 5–6.

41. Naison, "Remaking America: Communists and Liberals in the Popular Front," in *New Studies in the Politics and Culture of U.S. Communism*, 69.

42. Denning, *The Cultural Front*, xix. Following Denning, I capitalize Popular Front as the name of the "democratic social movement"; the "cultural front," which is not capitalized, marks the encounter between the Popular Front and "the modern cultural apparatuses of mass entertainment and education" (xviii).

43. Ibid., 58.

44. Ibid., 163–64.

45. Ibid., 59.

46. Ibid., 59–60.

47. See Senate Committee on Government Operations, Permanent Subcommittee on Investigations, *State Department Teacher-Student Exchange Program*, "Testimony of Aaron Copland," May 26, 1953, 83rd Congress, 1st sess., http://www.access.gpo.gov/congress/senate/senate12cp107.html.

48. Pollack, *Copland*, 273; see also See C & P I, 192–94.

49. Arthur V. Berger, "The Young Composers' Group," *Trend* 2, no. 1 (1933): 26.

50. Ibid., 27–28.

51. On the Composers Collective, see Richard Reuss, *American Folk Music and Left-Wing Politics, 1927–1957*, ed. Joanne C. Reuss (New York: Scarecrow Press, 2000), 44–49, 67–69; Zuck, *A History of Musical Americanism*, 115–38; Carol J. Oja, "Marc Blitzstein's *The Cradle Will Rock* and Mass-Song Style of the 1930s," *The Musical Quarterly* 73 (1989): 445–75; and David King Dunaway, "Unsung Songs of Protest: The Composers Collective of New York," *New York Folklore* 5, nos. 1–2 (1979): 1–19. On the Workers Music League see "History of the Workers Music League" and "Platform of the Workers Music League," *The Worker Musician* 1, no. 1 (1932): 6.

52. See "Music," *Daily Worker*, February 22, 1936; Zuck, *A History of Musical Americanism*, 116. According to Reuss, the Collective was founded in February 1932 (*American Folk Music and Left-Wing Politics*, 44). The composer and musicologist Norman Cazden recalled the Collective as having first formed in late 1931; see Dunaway, "Unsung Songs of Protest," 1. According to Henry Leland Clark, a member of the Collective, the organization "grew out of a seminar in the writing of mass songs organized in 1933." See Clark, "Composers' Collective of New York," *Grove Music Online*, ed. Laura Macy, http://www.grovemusic.com.

53. "The Composers' Collective of N. Y.," *Unison* 1, no. 2 (1936), 2.

54. Richard Reuss describes the *Music Vanguard* as the "semi-independent journal" of the Composers Collective (Reuss, *American Folk Music and Left-Wing Politics*, 67).

55. "Introduction," *Music Vanguard* 1, no. 1 (1935): 1.

56. Ibid., 2.

57. Copland, "A Note on Young Composers," *Music Vanguard* 1, no. 1 (1935): 14–16; repr. in *Aaron Copland: A Reader*, ed. Richard Kostelanetz (New York: Routledge, 2004), 126–27.

58. Copland, "A Note on Young Composers," *Music Vanguard*, 15.

59. Ibid., 16.

60. Earl Browder, "Communism and Literature," address before the League of American Writers, April 26, 1935, in *Communism and Culture* (New York: Workers Library Publishers, 1941), 5.

61. Ibid., 6–7.

62. Pollack, *Copland*, 278.

63. Aaron Copland to Israel Citkowitz, [September] 1934, CCLC; and CCLC online, digital ID copland corr0190; also quoted in C & P I, 229, and Pollack, *Copland*, 277.

64. See Federal Writers' Project, *New York City Guide* (New York: Random House, 1939), 198–99.

65. Such works as *The Second Hurricane* (1936), *The City* (1939), *Quiet City* (1939), and *Letter from Home* (1944) remain attached to an urban sensibility.

66. Harold Clurman to Copland, September 13, 1934, CCLC.

67. Denning, *The Cultural Front*, 284.

68. On the proletarian avant-garde, see ibid., 64–67.

69. Ibid., 66.

70. Reuss, *American Folk Music and Left-Wing Politics*, 64.

71. "Platform of the Workers Music League," 6.

72. Charles Seeger, "On Proletarian Music," *Modern Music* 11, no. 3 (1934): 123–24.

73. "Platform of the Workers Music League," 6.

74. Foreword, *Workers Song Book* (New York: Workers Music League, 1934), emphasis original.

75. Copland, "Workers Sing!" *New Masses*, June 5, 1934, 28; repr. *Aaron Copland: A Reader*, 88.

76. On the connection between these traits and the mass-song style of the Collective, see Oja, "Marc Blitzstein's *The Cradle Will Rock*," 450–52.

77. See C & P I, 225. Comments from interview with Charles Seeger, as quoted in C & P I, 225.

78. Arthur Berger, "Copland and the Audience of the Thirties," *Partisan Review* 68 (2000), 570–71.

79. See Oja, "Marc Blitzstein's *The Cradle Will Rock*," 447–48.

80. Ashley Pettis, "Second Workers' Music Olympiad," *New Masses*, May 22, 1934, 29.

81. Pettis, "Marching With a Song," *New Masses*, May 1, 1934, 15.

82. Carl Sands [Charles Seeger], "Copeland's [*sic*] Music Recital at Pierre Degeyter Club," *Daily Worker*, March 22, 1934, CCLC. See also Pollack, *Copland*, 274–75.

83. Arthur Berger describes the *Piano Variations* as in Copland's "esoteric style— 'esoteric,' that is to say, in a relative sense or in the eyes of the broader musical public." Outside modern music circles, Berger continues, the work "was regarded as somewhat freakish and inaccessible. . . . To this day it is considered forbidding and its appeal is confined to relatively few" (*Aaron Copland* [New York: Oxford University Press, 1953], 25).

84. Sands, "Copeland's [*sic*] Music Recital at Pierre Degeyter Club."

85. Ibid.

86. Oja, *Making Music Modern*, 245–48.

87. Copland, "Music Since 1920," *Modern Music* 5, no. 3 (1928): 20.

88. See Aaron Copland, review of *Discoveries of a Music Critic*, by Paul Rosenfeld, *New Republic*, April 15, 1936, 291.

89. Aaron Copland, "Survey of Contemporary Music," lecture delivered at the Toledo Museum of Art, January 16, 1940, typescript, CCLC.

90. On Stravinsky as a reactionary, see in particular Richard Taruskin, "Back to Whom? Neoclassicism as Ideology," *19th-Century Music* 16 (1993): 290–93.

91. Program note for performance of the *Piano Variations* by John Kirkpatrick at Town Hall, March 26, 1940, CCLC.

92. O.T., review of *Piano Variations*, January 29, 1936, CCLC.

93. David K. Dunaway, "Charles Seeger and Carl Sands: The Composers' Collective Years," *Ethnomusicology* 24 (1980): 164.

94. Seeger, "On Proletarian Music," 124–25.

95. Copland, "Workers Sing!" 29.

96. "The Composers' Collective of N.Y.," 2.

97. In late 1936 and early 1937, Copland drafted a choral work on Langston Hughes's poem, "Ballad of Ozie Powell." Powell was one of nine young, black men accused of rape and known as the Scottsboro Boys. Their cause was adopted by the Popular Front and the Communist Party. See Pollack, *Copland*, 312–13; also Beth E. Levy, "Frontier Figures: American Music and the Mythology of the American West, 1895–1945" (Ph.D. diss., University of California, Berkeley, 2002), 258–71. On the Scottsboro case see James E. Goodman, *Stories of Scottsboro* (New York: Pantheon, 1994).

98. Pollack, *Copland*, 296.

99. Aaron Copland, text for WNCN radio program "Aaron Copland Comments," December 9, 1968, typescript, CCLC.

100. Berger, *Aaron Copland*, 28.

101. Ibid., 29.

102. See Denning, *The Cultural Front*, 367–68; Morgan Y. Himelstein, *Drama Was a Weapon: The Left-Wing Theater in New York, 1929–1941* (New Brunswick, N.J.: Rutgers University Press, 1963), 155–60.

103. Harold Clurman to Copland, May 24, 1932, CCLC.

104. Howard Pollack has likewise observed that the juxtaposition of movements "strikes one as dialectical" (Pollack, *Copland*, 297). My thanks to Wayne Shirley for pointing out the design of the orchestration.

105. A sketch page among the manuscripts for *Elegies* is titled "Elegy for Hart Crane." Although the sketch is dated February 1932, perhaps the dedication was added after the poet committed suicide in April 1932. *Elegies* was later withdrawn from the composer's catalogue.

106. "Sidewalks of New York" is included on *Music of the Carousel*, Smithsonian Folkways Recordings, FW06128, 1961.

107. Robert A. Slayton, *Empire Statesman: The Rise and Redemption of Al Smith* (New York: Free Press, 2001), 222–24.

108. Ibid., 170–88.

109. Ibid., 311–13.

110. Ibid., 315–16.

111. Edmund Wilson, "Progress and Poverty," *New Republic*, May 20, 1931; repr., "May First: The Empire State Building, Life on the Passaic River," *The American Earthquake: A Chronicle of the Roaring Twenties, the Great Depression, and the Dawn of the New Deal* (1958; repr., New York: Da Capo, 1996), 293–94. The off-color quip does not appear in the original article.

112. "League is Formed to Scan New Deal, 'Protect Rights,'" *New York Times*, August 23, 1934, 1. See also Slayton, *Empire Statesman*, 376–89; Christopher M. Finan, *Alfred E. Smith: The Happy Warrior* (New York: Hill & Wang, 2002), 308–11; George Wolfskill, *The Revolt of the Conservatives: A History of the American Liberty League, 1934–1940* (Boston: Houghton Mifflin, 1962).

113. Tammany Hall had originally been located on East 14th Street. In 1927 that building was sold, and the following year plans for a new headquarters were announced. The new Tammany Hall, located on the northeast corner of Union Square, was under construction during the presidential election. Completed in 1929, it housed the offices of the Democratic County Committee.

114. Harold Clurman to Copland, July 31, 1934, CCLC.

115. See Reuss, *American Folk Music and Left-Wing Politics*, 59–66; on socialist realism see, for example, Malcolm H. Brown, ed., *Russian and Soviet Music: Essays for Boris Schwarz* (Ann Arbor, Mich.: UMI Research Press, 1984); Hans Gunther, ed., *The Culture of the Stalin Period* (New York: St. Martin's Press, 1990); M. Parkhomenko and A. Miasnikov, *Socialist Realism in Literature and Art: A Collection of Articles*, trans. C. V. James (Moscow: Progress Publishers, 1971); Regine Robin, *Socialist Realism: An Impossible Aesthetic*, trans. Catherine Porter (Stanford, Cal.: Stanford University Press, 1992); Pauline Fairclough, "The 'Perestroyka' of Soviet Symphonism: Shostakovich in 1935," *Music & Letters* 83 (2002): 259–74.

116. Reuss, *American Folk Music and Left-Wing Politics*, 66–67. The foreword to the second *Workers Songbook* (which included Copland's song) noted that the collection was "a definite advance over the first book" and singled out as "particular noteworthy" the inclusion of "satirical songs in the American folk style aimed at the 'best' personalities of American Capitalism." Foreword, *Workers Songbook 2* (New York: Workers Music League, 1935).

117. According to Reuss, "the American communist movement's rapidly developing admiration for folk culture was neither dictated from nor controlled by Moscow" although "there certainly was a correlation" *(American Folk Music and Left-Wing Politics*, 57). Moreover, he demonstrates that "well before Gorky started removing the stigma from folk music (in Communist eyes, at least) in his talk to the Writers' Congress in 1934, the American [Composers] collective had begun changing its own position on the subject" (ibid., 66). See also George Maynard, "Music Appreciation among Workers," *Daily Worker*, January 13, 1934; Lan Adomian, "What Songs Should Workers' Choruses Sing?" *Daily Worker*, February 7, 1934, and Zuck, *A History of Musical Americanism*, 139–54.

2. Expanding America

1. Aaron Copland to John Kirkpatrick, June 22, 1932, as quoted in C & P I, 208.

2. Copland completed a draft full score of *Statements* in June 1934, but "Dogmatic" was not finished until 1935. A two-piano score of *El Salón México* was completed in 1934 and premiered by Copland and John Kirkpatrick on October 11, 1935 at the New School for Social Research on an all-Copland program. The orchestral version was completed in 1936.

3. Copland, "Composer from Brooklyn," *Magazine of Art* (1939); repr., *Our New Music: Leading Composers in Europe and America* (1941; rev. and enlarged ed. *The New Music, 1900–1960*, New York: W. W. Norton, 1968), 160.

4. C & P I, 247. The orchestral version of *El Salón México* was premiered by Carlos Chávez and the Orquesta Sinfónica de México on August 27, 1937. On September 12, 1937, the work was performed again on a free concert for workers (advertised as *"concierto gratuito para trabajadores"*). Under the direction of Eugene Ormandy, the Minneapolis Symphony premiered just two of the six movements of *Statements for Orchestra* for NBC radio in 1936, and on a subsequent symphony program later that year, only the final two movements were performed. The complete work was premiered by the New York Philharmonic (conducted by Dimitri Mitropoulos) on January 7, 1942—seven years after the piece was completed. See C & P I, 236.

Chávez and the Orquesta Sinfónica de México gave the world premiere of the *Short Symphony* (1933) in November 1934. Copland's arrangement, the Sextet, was performed in the United States in 1939, but the *Short Symphony* waited for its U.S. premiere until 1944, when Leopold Stokowski conducted the NBC Symphony on a radio broadcast. In 1957 Leonard Bernstein conducted the Philharmonic in the U.S. concert premiere. See C & P I, 211–12.

5. C & P I, 248.

6. Copland, "The Composers of South America," in *Copland on Music* (New York: W. W. Norton, 1963), 203.

7. On "pan-ethnic Americanism" in the Popular Front, see Michael Denning, *The Cultural Front: The Laboring of American Culture in the Twentieth Century* (London: Verso 1997), 130.

8. For a thoroughgoing discussion of Copland's friendship with Chávez as well as with other Latin American composers, see Pollack, *Copland*, 216–33; also Robert Parker, "Copland and Chávez: Brothers in Arms," *American Music* 5 (1987): 433–44.

9. Copland, "Carlos Chávez—Mexican Composer," *New Republic* (1928); repr. in *American Composers on American Music*, ed. Henry Cowell (Palo Alto, Calif.: Stanford University Press, 1933), 106.

10. Copland to Carlos Chávez, October 31, 1928, CCLC.

11. Copland to Chávez, August 15, 1930, CCLC.

12. Copland, "Carlos Chávez—Mexican Composer," in *American Composers on American Music*, 102–3, 105.

13. Ibid.: "exemplifies the complete overthrow," 102–3; "the first authentic signs," 106.

14. Copland to Chávez, December 16, 1933, CCLC.

15. Ibid.

16. Carlos Chávez, "The Function of the Concert," *Modern Music* 15, no. 2 (1938): 75.

17. Copland, "Composer from Brooklyn," 161.

18. Copland, "Mexican Composer," *New York Times*, May 9, 1937.

19. Copland to Arthur Berger, September 8, 1944, CCLC; see also Pollack, *Copland*, 227.

20. Moreover, Copland may have even been inspired to compose for films by Revueltas's example. In 1935, Revueltas wrote the score for Paul Strand's *The Wave*. As

a friend of the composer and the filmmaker, Copland went to see *The Wave* when it opened in New York in 1937; that same year he began to look for movie work, and in 1939 he composed his first film score, for Ralph Steiner's documentary *The City* (see Pollack, *Copland*, 337–39). Copland's knowledge of Revueltas's music should qualify the notion that Copland's forays into film composition were directly inspired by Virgil Thomson's works (Virgil Thomson, *American Music Since 1910* [New York: Holt, Rinehart and Winston, 1970], 55–56). Thomson claims credit for a host of Copland's musical doings in the 1930s and 1940s that also might be credited to his engagement with Latin American music and the music of Chávez and Revueltas. In any event, the influence of Mexico and Mexican composers was certainly decisive on Copland's developing an accessible melodic style.

21. John Dewey, *Art as Experience* (1934; repr., New York: Perigee, 1980), 3.

22. Stuart Chase, *Mexico: A Study of Two Americas* (New York: Macmillan, 1931). Diego Rivera provided the illustrations and had also illustrated a previous volume on Mexico, Carleton Beals's *Mexican Maze* (N.p.: Book League of America, 1931). For discussions of Chase's book and its significance, see Warren Susman, *Culture as History: The Transformation of American Society in the Twentieth Century* (New York: Pantheon Books, 1984), 155–56; also Richard H. Pells, *Radical Visions and American Dreams: Culture and Social Thought in the Depression Years* (1973; repr., Middletown, Conn.: Wesleyan University Press, 1984), 101–02; and Helen Delpar, *The Enormous Vogue of Things Mexican: Cultural Relations Between the United States and Mexico, 1920–1935* (Tuscaloosa: University of Alabama Press, 1992), 68–70.

23. Chase's study of Tepoztlán was not the first; Robert Redfield had studied the same village for his 1930 book, *Tepoztlán, A Mexican Village: A Study of Folk Life* (Chicago: University of Chicago Press, 1930).

24. Robert and Helen Lynd, *Middletown: A Study in Contemporary American Culture* (New York: Harcourt, Brace, 1929); see also Pells, *Radical Visions*, 25–27. The model for Middletown was Muncie, Indiana.

25. Chase, *Mexico*, 17.

26. Luis Sandi, "Music in Mexico, 1934," *Modern Music* 12, no. 1 (1934): 39.

27. Waldo Frank, *The Re-Discovery of America* (New York: Duell, Sloan and Pearce, 1929), 268, 269.

28. On such stereotypes during the era of "Good Neighbor" diplomacy (1933–45), see Fredrick B. Pike, "Latin America and the Inversion of United States Stereotypes in the 1920s and 1930s: The Case of Culture and Nature," *The Americas* 42 (1985–86): 131–62.

29. Chapters 7 through 11 of Chase's *Mexico* are titled "Machineless Men."

30. Ibid.: "Tepoztlán is far more American," 15; "the art of living," 327; "there are certain features," 326.

31. Waldo Frank, *America Hispana: A Portrait and a Prospect* (New York: Charles Scribner's Sons, 1931), 231.

32. Ibid., 231–32.

33. John Dewey traveled to Mexico City in the summer of 1926 and again in 1937 to meet Leon Trotsky after the Moscow trials. Terry A. Cooney, *Balancing Acts: American Thought and Culture in the 1930s* (New York: Twayne Publishers, 1995), 146–47.

34. Pollack, *Copland*, 223.

35. Copland to his parents, September 10, 1932; and September 29, 1932, CCLC.

36. Copland to Virgil Thomson, December 5, 1932, as quoted in C & P I, 214.

37. Copland to his parents, September 10, 1932, CCLC.

38. Copland to Mary Lescaze, January 13, 1933, CCLC; see also Pollack, *Copland*, 225.

39. Jesús Flores y Escalante, *Salón México: Historia Documental y Gráfica del Danzón en México* (Mexico City: Asociación Mexicana de Estudios Fonográficos, 1993), 106. Translation by Jesús A. Ramos Kittrell.

40. Flores y Escalante, *Salón México*, 110. According to Flores y Escalante, the murals were actually by José Gómez Rosas (324).

41. Copland, "The Story Behind *El Salón México*," *Victor Record Review* 1, no. 12 (1939): 4–5; also quoted in C & P I, 245.

42. Copland, "The Story Behind *El Salón México*," 4.

43. Kenneth Burke, "Revolutionary Symbolism in America," in *American Writer's Congress*, ed. Henry Hart (New York: International Publishers, 1935), 87–93. Denning describes Burke as "the foremost rhetorical theorist of the Popular Front" (*The Cultural Front*, 124) and explores the radical potential of "the people" as a symbolic construction (123–24). Out of the first American Writers' Congress grew the League of Writers, a new organization with which Copland was connected. He gave a speech at its invitation on December 9, 1935, then joined (with Burke) the League-sponsored Committee of Professional Groups for Browder and Ford (the Communist Party presidential ticket) in 1936. Copland's typescript remarks from a 1940 radio broadcast offer a suggestive echo of Burke's 1935 address. Both Copland and Burke use the striking metaphor of a lawyer's brief: the propagandizing artist "speaks in behalf of his cause," Burke wrote, "not in the ways of a lawyer's brief, but by the sort of things he associates with it" (91). Copland, defending his simplified musical style, explained that "music's advance can't be plotted out like a lawyer's brief. In any event, we have come to the end of a musical time in which the composer and his public did not talk the same language" (Copland, typescript radio address for WABC, May 26, 1940, CCLC).

44. Burke, "Revolutionary Symbolism," 89.

45. Ibid., 90.

46. Ibid., 91.

47. See Denning, *The Cultural Front*, 124. Denning distinguishes between multiple, competing forms of "populism" in the thirties and forties (124–29), arguing that the populist rhetoric of the Front does not represent a softening of the radical position.

48. Burke, "Revolutionary Symbolism," 90.

49. Frances Toor, ed. *Cancionero Mexicano* (Mexico City: Mexican Folkways, 1931), and Rubén M. Campos, *El Folklore y la Musica Mexicana* (Mexico City: Publicaciones de la Secretaria de Educacion Publica, 1928). See Pollack, *Copland*, 298–303.

50. Copland, "The Story Behind *El Salón México*," 5.

51. The antibourgeois stance of the avant-garde and the use of folk sources in radical politics is discussed in Raymond Williams, "The Politics of the Avant-Garde,"

in *The Politics of Modernism: Against the New Conformists* (London: Verso, 1997), 52–61.

52. Denning, *The Cultural Front*, 125.

53. Kenneth Burke, *Permanence and Change: An Anatomy of Purpose* (1935; 2nd rev. ed., Indianapolis: Bobbs-Merrill, 1965), 111–24; also Denning, *The Cultural Front*, 122–23.

54. Burke, *Permanence and Change*, 112.

55. Ibid. "Class-consciousness is a social therapeutic because it is *reclassification-consciousness*. It is a new perspective that realigns something so profoundly ethical as our categories of allegiance. By this reinterpretative schema, members of the same race or nation who had formerly thought of themselves as *allies* become *enemies*, and members of different races or nations who had formerly thought of themselves as *enemies* become *allies*" (113).

56. Ibid., 112.

57. Williams, "The Politics of the Avant-Garde," 58.

58. Frances Toor groups the song under the heading "canciones revolucionarias" (Toor, *Cancionero Mexicano*). See also Pollack, *Copland*, 625–26, n. 25.

59. "El Mosco" is found in Campos, *El Folklore y la Musica Mexicana*.

60. Gayle Murchison draws on Gerard Béhague's work to classify this rhythm as *sesquialtera*. See Murchison, "Nationalism in William Grant Still and Aaron Copland Between the Wars: Style and Ideology" (Ph.D. diss., Yale University, 1998), 389.

61. Frank, *America Hispana*, 238.

62. Warren Storey Smith, "Copland's Newest Symphony," review of *El Salón México*, the Boston Symphony Orchestra (Koussevitzky), *Boston Post*, October 15, 1938, 8.

63. The term is borrowed from Denning, *The Cultural Front*, 130. On ethnicity and Americanism, see ibid., 128–32.

64. Henry A. Wallace, "Pan America," *New York Times*, July 9, 1939, magazine section; repr. *Democracy Reborn*, ed. Russell Lord (New York: Reynal & Hitchcock, 1944), 159

65. As quoted in Wallace, *Democracy Reborn*, 173.

66. J. Manuel Espinosa, *Inter-American Beginnings of U. S. Cultural Diplomacy, 1936–48* (Washington, D.C.: Department of State Publications, 1976), 89–107; Irwin F. Gellman, *Roosevelt and Batista: Good Neighbor Diplomacy in Cuba, 1933–1945* (Albuquerque: University of New Mexico Press, 1973).

67. See Gellman, *Good Neighbor Diplomacy*, 145–55.

68. Letter from Edward G. Trueblood to Copland, April 17, 1941, CCLC.

69. Minutes of the meeting of the State Department Division of Cultural Relations Committee on Music, November 20, 1940, CCLC. Also Espinosa, *Inter-American Beginnings of U.S. Cultural Diplomacy*, 175–76.

70. Henry Allen Moe to Copland, June 6, 1941, CCLC.

71. See Pollack, *Copland*, 228–33; also C & P I, 323–29.

72. Excerpts from Copland's diaries are published in C & P I, 324–29; Copland, "The Composers of South America," *Modern Music* 19 (1942): 75–82.

73. Copland, "Report of South American Trip, August 19–December 13, 1941," 9, typescript, CCLC. See also Copland, "The Composers of South America," *Modern Music* 19 (1942); repr. in *Copland on Music*, 210.

74. Copland, "Report of South American Trip," 33.

75. Ibid., 35.

76. Ibid., "extremely cordial," 34; "brutally frank," 35.

77. Ibid., 35.

78. Ibid., 35–36.

79. Beals, *The Crime of Cuba*, 4th printing (Philadelphia: J. B. Lippincott, 1934), 7.

80. Beals, "Aftermath," in *The Crime of Cuba*, 468.

81. Beals's earlier works on Mexico include *Brimstone and Chili: A Book of Personal Experiences in the Southwest and in Mexico* (New York: Knopf, 1927); *Mexico: An Interpretation* (New York: B. W. Huebsch, 1923); and *Mexican Maze*. See also Delpar, *The Enormous Vogue of Things Mexican*, 30–32.

82. Gellman, *Roosevelt and Batista*, 180–81.

83. Ibid., 186.

84. Copland to Leonard Bernstein, [April–May 1941], Leonard Bernstein Collection, Music Division, Library of Congress.

85. Copland, "Report of South American Trip," 41.

86. Pollack, *Copland*, 375–76.

87. Note to conductors, found in ARCO 50–A, CCLC; see also the preface to the published piano score, Boosey & Hawkes, 1949.

88. Emilio Grenet, *Popular Cuban Music*, trans. R[uby Hart] Phillips (Havana: Carasa, 1939), xviii.

89. Copland, as quoted by Phillip Ramey, liner notes, *The Copland Collection: Orchestral and Ballet Works, 1936–1948* (Sony Classical, compact disc SM3K 46559, 1990), 9.

90. Ibid.

91. Burke, *Permanence and Change*, 115.

92. Ibid., 119–20.

93. Ibid., 115

94. Ibid.

95. Copland, Latin American diary (September–October 1963), entries of September 13, September 24, and October 2, CCLC.

96. See Pollack, *Copland*, 206–7.

97. As quoted in ibid., 232–33.

98. Copland to Leonard Bernstein, August 11, 1944, CCLC.

99. Copland to Bernstein, August 25, 1944, CCLC.

3. Creating Community

1. Casey Nelson Blake, *Beloved Community: The Cultural Criticism of Randolph Bourne, Van Wyck Brooks, Waldo Frank, and Lewis Mumford* (Chapel Hill: University of North Carolina Press, 1990), 2.

2. Ibid., 295.

3. Ibid., 289–90.

4. Randolph Bourne, "Trans-national America" (1916), as quoted in Blake, *Beloved Community*, 2.

5. On the Young Pioneers and the Communist children's movement, see Paul C. Mishler, *Raising Reds: The Young Pioneers, Radical Summer Camps, and Communist Political Culture in the United States* (New York: Columbia University Press, 1999).

6. See Gayle Murchison, "Nationalism in William Grant Still and Aaron Copland Between the Wars: Style and Ideology" (Ph.D. diss., Yale University, 1998), 343–44.

7. Stephen Hinton explores the aesthetic and political stance behind *Gebrauchsmusik* as opposed to "musical autonomy" in the entry "Gebrauchsmusik" in *New Grove Online*, ed. Laura Macy, http://www.grovemusic.com.

8. Pollack, *Copland*, 67–68.

9. On *Gebrauchsmusik* and *neue Sachlichkeit*, see Stephen Hinton, *The Idea of Gebrauchsmusik: A Study of Musical Aesthetics in the Weimar Republic (1919 to 1933) with Particular Reference to the Works of Paul Hindemith* (New York: Garland, 1989).

10. Paul Rosenfeld, "Copland's Play Opera," *One Act Play Magazine* 2 (December 1938): 603.

11. See Harvey Klehr, *The Heyday of American Communism: The Depression Decade* (New York: Basic Books, 1984), 204, 320; also Earl Robinson, *Ballad of an American: The Autobiography of Earl Robinson*, with Eric A. Gordon (Lanham, Md.: Scarecrow Press, 1998), 39–41.

12. Pollack, *Copland*, 303–4.

13. Aaron Copland, "Baden-Baden," *Modern Music* 5, no. 1 (1927); repr. *Copland on Music* (New York: W. W. Norton, 1963), 185.

14. Marc Blitzstein, "Popular Music—An Invasion: 1923–1933," *Modern Music* 10 (1933): 101.

15. Marc Blitzstein, "Weill Score for *Johnny Johnson*," *Modern Music* 14 (1936): 44. Blitzstein revised his opinion of Weill after hearing him talk to the Group Theatre during the summer of 1936. He greatly admired *Johnny Johnson*, and though he had once thought *Die Driegroschenoper* a "mistaken success," his adaptation of *The Threepenny Opera* was a commercial and critical triumph. See Eric A. Gordon, *Mark the Music: The Life and Work of Marc Blitzstein* (New York: St. Martin's Press, 1989), 124–25, and 135; also Kim H. Kowalke, "*The Threepenny Opera* in America," in *Kurt Weill: "The Threepenny Opera*," ed. Stephen Hinton (Cambridge: Cambridge University Press, 1990), 78–119.

16. Blitzstein, "Popular Music," 101.

17. From the transcript of the composers' conference at Yaddo in 1932, CCLC. Also quoted in Pollack, *Copland*, 307.

18. Copland, *Our New Music: Leading Composers in Europe and America* (1941; rev. and enlarged ed. *The New Music, 1900–1960*, New York: W. W. Norton, 1968), 82.

19. Copland's letters reached Cowell at the San Quentin State Penitentiary, where he was incarcerated on a morals charge.

20. Henry Cowell to Copland, October 23, 1936, CCLC.

21. Copland, autograph notes on *The Second Hurricane*, CCLC.

22. Ibid.

23. See C & P I, 251–57; also Eric A. Gordon, *Mark the Music*, 138–39.

24. On the settlement movement in general, see Allen F. Davis, *Spearheads for Reform: The Social Settlements and the Progressive Movement, 1890–1914* (New York: Oxford University Press, 1970). The history of the Henry Street Settlement in particular is documented in three books by two of its directors, Lillian D. Wald, *The House on Henry Street* (New York: Henry Holt, 1915) and *Windows on Henry Street* (Boston: Little, Brown, 1934); Helen Hall, *Unfinished Business in Neighborhood and Nation* (New York: Macmillan, 1971).

25. John Reed, "East Side Exiles Stirred by Russian Envoy's 'Welcome Home': Orthodox and Jews Alike Jubilant Over Bakhmetieff's Message to Crowds that Swarmed Around Henry Street Settlement," *The Evening Mail*, July 11, 1917, as quoted in Marjorie N. Feld, "'An Actual Working Out of Internationalism': Russian Politics, Zioinism, and Lillian Wald's Ethnic Progressivism," *Journal of the Gilded Age and Progressivism* 2 (2003): 24.

26. See Shannon Louise Green, "'Art for Life's Sake': Music Schools and Activities in U.S. Social Settlement Houses, 1892–1942" (Ph.D. diss., University of Wisconsin-Madison, 1998), 21–52.

27. On the *Lehrstück*, see Stephen Hinton, "Lehrstück: An Aesthetics of Performance," *Hindemith-Jahrbuch* 22 (1993): 68–96.

28. Copland also served as a member of the board. See Robert Francis Egan, "The History of the Music School of the Henry Street Settlement" (Ph.D. diss., New York University, 1967), 294, 308.

29. On Brecht, the genre of *Lehrstück*, and *Der Jasager*, see in particular W. Anthony Sheppard, *Revealing Masks: Exotic Influences and Ritualized Performance in Modernist Music Theater* (Berkeley: University of California Press, 2001), 83–95.

30. Edwin Denby, "A Good Libretto," *Modern Music* 13 (1936): "a good poet," 21; "It is in the Informative," 20.

31. Edwin Denby, as quoted in C & P I, 259.

32. *New York Times*, January 25, 1937, and January 26, 1937.

33. *New York Times*, April 1, 1937; *New York Herald Tribune*, April 1, 1937.

34. Michael Denning, *The Cultural Front: The Laboring of American Culture in the Twentieth Century* (London: Verso, 1997), 118–20.

35. See James Curtis, *Mind's Eye, Mind's Truth: FSA Photography Reconsidered* (Philadelphia: Temple University Press, 1989), 45–69.

36. See Laura Browder, *Rousing the Nation: Radical Culture in Depression America* (Amherst: University of Massachusetts Press, 1998), 119–21.

37. Ibid., 131.

38. Wald, *Windows on Henry Street*, 338.

39. Typescript scenario, CCLC.

40. See Mishler, *Raising Reds*, 111.

41. Script, *The Second Hurricane*, CCLC.

42. Lionel Trilling, "Greatness with One Fault in It," *Kenyon Review* 4 (1942): 99. See also Paula Rabinowitz, *They Must Be Represented: The Politics of Documentary* (London: Verso, 1994), 43–46. As Rabinowitz observes, Trillings's comment seems

akin to Georg Lukács's analysis of bourgeois consciousness. See Lukács, *History and Class Consciousness: Studies in Marxist Dialectics*, trans. Rodney Livingstone (London: Merlin Press, 1971).

43. Edwin Denby to Copland, undated, CCLC.

44. Denby to Copland, undated, CCLC.

45. *Series of Old American Songs*, ed. S. Foster Damon (Providence: Brown University Library, 1936). Copland later used additional songs from this collection in *Lincoln Portrait* and the two sets of *Old American Songs* (1950, 1952).

46. On the left-wing interest in American folk song, see Barbara A. Zuck, *A History of Musical Americanism* (Ann Arbor: UMI Research Press, 1980); Robbie Lieberman, *"My Song is My Weapon": People's Songs, American Communism, and the Politics of Culture, 1930–50* (Urbana: University of Illinois Press, 1989); Robert Cantwell, *When We Were Good: The Folk Revival* (Cambridge, Mass.: Harvard University Press, 1996); Richard A. Reuss, with JoAnne C. Reuss, *American Folk Music and Left-Wing Politics, 1927–1957* (Lanham, Md.: Scarecrow Press, 2000).

47. "The League Looks Ahead," *Unison* 1, no. 1 (1936): 1. On the American Music League, see Zuck, *Musical Americanism*, 137–38.

48. David King Dunaway, "Unsung Songs of Protest: The Composers Collective of New York," *New York Folklore* 5, nos. 1–2 (1979): 13; Ann M. Pescatello, *Charles Seeger: A Life in American Music* (Pittsburgh: University of Pittsburgh Press, 1992), 136–72.

49. See Pescatello, *Charles Seeger*, 154–59; John A. Lomax, "1939 Annual Report: Excerpt from the Archive of American Folk-Song Annual Report, 1928–39," The John and Ruby Lomax Southern States Recording Trip, Library of Congress, http://memory.loc.gov/ammem/, digital ID afcss 39 ar0001.

50. Cantwell, *When We Were Good*, 100.

51. As Pollack notes, Denby altered the original text ("sweet praise to high Heaven"). See Pollack, *Copland*, 308.

52. Rosenfeld, "Copland's Play Opera," 604.

53. William Stott, *Documentary Expression and Thirties America* (Chicago: University of Chicago Press, 1973), 8.

54. Rahv, "The Cult of Experience in American Writing," as quoted in Stott, *Documentary Expression*, 39.

55. Copland to Carlos Chávez, May 18, 1937, CCLC.

56. Ibid.

57. "Production Notes" to *The Second Hurricane*.

58. Virgil Thomson, "In the Theatre," *Modern Music* 15 (1938): 113.

59. Copland, typescript remarks, June 11, 1942, CCLC. These were presumably offered in connection with a performance of *The Second Hurricane* broadcast on WOR the same day.

60. Ibid.

61. *The Second Hurricane*, narrator's script for performance at the Museum of Modern Art, January 26, 1961, CCLC.

62. Harold Clurman to Copland, June 2, 1936, CCLC.

63. Copland to Carlos Chávez, June 2, 1937, CCLC.

64. William Alexander, *Film on the Left: American Documentary Film from 1931 to 1942* (Princeton, N.J.: Princeton University Press, 1981), 249.

65. On the compositional history of Copland's score, see Claudia Widgery, "The Kinetic and Temporal Interaction of Music and Film: Three Documentaries of 1930's America" (Ph.D. diss., University of Maryland, College Park, 1990), 256–93; also Alfred Williams Cochran, "Style, Structure, and Tonal Organization in the Early Film Scores of Aaron Copland" (Ph.D. diss., Catholic University, 1986), 9–115.

66. Colin McPhee composed scores for *Mechanical Principles* and *H₂O*; Blitzstein wrote the music for *Surf and Seaweed*. On the Copland-Sessions concerts, see Carol J. Oja, "The Copland-Sessions Concerts and Their Reception in the Contemporary Press," *The Musical Quarterly* 65 (1979): 212–29. Copland's music for documentary film is discussed by Neil Lerner in "The Classical Documentary Score in American Films of Persuasion: Context and Case Studies, 1935–1945" (Ph.D. diss., Duke University, 1997); also "Aaron Copland, Normal Rockwell, and the 'Four Freedoms': The Office of War Information's Vision and Sound in *The Cummington Story* (1945)," in *Copland and His World*, ed. Carol J. Oja and Judith Tick (Princeton, N.J.: Princeton University Press, 2005).

67. Ralph Steiner as quoted in Russell Campbell, *Cinema Strikes Back: Radical Filmmaking in The United States, 1930–1942* (Ann Arbor: UMI Research Press, 1978), 118. On the Nykino, see in particular Alexander, *Film on the Left*, 65–145.

68. Alexander, *Film on the Left*, 145.

69. Ibid., 148.

70. Ibid., 178–85.

71. Ibid., 249–52.

72. On Mumford, *The City*, and the genesis of the film, see Howard Gillette Jr., "Film as Artifact: *The City* (1939)," *American Studies* 18, no. 2 (1977): 71–85.

73. On the Regional Planning Association of America, see Robert Wojtowicz, *Lewis Mumford and American Modernism: Eutopian Theories for Architecture and Urban Planning* (Cambridge: Cambridge University Press, 1996), 113–60; and Mark Luccarelli, *Lewis Mumford and the Ecological Region: The Politics of Planning* (New York: Guilford Press, 1995), 75–164.

74. Lewis Mumford, *The Culture of Cities* (New York: Harcourt, Brace, 1938), 491.

75. Ibid., 347.

76. Ibid., 354.

77. Luccarelli, *Lewis Mumford and the Ecological Region*, 41–42.

78. Mumford, The Culture of Cities, 348.

79. On the dialectical argument in *Technics and Civilization*, for example, see Wojtowicz, *Lewis Mumford and American Modernism*, 99–100. On Mumford's history of technology as opposed to Marx's dialectical materialism, see Rosalind Williams, "Lewis Mumford as a Historian of Technology in *Technics and Civilization*," in *Lewis Mumford: Public Intellectual*, ed. Thomas P. Hughes and Agatha C. Hughes (New York: Oxford University Press, 1990), 43–65.

80. Mumford, *The Culture of Cities*, 401.

81. Ibid., 6.

82. Typescript scenario of *The City* from Civic Films, 2, CCLC.

83. Lewis Mumford, *Sticks and Stones* (1925; 2nd rev. ed., New York: W. W. Norton, 1955), 14.

84. Pollack, *Copland*, 338.

85. Mumford, *Sticks and Stones*, 18.

86. Mumford, *The Culture of Cities*, 143.

87. Ibid., 228.

88. Typescript scenario, 2, CCLC.

89. On the greenbelt towns, see Joseph L. Arnold, *The New Deal in the Suburbs: A History of the Greenbelt Town Program, 1935–1954* (Columbus: Ohio State University Press, 1971).

90. Typescript scenario, 3, CCLC.

91. Mumford, *The Story of Utopias* (New York: Boni and Liveright, 1922), 268, 269.

92. Bill Nichols, *Representing Reality: Issues and Concepts in Documentary* (Bloomington: Indiana University Press, 1991), 32–38.

93. As quoted in Alexander, *Film on the Left*, 248.

94. A point made by Charles Keil, "American Documentary Finds Its Voice: Persuasion and Expression in *The Plow That Broke the Plains* and *The City*," in *Documenting the Documentary: Close Readings of Documentary Films and Video*, ed. Barry Keith Grant and Jeannette Sloniowski (Detroit, Mich.: Wayne State University Press, 1998), 127.

95. See Paul Arthur, "Jargons of Authenticity (Three American Moments)," in *Theorizing Documentary*, ed. Michael Renor (New York: Routledge, 1993), 112; and Keil, "American Documentary Finds Its Voice," 127.

96. On the agrarian myth see especially Richard Hofstadter, *The Age of Reform: From Bryan to F.D.R.* (New York: Vintage Books, 1955), 23–59.

97. Henwar Rodakiewicz, "Treatment of Sound in *The City*," in *The Movies as Medium*, ed. Lewis Jacobs (New York: Farrar, Straus & Giroux, 1970), 280.

98. Mumford, *The Story of Utopias*, 181.

99. Rodakiewicz, "Treatment of Sound in *The City*," 280.

100. On this segment, see Widgery, "The Kinetic and Temporal Interaction of Music and Film," 311–14.

101. On Copland and the pastoral trope, particularly in film, see Neil Lerner, "Copland's Music of Wide Open Spaces: Surveying the Pastoral Trope in Hollywood," *The Musical Quarterly* 85 (2001): 477–515.

102. Rodakiewicz, "Treatment of Sound in *The City*," 281–84.

103. Ibid., 284.

104. See Widgery, "The Kinetic and Temporal Interaction of Music and Film," 310.

105. Rodakiewicz, "Treatment of Sound in *The City*," 285.

106. Ibid.

107. Keil, "American Documentary Finds Its Voice," 128–29.

108. Widgery notes that the outlines for sound allocation in part 3 initially included only narration and that Copland may have added music at a late date in the

film's production. The distribution of sound Copland sketched in the margins of the final outline suggests that he intended fewer repetitions of the flowing melody ("The Kinetic and Temporal Interaction of Music and Film," 285–87).

109. Richard Griffith, "Films at the Fair," *Films* 1 (1939): 63–64.

110. Rodakiewicz, "Treatment of Sound in *The City*," 282; see also Alexander, *Film on the Left*, 250.

111. Alexander, *Film on the Left*, 251.

112. Rodakiewicz, "Treatment of Sound in *The City*," 282.

113. Alexander, *Film on the Left*, 251–52.

114. On this point, see in particular Arthur, "Jargons of Authenticity (Three American Moments)," 108–34.

115. Mumford, "New Homes for a New Deal III: The Shortage of Dwellings and Direction," *New Republic*, February 28, 1934, 69–72; Wojtowicz, *Lewis Mumford and American Modernism*, 132–33.

116. Mumford, *The Culture of Cities*, 391–92.

117. Ibid., 354–55.

118. Ibid., 355.

119. Blake, *Beloved Community*, esp. 281–83.

120. Neil Lerner is nonetheless right to observe that "the 'paradise' envisioned in *The City* still has the imperfections of racial segregation and the secondary status of women" ("Wide Open Spaces," 511, n. 47). This is also clearly a Christian community.

4. "The Dancing of an Attitude"

1. Kenneth Burke, *The Philosophy of Literary Form: Studies in Symbolic Action* ([Baton Rouge:] Louisiana State University Press, 1941), 1.

2. Ibid., 9.

3. Neil Lerner, "Copland's Music of Wide Open Spaces: Surveying the Pastoral Trope in Hollywood," *The Musical Quarterly* 85 (2001): 503. *Appalachian Spring*, discussed in the following chapter, is associated with pioneering and the frontier—both linked in turn to the West. See Robert G. Athearn, *The Mythic West in Twentieth Century America* (Lawrence: University Press of Kansas, 1986), 12.

4. Lerner, "Copland's Music of Wide Open Spaces," 501.

5. On the nostalgic force of *Billy the Kid* and hegemonic implications of *Rodeo*, see Beth E. Levy, "Frontier Figures: American Music and the Mythology of the American West, 1895–1945" (Ph.D. diss., University of California, Berkeley, 2002), 285–339.

6. Kenneth Burke, *Counter-Statement* (New York: Harcourt, Brace, 1931), 206.

7. Claude Lévi-Strauss, "The Structural Study of Myth," *Structural Anthropology*, trans. Claire Jacobson and Brooke Grundfest Schoepf (New York: Basic Books, 1963), 206–31.

8. David Hamilton Murdoch, *The American West: The Invention of a Myth* (Reno: University of Nevada Press, 2001), 20.

9. Ibid., 21.

10. Ibid., 21.

11. United States Census Office, Eleventh Census, 1890, *Extra Census Bulletin*, no. 2: *Distribution of Population According to Density, 1890* (Washington, D.C.: U.S. Government Printing Office, 1891); as quoted in Frederick Jackson Turner, *The Frontier in American History* (New York: Henry Holt, 1920), 1.

12. Turner, "The Significance of the Frontier in American History," first delivered at the meeting of the American Historical Association in Chicago, July 12, 1893, and published in the *Proceedings of the State Historical Society of Wisconsin* (December 14, 1893; repr. in *The Frontier in American History*, 1–38). Citations refer to the reprinted edition.

13. Turner, *The Frontier in American History*, 2–3

14. Ibid., 30.

15. Ibid. Turner described Jefferson as "the first prophet of American democracy" and connected his "gospel" to "the Western influence." In his 1903 article "Contributions of the West to American Democracy," Turner argues that "Jefferson's 'Notes on Virginia' reveals clearly his conception that democracy should have an agricultural basis, and that manufacturing development and city life were dangerous to the purity of the body politic. Simplicity and economy in government, the right of revolution, the freedom of the individual, the belief that those who win the vacant lands are entitled to shape their own government in their own way, —these are all parts of the platform of political principles to which he gave his adhesion, and they are all elements eminently characteristic of the Western democracy into which he was born" (Turner, "Contributions of the West to American Democracy," 1903; in *The Frontier in American History*, 250).

On the persistent linkage between open land and democratic values in the nineteenth century, see in particular Henry Nash Smith, *Virgin Land: The American West as Symbol and Myth* (Cambridge, Mass.: Harvard University Press, 1950). Smith argues that the "image of an agricultural paradise in the West, embodying group memories of an earlier, simpler and, it was believed, a happier state of society, long survived as a force in American thought and politics" (124). See also, David M. Wrobel, *The End of American Exceptionalism: Frontier Anxiety from the Old West to the New Deal* (Lawrence: University Press of Kansas, 1993), 5; Murdoch, *The American West*, 17–18.

16. Turner, *The Frontier in American History*, 32.

17. Ibid.

18. "Bearing in mind the far-reaching influence of the disappearance of unlimited resources open to all men for the taking, and considering the recoil of the common man when he saw the outcome of the competitive struggle for these resources as the supply came to its end over most of the nation, we can understand the reaction against individualism and in favor of drastic assertion of the powers of government. Legislation is taking the place of the free lands as the means of preserving the ideal of democracy. But at the same time it is endangering the other pioneer ideal of creative and competitive individualism. . . . It would be a grave misfortune if these people so rich in experience, in self-confidence and aspiration, in creative genius, should turn to some Old World discipline of socialism or plutocracy, or despotic rule, whether by

class or by dictator" (Turner, "The West and American Ideals," 1914; in *The Frontier in American History*, 307).

19. Wrobel, *The End of American Exceptionalism*, 122–42; also, Steven Kesselman, "The Frontier Thesis and the Great Depression," *Journal of the History of Ideas* 29 (1968): 253–68.

20. *The Public Papers and Addresses of Franklin D. Roosevelt*, vol. 1, *The Genesis of the New Deal, 1928–1932* (New York: Random House, 1938), 746.

21. Ibid., 746–47.

22. Ibid., 750.

23. Stuart Chase, *A New Deal* (New York: Macmillan: 1936), 66.

24. Henry A. Wallace, *New Frontiers* (New York: Reynal & Hitchcock, 1934), 11.

25. Ibid., 271.

26. Ibid., 274.

27. Ibid., 277.

28. Walter Prescott Webb, *Divided We Stand: The Crisis of a Frontierless Democracy* (New York: Farrar & Rinehart, 1937), as quoted in Steven Kesselman, "The Frontier Thesis and the Great Depression," *Journal of the History of Ideas* 29 (1968): 258.

29. *League of Professional Groups for Foster and Ford, Culture and the Crisis: An Open Letter to the Writers, Artists, Teachers, Physicians, Engineers, Scientists and Other Professional Workers of America* (New York: Workers Library Publishers, 1932), 7; see also Kesselman, "The Frontier Thesis and the Great Depression," 259.

30. While in Mexico as an agent of the Comintern in 1922, Fraina disappeared, only to resurface nearly ten years later under a new name. He was a principal author of the radical tract *Culture and the Crisis* and active in the League of Professional Groups for Foster and Ford. But Corey objected to the Bolshevik control of the CPUSA; he eventually quit the Party and resigned from the League. See Michael Denning, *The Cultural Front: The Laboring of American Culture in the Twentieth Century* (London: Verso, 1997), 99 and 102.

31. Lewis Corey, *The Decline of American Capitalism* (New York: Covici Friede, 1934), 49; see also Kesselman, "The Frontier Thesis and the Great Depression," 259–60.

32. Corey, *The Decline of American Capitalism*, 51.

33. Ibid., 51–52 and 515–40.

34. Ibid., 521.

35. Ibid., 518.

36. On Burke, see in particular Jack Selzer, *Kenneth Burke in Greenwich Village: Conversing with the Moderns, 1915–1931* (Madison: University of Wisconsin Press, 1996); also Daniel Aaron, *Writers on the Left: Episodes in American Literary Communism* (New York: Harcourt, Brace & World, 1961), 287–92.

37. Burke, *Counter-Statement*, 136–37.

38. Ibid., 137–38.

39. Ibid., 138.

40. Ibid., 137.

41. Ibid., 139.

42. Ibid., 141–42.

43. Ibid., 145.

44. Ibid.: "could never triumph," 143; "perfecting the means," 146–47.

45. Ibid., 150.

46. Ibid.: "politically and economically," 149; "to formulate," 150.

47. Ibid., 146–47.

48. On the Ballet Caravan, see Lincoln Kirstein, *Mosaic: Memoirs* (New York: Farrar, Straus & Giroux, 1994).

49. As quoted in Pollack, *Copland*, 316. In C & P I (280), Loring recalls that Kirstein gave him a book titled *The Life and Times of William Bonney*, but no such work exists.

50. The following lists original publication information; many of these volumes were reprinted, even multiple times. Agnes C. Laut, *Pilgrims of the Santa Fe* (New York: Frederick A. Stokes, 1931); John Lomax, *Cowboy Songs and Other Frontier Ballads* (New York: Sturgis & Walton, 1910); J. B. Priestley, *The Doomsday Men: An Adventure* (London: Heinemann, 1938); Owen Wister, *The Virginian: A Horseman of the Plains* (New York: Macmillan, 1902); Theodore Roosevelt, *Ranch Life and the Hunting Trail* (New York: Century, 1888).

51. Loring's notebooks are now found in the Dance Division of the New York Public Library.

52. On Roosevelt and Wister, see especially G. Edward White, *The Eastern Establishment and the Western Experience: The West of Frederic Remington, Theodore Roosevelt, and Owen Wister* (Austin: University of Texas Press, 1989); also Murdoch, *The American West*, 63–80.

53. White, *The Eastern Establishment and the Western Experience*, 31–51.

54. Stephen Tatum, *Inventing Billy the Kid: Visions of the Outlaw in America, 1881–1981* (Albuquerque: University of New Mexico Press, 1982), 40–66.

55. Ibid., 63.

56. Ibid., 63–66.

57. Ibid., 89–90.

58. Ibid., 103.

59. Walter Noble Burns, *The Saga of Billy the Kid* (New York: Grosset & Dunlap, 1926), 55.

60. Ibid., 56.

61. Tatum, *Inventing Billy the Kid*, 104.

62. Burns, *The Saga of Billy the Kid*: "life closed the past," 54; exemplifies bravado, 105.

63. Narration for Omnibus broadcast of *Billy the Kid*, November 8, 1953, Loring Papers, NYPL.

64. Kirstein, "Blast at Ballet" (1937; repr. in *Three Pamphlets Collected*, New York: Dance Horizons, 1967), 46–47.

65. Jessica Burr discussed the striking timbres of this opening in "Open Fifths, Open Prairie, and the Opening of *Billy the Kid*," Sonneck Society annual meeting, March 7, 1997.

66. The sketches for *Billy the Kid* are available at CCLC online. The sketches dated November and December 1934 and March 1935 are found on image 54; August 1935,

image 56; titled *Radio Serenade*, images 57 and 60; April and May 1937, images 60 and 59.

67. Loring, choreographic notes for *Billy the Kid*, Loring Collection, NYPL. Levy offers a insightful reading of this opening ("Frontier Figures," 297–303).

68. Pollack, *Copland*, 321. Copland apparently reminded the choreographer that "America the Beautiful" ("My Country 'Tis of Thee") is in triple meter.

69. On the Dust Bowl migration, see James N. Gregory, *American Exodus: The Dust Bowl Migration and Okie Culture in California* (New York: Oxford University Press, 1991).

70. James Curtis, *Mind's Eye, Mind's Truth: FSA Photography Reconsidered* (Philadelphia: Temple University Press, 1989), 6.

71. Ibid.

72. Paul S. Taylor, "Again the Covered Wagon," *Survey Graphic* (July 1935), 349.

73. Ibid., 350.

74. On racial populism in *The Grapes of Wrath* see Denning, *The Cultural Front*, 260–69.

75. A point also noted by Levy, "Frontier Figures," 312–13.

76. The term medley is used here as a specific form of musical borrowing; see J. Peter Burkholder, "The Uses of Existing Music: Musical Borrowing as a Field," *Notes* 50 (1998): 851–70. Elsewhere in *Billy the Kid*, Copland quotes "The Dying Cowboy" and "Trouble for the Range Cook." Gayle Murchison notes a similarity between the *jarabe* tune and "Trouble for the Range Cook"; although some of the contours are similar, Copland's tune is so altered that it is difficult to identify securely the *jarabe* as a borrowing. See Gayle Murchison, "Nationalism in William Grant Still and Aaron Copland between the Wars: Style and Ideology" (Ph.D. diss., Yale University, 1998), 411–13.

77. C & P II, 278.

78. *The Lonesome Cowboy: Songs of the Plains and Hills*, comp. John White and George Shackley (New York: George T. Worth, 1930). Copland also consulted a second collection: *Songs of the Open Range*, ed. Ina Sires, and sheet music edited by John Lomax and Oscar J. Fox. The discovery of these sources was first reported in Elizabeth Bergman [Crist], "Perspectives on Aaron Copland's Folk Song Borrowings," Sonneck Society annual meeting, March 23, 1996; and Jessica Burr, "Arranging 'Git Along, Little Doggies': A Case Study Using Aaron Copland's Songbooks," American Musicological Society annual meeting, November 4, 1999. Multiple versions of songs are found in these volumes, all of which are preserved in the Copland Collection, and the settings in *Billy* seem in some instances to conflate the tunes as variously presented. See Pollack, *Copland*, 320.

79. See Gregory, *American Exodus*, 154–69.

80. Roosevelt, *Ranch Life and the Hunting Trail*, as quoted by Loring.

81. *The Lonesome Cowboy: Songs of the Plains and Hills*, 4.

82. Loring, scenario for *Billy the Kid*, typescript, Loring Collection, NYPL.

83. Ibid.

84. Ibid.

85. Ibid.

86. Pollack, *Copland*, 322.

87. Loring, scenario for *Billy the Kid*.

88. On the different between the opening and closing processions, see Paul Hodgins, *Relationships Between Score and Choreography in Twentieth-Century Dance: Music, Movement and Metaphor* (Lewiston, N.Y.: Edwin Mellen Press, 1992), 162.

89. Tatum, *Inventing Billy the Kid*, 106.

90. Program notes for *Billy the Kid*, November 3, 1941, Loring Collection, NYPL.

91. As quoted in C & P I, 356.

92. This story line, as described in an undated typescript in the Agnes de Mille Collection, NYPL, differs slightly from the original scenario held in the Copland Collection but reflects the final choreography of the ballet. My description of the ballet is based on two recorded performances: a televised performance by the Ballet Theater in 1953 for Omnibus and 1976 staging by the American Ballet. There are small differences between the two, but I have confined my observations to points of commonality. My thanks to Anderson Ferrell and Jonathan Prude for granting me access to view and permission to quote the papers of Agnes de Mille.

93. On the genesis of *Rodeo* as a dance, see Barbara Barker, "Agnes de Mille, Liberated Expatriate, and *The American Suite, 1938*," *Dance Chronicle* 19 (1996): 113–50. Wayne Shirley has discovered that the piece for band was to be an introduction to the final march in *From Sorcery to Science*.

94. ARCO 47.1, misleadingly designated in the Copland Collection as "rough sketches" but indeed a pencil short score, CCLC. See also CCLC online, digital ID copland sket0021.

95. Ira Ford, *Traditional Music of America* (New York: E. P. Dutton, 1940) and *Our Singing Country: A Second Volume of American Ballads and Folk Songs*, collected and compiled by John A. Lomax and Alan Lomax, music edited by Ruth Crawford Seeger. See Pollack, *Copland*, 367. Pollack credits Jessica Burr with having discovered "Gilderoy" and "Tip Toe, Pretty Betty Martin"; the latter is not in the suite, only the complete ballet (635, n. 28).

96. Pollack, *Copland*, 367.

97. Levy, "Frontier Figures," 330.

98. Pollack, *Copland*, 367.

99. Agnes de Mille, "An American Ballet," typescript scenario for *Rodeo* (1942), CCLC.

100. Levy (following Marcia Siegel) sees *Rodeo* as "a ballet in which traditional gender roles are forcefully, even violently reinforced" (Levy, "Frontier Figures," 327; see also Marcia Siegel, *The Shapes of Change: Images of American Dance* [Boston: Houghton Mifflin, 1979], 125–31).

101. On Copland's sexuality, see Pollack, "Personal Affairs," in *Copland*, 234–56. For interpretations of Copland's sexuality in his music, see Nadine Hubbs, *The Queer Composition of America's Sound: Gay Modernists, American Music, and National Identity* (Berkeley: University of California Press, 2004); David Metzer, "'Spurned Love': Eroticism and Abstraction in the Early Works of Aaron Copland," *Journal of Musicology* 15 (1997): 417–43; David Schiff, "Who Was That Masked Composer?" *Atlantic*

Monthly, January 2000, 116–21; Daniel E. Mathers, "Expanding Horizons: Sexuality and the Re-zoning of *The Tender Land*," in *Copland Connotations: Studies and Interviews*, ed. Peter Dickinson (Rochester, N.Y.: Boydell Press, 2002), 103–17. Mathers reveals the ways in which the ostensibly heterosexual coming-of-age story in *The Tender Land* can be read from a queer perspective.

102. Carol Easton, *No Intermissions: The Life of Agnes de Mille* (Boston: Little, Brown, 1996), 249. As Levy notes, "In less than half an hour, [the Cowgirl] acts out one of the country's most striking demographic shifts during the forties, when women temporarily swelled the work force" ("Frontier Figures," 329–30).

103. Stacy Wolf, *A Problem Like Maria: Gender and Sexuality in the American Musical* (Ann Arbor: University of Michigan Press, 2002), 49; on the tomboy, see also Barbara Creed, "Lesbian Bodies: Tribades, Tomboys, and Tarts," in *Sexy Bodies: The Strange Carnalities of Feminism*, ed. Elizabeth Grosz and Elspeth Probyn (New York: Routledge, 1995), 86–103.

104. Wolf, *A Problem Like Maria*, 50.

105. Easton, *No Intermissions*, 75.

106. De Mille wrote "at length about dancers and sex," Easton notes, "often in terms of sublimation and control" (ibid., 117). See also Agnes de Mille, "Ballet and Sex," in *Dance to the Piper* (Boston: Little, Brown, 1952), 63–71; *And Promenade Home* (Boston: Little, Brown, 1958), 226; see also Barbara Barker, "Agnes de Mille's Heroines of the Forties," in *Proceedings of the Twelfth Annual Conference of the Society of Dance History Scholars* (Riverside, Cal.: Society of Dance History Scholars, 1989), 143.

107. Easton, *No Intermissions*, 96–99.

108. Ibid., 98.

109. Sally Banes, *Dancing Women: Female Bodies on the Stage* (New York: Routledge, 1998), 192.

110. Wolf, *A Problem Like Maria*, 32.

111. As Wolf explains, such queer interpretations do not necessarily rely on the intent of the composer, librettist, or even performers but may be constructed by the "queer" or "lesbian" spectator engaged in a non-normative reading (23–26). See also Alexander Doty, "There's Something Queer Here," in *Out in Culture: Gay, Lesbian, and Queer Essays on Popular Culture*, ed. Corey K. Creekmur and Alexander Doty (Durham, N.C.: Duke University Press, 1995), 71–90. The emphasis on readings made possible by the work but realized only by the spectator is crucial here, given the ease with which *Rodeo* might be said to reflect de Mille's and Copland's own sexualities. The issue of intent seems to be the bone of contention between David Schiff and Vivian Perlis in an exchange about *Rodeo* in the *Atlantic Monthly*. Ignoring the possibility that the Cowgirl may be related to a "lesbian" identity (which I place in quotations to indicate that the specific sexual choice is not so much at stake as the oppositional stance toward a heteronormative construction of gender), Schiff suggests that "if we view the sexually ambiguous figure of the tomboy as a woman, her capitulation seems politically incorrect, as feminist critics have noted. But think of the cowgirl as a closeted homosexual male, as Copland may have, and the story takes on a very different feeling" (David Schiff, "Who Was That Masked Composer?" 120). Vivian Perlis responds: "Schiff is on the mark when he writes that in *Rodeo* the story

'takes on a very different feeling' when one thinks of 'the cowgirl as a closeted homo-sexual male, as Copland may have.' Very different indeed! This is pure (and pretty far-fetched) speculation. I would bet it never occurred to Copland to think of Agnes De Mille's cowgirl as 'a closeted homosexual male'" (Letter to the Editor, *Atlantic Monthly*, April 2000, 16).

112. Wolf, *A Problem Like Maria*, 23.

113. De Mille, scenario, Agnes de Mille Papers, NYPL.

114. De Mille, "An American Ballet," CCLC. Levy likewise recognizes this inter-lude as a moment in which the Cowgirl "appreciates the self-sufficiency of her rela-tionship with her surroundings and exults in it" (Levy, "Frontier Figures," 336).

115. De Mille, scenario, Agnes de Mille Papers, NYPL.

116. Banes, *Dancing Women*, 193.

117. Ibid.

118. De Mille, "An American Ballet," CCLC.

119. De Mille, scenario, Agnes de Mille Papers, NYPL.

120. Banes, *Dancing Women*, 193.

121. Having noted the apparently unique position of *Rodeo* as a thoroughly folk-like score, Howard Pollack nevertheless hears "Copland's inimitable personality at each turn" (Pollack, *Copland*, 367).

122. "Bonaparte's Retreat" (p. 129) is indexed in Ford's collection as one of seven "tunes with the violin discorded." Judith Tick observes that "Copland plays with the concert sound of a classical orchestra tuning up and, at the same time, the vernacu-lar 'discorded' tuning of rural Anglo-American fiddles, where the instrument's four strings are retuned to sound only one interval of a fifth. In the Lomax collection *Our Singing Country*, Copland learned about discorded tunings from the transcription of the fiddle tune 'Bonyparte.'" See Judith Tick, "The Music of Aaron Copland," in *Aaron Copland's America: A Cultural Perspective* (New York: Watson-Guptill, 2000), 156. The recording and transcription of Stepp's performance use the tuning DADD, as does the tune in Ford's *Traditional Music of America*.

123. Ford, *Traditional Music of America*, 21.

124. On Fiddler Bill and "Bonaparte's Retreat," see Stephen Wade, "The Route of 'Bonaparte's Retreat': From 'Fiddler Bill' Stepp to Aaron Copland," *American Music* 18 (2000): 343–69; Seeger's transcription of the tune as performed by Stepp in 1937 is found in *Our Singing Country*, p. 55.

125. Not "Hop Light Ladies," which Wade erroneously suggests that Pollack iden-tifies (Wade, "The Route of 'Bonaparte's Retreat,'" 363 and 369, n. 70). "Hop Up, My Ladies" appears in *Our Singing Country* (p. 58). The tune is also known as "Hop Light, Ladies" and "Miss McCloud's Reel." But this is not the same melody as "McLeod's Reel" as found in Ford's volume and Copland's score.

126. Pollack, *Copland*, 371.

127. Banes, *Dancing Women*: "happy ending," 193; "inhabits a world," 192–93.

128. In *Shapes of Change*, Siegel argues that "the moral purpose of [de Mille's] ballet is to show the error in being a nonconformist" (128); Levy considers Siegel's interpretation in "Frontier Figures" (328–34), concluding that "the imagery of the American West offered a haven for social and sexual aberrance, but also a site where

patriarchal visions of social and moral order could be vigorously (and even violently) reinforced" (339).

5. In Wartime

1. Harvey Klehr, *The Heyday of American Communism: The Depression Decade* (New York: Basic Books, 1984), 398–409. On the CPUSA during the war years, see Maurice Isserman, *Which Side Were You On? The American Communist Party during the Second World War* (Urbana: University of Illinois Press, 1993). Richard Pells, *The Liberal Mind in a Conservative Age: American Intellectuals in the 1940s and 1950s* (New York: Harper & Row, 1985), 8.

2. On the reactions to the Moscow trials and the pact, see Judy Kutulas, *The Long War: The Intellectual People's Front and Anti-Stalinism, 1930–1940* (Durham, N.C.: Duke University Press, 1995), 106–31 and 164–85.

3. Harold Clurman to Copland, August 28, 1939, CCLC.

4. Hitler launched Operation Barbarossa, an attack on the Soviet Union, on June 22, 1941. Ralph B. Levering identifies the turning point in American sentiment toward Russia as Winston Churchill's speech that same day (broadcast on NBC radio), in which he argued that Germany was the greater threat. See Levering, *American Opinion and the Russian Alliance* (Chapel Hill: University of North Carolina Press, 1976), 39–53.

5. Aaron Copland, "The Musical Scene Changes," *Twice A Year* 5–6 (1940–41), 343.

6. Ibid., 342.

7. Michael Denning, *The Cultural Front: The Laboring of American Culture in the Twentieth Century* (London: Verso, 1997), 24.

8. The CPUSA was officially disbanded in May 1944, immediately reconstituted as the Communist Political Association, and then organized as an official political party in 1945.

9. Denning, *The Cultural Front*, 168.

10. André Kostelanetz to Copland, December 18, 1941, CCLC.

11. On the *Lincoln Portrait* commission, see C & P I, 341–43.

12. On Whitman, see Alan M. Wald, *Exiles from a Future Time: The Forging of the Mid-Twentieth-Century Literary Left* (Chapel Hill: University of North Carolina Press, 2002), 36–37; Bryan K. Garman, "'Heroic Spiritual Grandfather': Whitman, Sexuality, and the American Left, 1890–1940," *American Quarterly* 52 (2000): 90–126. On Lincoln and the Popular Front, see Charles C. Alexander, *Here the Country Lies: Nationalism and the Arts in Twentieth-Century America* (Bloomington: Indiana University Press, 1980), 194.

13. "Address of the International Working Men's Association to Abraham Lincoln, President of the United States of America," presented to U.S. Ambassador Charles Francis Adams, January 28, 1865, in Karl Marx and Frederick Engels, *The Civil War in the United States*, ed. Richard Enmale (New York: International Publishers, 1937), 281.

14. Earl Browder, *What is Communism?* (New York: Vanguard Press, 1936): "to lead to victory," 17; *"We are the Americans,"* 19 (emphasis original); "prophetic lines," 21.

15. "'Free, Prosperous, Happy. . .': The Text of the Communist Election Platform," *New Masses*, July 14, 1936: "to fight for," 17; "The Communist Party," 19. Copland supported the Communist ticket in 1936.

16. Law took command in March 1937 after Robert Merriam was wounded in battle. On American involvement in the Spanish Civil War, see in particular Arthur H. Landis, *The Abraham Lincoln Brigade* (New York: Citadel Press, 1967), and Peter N. Carroll, *The Odyssey of the Abraham Lincoln Brigade: Americans in the Spanish Civil War* (Stanford, Cal.: Stanford University Press, 1994).

17. On the linkage of Roosevelt and Lincoln, see Alfred Hayworth Jones, *Roosevelt's Image Brokers: Poets, Playwrights, and the Use of the Lincoln Symbol* (Port Washington, N.Y.: Kennikat Press, 1974).

18. *The Public Papers and Addresses of Franklin D. Roosevelt*, vol. 3, *The Advance of Recovery and Reform, 1934* (New York: Random House, 1938), 422.

19. As quoted by Roosevelt in *The Public Papers and Addresses of Franklin D. Roosevelt*, vol. 5, *The People Approve, 1936* (New York: Random House, 1938), 222.

20. Merril D. Peterson, *Lincoln in American Memory* (New York: Oxford University Press, 1994), 311–47.

21. *The Public Papers and Addresses of Franklin D. Roosevelt*, 1938 vol., *The Continuing Struggle* (New York: Macmillan, 1941): "having fought," 41; dedicating the Peace Memorial, 419–21.

22. Jones, *Roosevelt's Image Brokers*, 71–72.

23. Barry Schwartz, "Memory as a Cultural System: Abraham Lincoln in World War II," *American Sociological Review* 61 (1996): 914–20.

24. Ibid., 912.

25. Carl Sandburg, "Lincoln–Roosevelt: How Two Presidents Sought Solutions of Similar Problems," *Today* 10 (February, 1934): 5.

26. See Pollack, *Copland*, 358; Alexander, *Here the Country Lies*, 194–95; and especially Peterson, *Lincoln in American Memory*, 311–73. Copland was not the last to draw on Lincoln's words or image. Among later works inspired by Abraham Lincoln are Herbert Elwell, *Lincoln: Requiem aeternam* (1946); Robert Palmer, *Abraham Lincoln Walks at Midnight* (1948); Ulysses Kay, *A Lincoln Letter* (1953); Roy Harris, *Abraham Lincoln Walks at Midnight* (1954) and Symphony No. 10: "Abraham Lincoln" (1965); Ferde Grofé, *Lincoln's Gettysburg Address* (1954); Vincent Persichetti, *A Lincoln Address* (1973); and Stephen Paulus, *The Long Shadow of Lincoln* (1994).

27. R. L. Duffus, "In the White House 1861–65," *New York Times*, February 8, magazine, 3.

28. "Pilgrimages Made to Lincoln's Tomb," *New York Times*, February 13, 1942, 14.

29. "President Lays Lincoln Wreath," *New York Times*, February 13, 1942, 14.

30. Earl Robinson, *Ballad of an American: The Autobiography of Earl Robinson*, with Eric A. Gordon (Lanham, Md.: Scarecrow Press, 1998), 68; also, Pollack, *Copland*, 358; C & P I, 226–27; Richard Taruskin, *The Oxford History of Western Music*, vol. 5, *The Early Twentieth Century* (New York: Oxford University Press, 2005), 670–71.

31. Lord Charnwood, *Abraham Lincoln* (1916; 17th repr., New York: Henry Holt, 1928).

32. Copland, text for WNCN radio program "Aaron Copland Comments," November 25, 1968, typescript, CCLC.

33. *The Life and Writings of Abraham Lincoln*, ed. Philip van Doren Stern (New York: Random House, 1940).

34. Copland, autograph notes for the narration of *Lincoln Portrait*, CCLC. One of the interpolated biographical phrases is drawn from Stern's essay. Stern quotes a lengthy description of Lincoln from William Henry Herndon's 1890 biography: "when standing erect," Herndon writes of Lincoln, "he was six feet four inches high" (William Henry Herndon, *Lincoln: The True Story of a Great Life*, 1890; as quoted in *The Life and Writings of Abraham Lincoln*, 73). Copland transcribed this description in his autograph notes for the narration, eventually changing "high" to "tall."

35. Carl Sandburg, *The People, Yes* (New York: Harcourt, Brace & World, 1936), 136–37.

36. Stern, "The Life of Abraham Lincoln," in *The Life and Writings of Abraham Lincoln*, 149.

37. Copland, autograph notes for the narration of *Lincoln Portrait*, CCLC; the first two sentences are found in *The Life and Writings of Abraham Lincoln*, 77; the concluding sentence on page 85.

38. S. Foster Damon's *Series of Old American Songs* (Providence, R.I.: Brown University Library, 1936).

39. *A Treasury of American Song*, comp. Olin Downes and Elie Siegmeister (New York: Howell, Soskin, 1940); Pollack, *Copland*, 633–34, n. 6. Copland also knew "Springfield Mountain" from a recording of the Old Harp Singers of Nashville. See Pollack, *Copland*, 358–59, and Copland, "Scores and Records," *Modern Music* 16 (1939): 186.

40. Neil Lerner, "Copland's Music of Wide Open Spaces: Surveying the Pastoral Trope in Hollywood," *The Musical Quarterly* 85 (2001): 482–83.

41. Pollack, *Copland*, 359.

42. My thanks to K. M. Knittel for this observation.

43. C & P I, 323–34.

44. On William "Bill" Adams (1887–1972) see Thomas A. DeLong, *Radio Stars: An Illustrated Biographical Dictionary of 953 Performers, 1920 through 1960* (Jefferson, N.C.: McFarland, 1996), 6.

45. Geer narrated *Lincoln Portrait* with the Boston Symphony Orchestra on March 26–27 and April 9–10 (in Boston) and in Brooklyn, New York City, and New Brunswick, N.J., during the interim.

46. On Geer, see Denning, *The Cultural Front*, 155 and 261; on the Mercury Theatre, 370–75. Copland wrote the incidental music for *Five Kings*, a redaction of Shakespeare devised by Orson Welles for the Mercury Theatre, but never produced (C & P I, 286–87).

47. William Schuman to Copland, March 31, 1943, CCLC.

48. Copland to Kostelanetz, April 8, 1943, CCLC.

49. Schwarzkopf narrated *Lincoln Portrait* in the wake of the first Gulf War on *Leonard Slatkin Conducts American Portraits*, Saint Louis Symphony Orchestra, Leonard Slatkin, conductor, compact disc, RCA Red Seal, 1992 (rec. September 15, 1991);

James Earl Jones is heard on *Portraits of Freedom*, Seattle Symphony, Gerard Schwarz, conductor, compact disc, Delos, 1993 (rec. June 8–10, 1992); Henry Fonda narrates with Copland conducting the London Symphony Orchestra, *Copland Conducts Copland*, compact disc, CBS Records Masterworks, 1988 (rec. 1968).

50. Program for Washington National Symphony performances on February 11, 12, and 13, 1969, CCLC.

51. Copland, interview with Phillip Ramey, June 1, 1971, in liner notes for *Copland Conducts Copland*.

52. Andre Kostelanetz, "When I Heard Lincoln's Words," *Parade*, February 12, 1956, CCLC.

53. Sketches for *Lincoln Portrait* are housed at the Harry Ransom Humanities Research Center, University of Texas at Austin, Austin, Texas.

54. On March 5, Copland wrote to Koussevitzky: "Dear Sergei Alexandrovitch: This is to confirm the conversation I had on the phone yesterday with Olga. I agree to make an orchestral arrangement of the Internationale, as you requested. I assume you want a plain version similar to that of the Star Spangled Banner which I have heard you use. I will give it to you when you are in New York next week. I suppose that is time enough to prepare it for performance in Washington. If you need it sooner, let me know" (CCLC online, copland corro292).

55. Kostelanetz, "When I Heard Lincoln's Words."

56. There is little evidence of Copland's reaction to the political and commercial appropriation of *Lincoln Portrait* in particular or his accessible music more generally. In August 1942, however, he wrote to William Schuman with some sense of rueful irony: "If you have nothing better to do, listen in on the afternoon of the 16th at 4:30, when Kostelanetz is broadcasting my Lincoln piece, for the greater glory of Coca-Cola" (Copland to Schuman, August 6, 1942, William Schuman Papers, NYPL).

57. Martha Graham as quoted in Anna Kisselgoff, "Copland on 'Appalachian' Beginnings," *New York Times*, December 17, 1975.

58. On Graham's politics, see in particular Ellen Graff, "Dancing Red: Art and Politics," in *Of, By, and For the People: Dancing on the Left in the 1930s*, ed. Lynn Garafola, *Studies in Dance History* 5 (1994), 7.

59. See Julia L. Foulkes, *Modern Bodies: Dance and American Modernism from Martha Graham to Alvin Ailey* (Chapel Hill: University of North Carolina Press, 2002), 120–22; Anna Kisselgoff, "Protest Themes Lurk in Graham's 1935 'Panorama,'" *New York Times*, February 8, 1999.

60. On *American Document*, see Graff, "Dancing Red," 8–9, and *Stepping Left: Dance and Politics in New York City, 1928–1942* (Durham, N.C.: Duke University Press, 1997), 124–30; Foulkes, *Modern Bodies*, 147–52; Susan Manning, "*American Document* and American Minstrelsy," in *Moving Words: Re-Writing Dance*, ed. Morris Gay (New York: Routledge, 1996), 183–202.

61. Eve Stebbins [Edna Ocko], "From Isadora to Picket Line Priscilla," *TAC* (July-August 1939), as quoted in "Reviewing on the Left: The Dance Criticism of Edna Ocko," ed. Stacey Prickett, in *Of, By, and For the People*, 100.

62. Pollack, *Copland*, 403.

63. Foulkes, *Modern Bodies*, 155.

64. The complex genesis and compositional history of *Appalachian Spring* has been well documented by Howard Pollack, *Copland*, 391–400; Marta Robertson, "Musical and Choreographic Integration in Copland's and Graham's *Appalachian Spring*," *The Musical Quarterly* 83 (1999): 6–26; and "'A Gift to Be Simple': The Collaboration of Aaron Copland and Martha Graham in the Genesis of *Appalachian Spring*" (Ph.D. diss., University of Michigan, 1992), 122–72; Wayne D. Shirley, "Ballet for Martha: The Commissioning of *Appalachian Spring*," *Performing Arts Annual* (1987): 102–33; and "Ballets for Martha: The Creation of *Appalachian Spring, Jeux de Printemps*, and *Hérodiade*," *Performing Arts Annual* (1988): 40–69; both reprinted as "For Martha," *Ballet Review* 27 (1999): 64–94. See also C & P II, 30–58.

65. The two scripts titled "NAME," one followed by a period, the other by a question mark, were both sent to Copland in the summer of 1943. The differences between all three drafts ("House of Victory," "Name.," and "Name?") are not significant to my interpretation, and so this account quotes only from "NAME?" It alone describes the final section, "The Lord's Day," in any detail. All three have autograph markings by Copland.

66. Copland was perhaps inspired by Graham to use a Shaker tune. In "House of Victory" Graham describes the simple staging of the ballet: "There will be no heavy construction; only the frame of a doorway, a platform of the porch, a Shaker rocking chair with a bone-like simplicity of line, and an old-fashioned rope swing."

67. As quoted in Robertson, "'A Gift to Be Simple,'" 174.

68. Ibid., 179, n. 11.

69. Program note for *Appalachian Spring* Suite, New York Philharmonic-Symphony, October 4, 1945; see also Robertson, "'A Gift to Be Simple,'" 181. The internal quotes in the program annotation indicate text originally published by Denby in the *New York Herald-Tribune*, May 15, 1945, one week after victory in Europe was declared. According to Robertson, Copland approved the synopsis.

70. The following description and interpretation of *Appalachian Spring* relies on the dance as captured on *Martha Graham in Performance* (West Long Branch, N.J.: Kultur, 1988). The performance on this video, in which Martha Graham dances the role of the Bride, was directed and photographed by Peter Glushanok and filmed in 1958. Cue numbers are those of the published suite for thirteen instruments. The suite omits some music in the ballet. Numbers for sections not in the suite are found in ARCO 55.3

71. Graham's *Frontier* (1935), which Robertson describes as "a choreographic sketch for *Appalachian Spring*," includes a similar miming of motherhood. Robertson, "'A Gift to Be Simple,'" 97.

72. On the difference between the variation set in the ballet and in the suite, see Robertson, "'A Gift to Be Simple,'" 272–78. Basically, in the ballet the final tutti variation arrives at the very end, separated from the four variations by the tumultuous sections "Fear in the Night," "Day of Wrath," and "Moment of Crisis." Also, the fourth variation of the ballet is the second in the suite.

73. Daniel Albright describes a similar phenomenon in Stravinsky's *Renard* (1922). See Albright, "Exhibiting Modernism: A View from the Air," in *Make It New: The Rise of Modernism*, ed. Kurt Heinzelman (Austin, Tex.: Harry Ransom Research Center, 2003), 56–57.

74. As Denning notes, "nothing seems more obvious than the 'populism' of the Popular Front." The determined invocation of "the 'people,'" he continues, "is generally understood to be a retreat from the radical 'proletarianism' of the early 1930s" (*The Cultural Front*, 124), but he argues forcefully against this position.

75. Waldo Frank, *Dawn in Russia: The Record of a Journey* (New York: Charles Scribner's Sons, 1932), 121.

76. Edmund Wilson, *Axel's Castle* (New York: Charles Scribner's Sons, 1931), 293.

77. John Dewey, *Impressions of Soviet Russia and the Revolutionary World* (New York: New Republic, 1929), 31.

78. Eugene Braudo, "The Russian Panorama," *Modern Music* 10, no. 2 (1933): 79, 83.

79. Ashley Pettis, "Forecast & Review: Musical Flashlights from Moscow," *Modern Music* 10, no. 1 (1932): 51.

80. C & P I, 56.

81. See *We Proudly Present: The Story of the National Council of American-Soviet Friendship, 1943–1953* (New York: National Council of American-Soviet Friendship, n.d.); also Pollack, *Copland*, 281–82; J. D. Parks, *Culture, Conflict and Coexistence: American-Soviet Cultural Relations, 1917–1958* (Jefferson, N.C.: McFarland, 1983), 65–68; Levering, *American Opinion and the Russian Alliance*, 125–27.

82. *Tribute to Russia* (New York: Congress of American-Soviet Friendship, n.d.); see also Levering, *American Opinion and the Russian Alliance*, 100–3.

83. *We Proudly Present*: "friendly relations," 11; "essential to winning," 14.

84. Pollack, *Copland*, 282. See also *We Proudly Present*, 15. Somewhat surprisingly, Copland is not noted among the "honor role of musicians, writers, directors, actors, dancers, who contributed their talents to American-Soviet affairs" (16). Leonard Bernstein, Roy Harris, Harold Clurman, and Agnes de Mille are included; significantly, however, it was Copland who was called to testify before the Senate Permanent Sub-Committee on Investigations, chaired by Senator Joseph McCarthy, in 1953. Copland is listed as "affiliated" with the National Council for Soviet-American Friendship in *Red Channels: The Report on Communist Influence in Radio and Television* (New York: American Business Consultants, 1950), 39–41.

85. Music Advisory Committee, Department of State, Sub-Committee on Musical Interchange with the U.S.S.R., revised minutes of meeting, February 11, 1944, typescript, CCLC.

86. Serge Koussevitzky, "Soaring Music," *New York Times*, March 5, 1939, World's Fair special section, 54. See also "Musical Art in the History of Life," typescript speech for 1939 World's Fair, Serge Koussevitzky Collection, Music Division, Library of Congress.

87. Copland, "Is There a Revolution in the Arts?" *Town Meeting* 5, February 19, 1940, 19.

88. "The Mission of Artists in the World Today," typescript, Koussevitzky Collection, Music Division, Library of Congress.

89. C & P II, 66; and "A Talk with Aaron Copland," interview by Phillip Ramey, in *New York Philharmonic Program*, November 20, 1980, 19.

90. See Hugo Leichtentritt, *Serge Koussevitzky: The Boston Symphony Orchestra and the New American Music* (Cambridge, Mass.: Harvard University Press, 1946), 179–81; in an issue of the *Information Bulletin of the Russian Embassy* (August 10, 1942) devoted to the Seventh Symphony, Koussevitzky described Shostakovich as "the bright torch of the Russian people" (as quoted in Leichtentritt, *Serge Koussevitzky*, 180). See also John H. Mueller, *The American Symphony Orchestra: A Social History of Musical Taste* (Bloomington: Indiana University Press, 1951), 226–27. Much ado was made in the press about the Seventh Symphony's circuitous route to the United States on microfilm. See, for instance, "Premiere of the Year," *Newsweek*, July 27, 1942, 66. The reception history of the symphony is documented in Terry Wait Klefstad, "The Reception in America of Dmitri Shostakovich, 1928–1946" (Ph.D. diss., University of Texas at Austin, 2003), 189–231; and Christopher H. Gibbs, "'The Phenomenon of the Seventh': a Documentary Essay on Shostakovich's 'War' Symphony," in *Shostakovich and his World*, ed. Laurel E. Fay (Princeton, N.J.: Princeton University Press, 2004).

91. Illustrating the public interest in Shostakovich's symphonies, CBS purchased the broadcast rights to the Eighth for the unheard of sum of $10,000. See "Shostakovich Sells Symphony for $10,000," *Life*, November 22, 1943, 43–44.

92. Copland, "The Musical Scene Changes," 341.

93. Copland, intermission talk, Stadium Concert, July 5, 1939, typescript, CCLC.

94. Ibid.

95. Copland, "From the '20s to the '40s and Beyond," *Modern Music* 20 (1943): 82.

96. C & P II, 68.

97. The eighteen fanfares, with their premiere dates, are: Bernard Wagenaar, *A Fanfare for Airmen* (October 9, 1942); Deems Taylor, *A Fanfare for Russia* (October 16 1942); Walter Piston, *A Fanfare for the Fighting French* (October 23, 1942); Henry Cowell, *A Fanfare to the Forces of Our Latin-American Allies* (October 30, 1942); Daniel Gregory Mason, *A Fanfare for Friends* (November 6, 1942); Paul Creston, *A Fanfare for Paratroopers* (November 27, 1942); Darius Milhaud, *Fanfare de la liberté* (December 11, 1942); William Grant Still, *A Fanfare for American Heroes* (December 18, 1942); Virgil Thomson, *Fanfare for France* (January 15, 1943); Morton Gould, *Fanfare for Freedom* (January 22, 1943); Leo Sowerby, *Fanfare for Airmen* (January 29, 1943); Harl McDonald, *Fanfare for Poland* (February 5, 1943); Bernard Rogers, *Fanfare for Commandos* (February 20, 1943); Anis Fuleihan, *Fanfare for the Medical Corps* (February 26, 1943); Felix Borowski, *Fanfare for the American Soldier* (March 5, 1943); Aaron Copland, *Fanfare for the Common Man* (March 12, 1943); Howard Hanson, *Fanfare for the Signal Corps* (April 2, 1943); Eugene Goossens, *Fanfare for the Merchant Marine* (April 16, 1943).

98. Eugene Goossens to Copland, August 30, 1942, CCLC. Note Goossens's use of the term *comradeship* rather than the more usual *camaraderie*.

99. Goossens to Copland, September 28, 1942, CCLC. See also C & P II, 368. Lidice was a Czechoslovakian town obliterated by the Nazis in June 1941, after which it became a favorite subject for artists concerned about the war. Copland frequently

struggled with titling his pieces; he drafted and redrafted titles for each movement of *Statements*, wrote out lists of possibilities for the *Short Symphony*, and even debated possible titles for the *Piano Variations* (see, for instance, CCLC online, copland sket0011, image 5).

100. The text is reproduced in *Vital Speeches*, January 15, 1941, 197–200. See also Neil Lerner, "Aaron Copland, Norman Rockwell, and the 'Four Freedoms': The Office of War Information's Vision and Sound in *The Cummington Story* (1945)," in *Copland and His World*, ed. Carol J. Oja and Judith Tick (Princeton, Princeton University Press, 2005).

101. Copland to Goossens, April 2, 1943, CCLC.

102. Henry A. Wallace, "The Price of Free World Victory: The Century of the Common Man," speech delivered to the Free World Association, Hotel Commodore, New York City, May 8, 1942; reprint in *Vital Speeches* 8 (June 1, 1942): 483–84.

103. Ibid.: "the supreme duty," 484; "for the common man," 483.

104. Henry R. Luce, "The American Century," *Life*, February 17, 1941; reprinted as a book of the same title (New York: Farrar and Rinehart, 1941) and in *Diplomatic History* 23 (1999): 159–71. On Luce's speech, see vol. 23, no. 2 of *Diplomatic History*, a special issue devoted to the concept of "the American Century"; also, Alan Brinkley, *Liberalism and Its Discontents* (Cambridge, Mass.: Harvard University Press, 1998), 107–8; and Denning, *The Cultural Front*, 43–44.

105. Luce, "The American Century," *Diplomatic History*, 165.

106. Ibid., 168.

107. Wallace, "The Price of Free World Victory," 484.

108. As quoted in Pollack, *Copland*, 360.

109. See Michael C. C. Adams, *The Best War Ever: America and World War II* (Baltimore: Johns Hopkins University Press, 1994), 76–79.

110. See ibid., 114–20; and Denning, *The Cultural Front*, 23–24.

111. Henry A. Wallace, *The Price of Free World Victory* (New York: L.B. Fischer, 1942); reprinted in Wallace, *The Century of the Common Man* (New York: Reynal & Hitchcock, 1943). The speech was excerpted in, among other periodicals, *Current History* 2 (July 1942): 385–91; *National Geographic Magazine*, August 1942, 276–80; *Independent Woman*, July 1942, 195–96; *New Republic*, May 25, 1942, 725–27; and *Scholastic: The American High School Weekly*, November 2, 1942, 14–15.

112. "Wallace's Free World Speech Has Wide Distribution," *Publishers' Weekly*, July 11, 1942, 103.

113. Goossens to Copland, November 17, 1942, CCLC.

114. Goosens to Copland, March 24, 1943, CCLC.

115. Copland to Goossens, April 2, 1943, CCLC.

116. "I meant my letter about your *Fanfare* to be both flattering and serious, for no one but a moron could mistake your piece for anything but what it is: a very solid, serious contribution. I wrote a *Fanfare for the Merchant Marine* for the last concert, and just because I brought in it a tune called 'The Roast Beef of England' a lot of people though I was trying to be funny. On the contrary, the piece had very tragic implications. I am glad you approved of my playing the piece around March 15th; it struck me as somehow very suitable." Goossens to Copland, April 26, 1943, CCLC.

117. Wallace, *The Price of Free World Victory*, 17.

118. Roosevelt needed to raise taxes to finance the American war effort. The 1942 Revenue Act represented a compromise between the president and the Congress that expanded the national tax base, with the result that more people paid income tax than ever before. See David M. Kennedy, *Freedom from Fear: The American People in Depression and War, 1929–1945* (New York: Oxford University Press, 1999), 624–25.

119. I have found no evidence of a performance in Boston before the first performance of the Symphony on October 18, 1946, and in New York City the *Fanfare* seems to have been played only once before the local premiere of the Third. The Copland-Perlis autobiography dates the New York premiere of the *Fanfare* to March 14, 1943, with George Szell and the Cincinnati Symphony (C & P II, 18). There is no documentation of this performance, however, and indeed the Cincinnati Symphony did not perform in New York at all in 1943. The first New York performance seems instead to have been on a Christmas program at Radio City (December 18, 1944) by Leopold Stokowski and the New York City Symphony.

120. Sincere thanks to James Hepokoski, whose work on and insights about the *Fanfare* in the symphony have influenced my analysis.

121. Concert Bulletin, 66th Season (1946–47), Boston Symphony Orchestra, October 18, 1946, 144, 146.

122. This is perhaps the tune that Leonard Bernstein described as "Because I'm Leaving Cheyenne" (also known as "Goodbye Old Paint"). The intervals are similar, but the theme might also be heard to evoke "Yankee Doodle." Copland steadfastly maintained that the Third Symphony did not contain any folksong quotations, except unconsciously, and without clear evidence to the contrary his opinion cannot be discounted. (Rarely, if ever, did he so purposefully conceal his borrowings.) Bernstein also noted the theme's chorale-like character, saying it "should be the Tanglewood hymn with words written to it to be sung every year at the closing ceremonies." As quoted in C & P I, 341; see also C & P II, 68.

123. C & P II, 68.

124. On the style of the mass song, see Carol J. Oja, "Marc Blitzstein's *The Cradle Will Rock* and Mass-Song Style of the 1930s," *The Musical Quarterly* 73 (1989): 450.

125. Kenneth Burke, *Permanence and Change: An Anatomy of Purpose* (1935; 2nd rev. ed., Indianapolis: Bobbs-Merrill, 1965), 249; on Burke's theory of symbolic action, see also Denning, *The Cultural Front*, 434–45.

126. Burke, *Permanence and Change*, 266.

127. On the compositional history of the Third Symphony, see Elizabeth Bergman Crist, "Aaron Copland's Third Symphony from Sketch to Score," *Journal of Musicology* 18 (2001): 377–405.

128. See Pells, *The Liberal Mind in a Conservative Age*.

Conclusion

1. Virgil Thomson, "Copland as Great Man," *New York Herald-Tribune*, November 24, 1946.

2. Thomson, "More About Copland's Third," *New York Herald-Tribune*, June 22, 1947.

3. In "Copland as Great Man" (1946), Thomson had written of the Third: "the nature of the work's expressivity is as plain as a newspaper editorial"; also Thomson, "More About Copland's Third" (1947).

4. Thomson, "More About Copland's Third."

5. Pollack, *Copland*, 283.

6. Aaron Copland, "Effect of the Cold War on the Artist in the United States," speech delivered at the Fine Arts Panel of the Cultural and Scientific Conference for World Peace, March 27, 1949, CCLC. See Jennifer L. DeLapp, "Copland in the Fifties: Music and Ideology in the McCarthy Era" (Ph.D. diss., University of Michigan, 1997), 93–100.

7. "Red Visitors Cause Rumpus," *Life*, April 4, 1949, 39–43.

8. See in particular Richard H. Pells, *The Liberal Mind in a Conservative Age: American Intellectuals in the 1940s and 1950s* (New York: Harper & Row, 1985).

9. On McCarthyism as a cultural movement, see Ellen Schrecker, *Many Are the Crimes: McCarthyism in America* (Princeton, N.J.: Princeton University Press, 1998).

10. Arthur J. Schlesinger, *The Vital Center: The Politics of Freedom* (1949; repr, Brunswick, N.J.: Transaction Publishers, 1998).

11. Ibid., 37–41.

12. On the New York Intellectuals, see John Patrick Diggins, *The Rise and Fall of the American Left* (New York: W. W. Norton, 1992), 210–17; also Judy Kutulas, *The Long War: The Intellectual People's Front and Anti-Stalinism, 1930–1940* (Durham, N.C.: Duke University Press, 1995), 4–14.

13. Clement Greenberg, "Avant-Garde and Kitsch," *Partisan Review* 6 (1939): 34–39; reprint in *Mass Culture: The Popular Arts in America*, ed. Bernard Rosenberg and David Manning White (Glencoe, Ill.: Free Press, 1957), 99. On Greenberg's aesthetic, see Erika Doss, *Benton, Pollack, and the Politics of Modernism: From Regionalism to Abstract Expressionism* (Chicago: University of Chicago Press, 1991), 363–416; Aaron Copland, "Composer from Brooklyn," *Magazine of Art* (1939); repr., *Our New Music: Leading Composers in Europe and America* (1941; rev. and enlarged ed. *The New Music, 1900–1960*, New York: W. W. Norton, 1968), 160.

14. Kutulas argues that "progressives were never able to bounce back after the People's Front collapsed. Some lost interest in politics; others joined the anticommunist crusade; most simply could not regain their passion. . . . They did not prosper. In part that was because they were older than anticommunists and perhaps legitimately past their primes. But it was also true that they could not coexist very easily with anticommunists, so once anticommunists triumphed, progressives gave way. . . . They were not entirely graceful about the process, but neither could they reverse the trends" (*The Long War*, 232–33).

15. Leonard Bernstein, "Aaron Copland at 70: An Intimate Sketch," in *Findings* (New York: Simon & Schuster, 1982), 290.

16. Copland, *The New Music*, 171.

17. Ibid., 161.

18. James Agee and Walker Evans, *Let Us Now Praise Famous Men* (Boston: Houghton Mifflin, 1941); see Pollack, *Copland*, 471–72.

19. Pollack, *Copland*, 473. In a notable queer reading of *The Tender Land*, Daniel E. Mathers finds "challenges to social and political norms" of 1950s America in "the opera's insistence on issues of individual identity, expression and self-acceptance" ("Expanding Horizons: Sexuality and the Re-zoning of *The Tender Land*," in *Copland Connotations: Studies and Interviews*, ed. Peter Dickinson [Rochester, N.Y.: Boydell Press, 2002], 126).

20. Whereas the chorus "The Promise of Living" closes act 1 of *The Tender Land* just before Laurie decides to leave the farm to see the world, in Bernstein's *Candide* (1956), following the original Voltaire (1759), the protagonist settles on a farm with his wife Cunégonde; there he famously declares, "il faut cultiver notre jardin," and the comic operetta closes with a climactic chorus, "Make Our Garden Grow," aptly described by Meryle Secrest as "Coplandesque" (*Leonard Bernstein: A Life* [New York: Alfred A. Knopf, 1994], 210).

21. Fred E. Busbey, "Aaron Copland and Inaugural Concert," January 16, 1953, 83rd Congress, 1st sess., *Congressional Record*, 99, pt. 9, appendix, 169. Busbey's remarks in the *Congressional Record* followed a report by Paul Hume in the *Washington Post* (January 15, 1953) announcing the cancellation. On this incident, see C & P II, 184–89; Pollack, *Copland*, 452–54; and DeLapp, "Copland in the Fifties," 123–29.

22. Busbey, "Aaron Copland and Inaugural Concert," A169–71. On information compiled about Copland by the U.S. government and the cancellation of *Lincoln Portrait*, see DeLapp, "Copland in the Fifties," 114–34. Many of these affiliations were also listed in *Red Channels: The Report on Communist Influence in Radio and Television* (New York: American Business Consultants, 1950), 39–41.

23. See C & P II, 186; Pollack, *Copland*, 452–53; DeLapp, "Copland in the Fifties," 132–33.

24. *Wieman v. Updegraff*, 344 U.S. 183 (1952) held as unconstitutional an Oklahoma law that required state employees to take a "loyalty oath" swearing that they were not affiliated with any Communist front or subversive organizations.

25. Copland to the League of Composers, February 9, 1953, Claire Reis Collection, NYPL.

26. Pollack, *Copland*, 454.

27. Copland's experience with McCarthyism is described in C & P II, 181–203; Pollack, *Copland*, 451–60; DeLapp, "Copland in the Fifties," 134–51.

28. Pollack, *Copland*, 457.

29. On instrumental music as an empty sign see Daniel K. L. Chua, *Absolute Music and the Construction of Meaning* (Cambridge: Cambridge University Press, 1999).

30. William Safire, "A Gioia to Behold," *New York Times*, editorial page, March 8, 2004.

Index